advance praise for

we hope you like this song

"Bree Housley tells a story that is touching, funny, and completely inspiring. Reading it, we can't help but think about our own resolutions, our own losses, and the friends and loved ones who've given meaning to our lives."

—Jeffrey Zaslow, bestselling author of *The Last Lecture* and *The Girls from Ames: A Story of Women and a Forty-Year Friendship*

"Bree's story is like an addictive power ballad for friendships between women. Her voice sings with a pleasing combination of ups, downs, out-loud laughter, and out-loud tears. You'll want to crank the volume on this one."

—Pam Thomas, award-winning director of *Sex and the City* and *Desperate Housewives*

"Housley has managed to write a book that's devastating, touching, and flat-out hilarious all at once. It's a great read, and Housley is a fine new voice."

—Michael Benoist, *GQ*

we hope you like this song

an overly honest story about friendship, death, and mix tapes

SEAL PRESS

For Shelly, Courtnee, and Eric: my best friends
Also for Hailey (when she grows up)

Author's Note: Although this book is based on true life experiences as I remember them, the names and certain identifying features of some people portrayed in it have been changed to protect their privacy . . . or to spare me embarrassment. —Bree Housley

Published by Seal Press
A Member of the Perseus Books Group
1700 Fourth Street
Berkeley, California

Photos courtesy of the author, except: title page and chapter backgrounds © Domini Dragoone, pg. 3 © Warner-Medlin, pg. 64 © Olan Mills (Davenport, Iowa), pgs. 206 and 209 © Devin David Photography-Chicago, pg. 237 Courtesy of Rogue Art Photography (Indianapolis, IN).

Library of Congress Cataloging-in-Publication Data

Housley, Bree, 1979-
We hope you like this song : an overly honest story about friendship, death, and mix tapes / Bree Housley.
p. cm.
ISBN 978-1-58005-431-7
1. Housley, Bree, 1979- 2. Bridgewater, Shelly Warner, 1979-2005. 3. Best friends—Iowa—Biography. 4. Bereavement. 5. Consolation. I. Title.
CT275.H6589A3 2012
977.7'034092—dc23
[B]
2012008699

9 8 7 6 5 4 3 2

Cover and interior design by Domini Dragoone
Printed in the United States of America | Distributed by Publishers Group West

Contents

bree,

Here is a little description to go along with the CD. You may have noticed that it is a musical tribute to our friendship. Here is why I chose the following songs:

How Much Is That Doggie in the Window — This classic started it all off. Our vocals started at a young age shortly after a choral concert. After the drinking fountain song, we sang this for hours. And our friendship blossomed.

Manic Monday — Our choreographic talents really appeared during the "Making of the Video" on this song. We spent days carefully planning each step of this oldie but goodie. And to think someone wrote "Bangles suck" on our dorm room door!

I Fall to Pieces — Although this is a Patsy Cline classic, nobody could belt out the tune quite like us. Our original facial expressions that we created to go with this song were impeccable. Who could've asked for cooler babysitters . . . ?

Hit Me with Your Best Shot — Not even Pat Benetar could match our vocals on this one. It takes me all the way back to high school . . . cruising around town . . . nothing brought us together quite like this one did.

Step by Step — New Kids! Need I say more?

Vibeology — We just couldn't get out of our choreographing stage, as this continued through our first year of college. I must say, this one was definitely a hit . . . good thing we performed for half our dorm floor!

If I Had a Million Dollars — The Barenaked Ladies concert was the best . . . brings me back to our macaroni and cheese days . . .

Play That Funky Music — Every time I hear this song from this day forward, I will forever think of you at a bar. Bet you're glad to hear that one . . . I'll make sure to pass that one to your kids one day!

Up in Here — This era reminds me of your gangsta side. I think this song is what prompted the creation of the Breester . . . could I be right?

Miami — My first trip ever . . . and I'll be coming down to see you there again soon. I had a great time and couldn't quit listening to this song before we left!

Tiny Dancer — Admit it, my lyrics were better than Elton's anyway.

I hope you like your CD! I know you'll miss Iowa sometimes, so I thought you could listen to this and think of all the fun times that are yet to be had!

B/F/F,
Shelly

glossary of friends

Shelly [shel-ee]

My inspiration. Best childhood friend from fourth grade until her death at age 25. Boy crazy, friend crazy, love crazy. She was an outgoing, hyper, spazz of a girl who would do anything for the people she loved. She ultimately proved this by giving up her life for her daughter, Hailey. She was a teacher, a sister, a wife, a friend, and a mother. A pregnancy condition called *preeclampsia* killed her. I would stab it in the face if I could.

BFF quality: Unconditional devotion, pre and post mortem.

Courtnee [kort-nee]

Older, wiser sister who means more to me than taffy. (Taffy means a lot to me.) She's a video editor, married to her high school sweetheart, Eric. She supported me through all the years of devastation following Shelly's death, proving her ultimate big sister prowess. Oh, plus she's my co-conspirator in this little adventure.

BFF quality: We share the same parents. And sometimes, it feels like we share the same brain.

Eric [er-ik]

He's the cool kid in class, slumming it with a nerd (i.e., my boyfriend). He hails from St. Louis where he went to an all-boys high school and attended "Mom Prom" (this is highly entertaining to me). He's a commercial photographer obsessed with sneakers, jackets, and gadgets.

BFF quality: True love. (Also: entertaining, handsome, understanding, smart, and athletic. But mostly, true love.)

Amy [ey-mee]

This one's from Indianapolis, though I met her in South Beach. We attended Miami Ad School together and became close friends out of necessity (we were the only non-exotically-beautiful Colombian girls in class). If I have an embarrassing admission, her ear is the first thing I grab.

BFF quality: Funny as shit.

Foxy [fok-see]

Also "Ami." This little lady has been by my side since high school. She's a fantastic singer/music enthusiast who never turns down an invite from a friend (even if it's a super lame invite). She's still holding out for her hero (thank you, Bonnie Tyler), but she's accumulated some hilarious stories getting there. She is my go-to friend for life.

BFF quality: More loyal than the definition of loyal. (i.e., If we were sassy teen sleuths, she'd be the Bess to my Nancy.)

Kerry [kar-ee]

We first bonded in an adult tap class. That's right, I said *adult* tap class. Please take time to imagine two full-grown women in leotards and high-heeled tap shoes, dancing to "Yakety-Yak." She's the catering manager of a classy Chicago hotel and has a talent for making any situation laugh-worthy. She, too, is still looking for the right guy, but spends the majority of her time flirting with gay men at the workplace.

BFF quality: Unpredictably amusing.

Christine [kri-steen]

She's the wise one of the group. She's comforting like a mother, albeit a mother who will get drunk with you and tell inappropriate stories about "shingles" in public. We were fatefully partnered through work as an art director/copywriter team when I moved to Chicago. She's married to a Russian named Oleg.

BFF quality: Ability to make you feel like you're always making the right decision. (Even when you're clearly not.)

Prologue:
when bree met shelly

Laverne and Shirley. Carrie and Miranda. Hillary Whitney and CC Bloom. Goose and Maverick? You bet your ass. Whether they're sipping martinis or flying motherfreaking jets, these pop culture pairs have effectively proven to the American public that soul mates are not just for the marrying kind. These characters demonstrate the caliber of friendship that every non-murdering human being yearns to find. As much as I adore these fictitious duos, I'm here to tell you it can happen in real life. The Cagney to my Lacey wasn't a made-up character from TV or film. Her name was Shelly Warner, and we're proof that BFFs really do exist.

Summer of 1989. The first photo Shelly and I ever took together. It's amazing how much I look like a forty-five-year-old woman trapped in a ten-year-old's body.

Shelly and I met in the pocket-size town of Walcott, Iowa, before we understood the importance of showers, clean teeth, and, well, personal hygiene in general. (Ironically, this tiny town is also the "World's Largest Truckstop." Need a T-shirt featuring a wolf or a woodland creature? Ring me.)

I cherish the day "the new girl" fluttered into Miss Siegel's homeroom class. It was in the fourth grade, that special time in life when the only thing that truly matters is friends—and maybe math. When Shelly's friendly blue eyes locked with my timid brown eyes, an odd version of love at first sight occurred. She was the popular blonde and was super cool. *I* was the mangy brunette and was super lame. She had a dazzling ponytail and perfectly tight rolled jeans. I had a dazzling mullet and badly hemmed culottes. (It wasn't the average business-up-front, party-in-the-back mullet, either. Nope, thanks to the bang perm kickin' it up front, this mullet partied all the time.) I'll never know what possessed a lovely social butterfly like Shelly to befriend a skittish moth like me. She had the world at her fingertips—everyone loved her. My fingertips were usually covered in Doritos cheese dust—no one really even knew I existed. I'm just glad she picked me as her favorite.

We spent our elementary school years doing kid stuff, like playing Barbies and freebasing Fun Dip. Her popularity grew by the day. She was already "going with" a boy by the end of fourth grade. I just had a secret crush. (And a massive boner for Chad Allen of *Our House* fame.)

Junior high was a different animal. We were exposed to a new species of girl. This species wore name-brand fashions. (Hello, Jordache. Pleasure to meet you, LA Gear.) There was suddenly pressure to be cool and say things like "bitchin!" Once again, Shelly's friend count multiplied like wet gremlins. Once again, she situated me on a pedestal above every one of them.

Our friendship carried on that way throughout high school. Her clump of friends grew bigger and bigger. My clump remained a clump. I didn't need a lot of friends; I had *her.* She had the energy of a wildebeest on Red Bull. Her laugh was loud enough to wake a town of bears in December. And only those of canine descent rivaled her loyalty. No one had a friendship as bulletproof as ours. (Evidence: Remember those pathetic couples that had senior class pictures taken together? See photo.) Shelly brought me out of my shell by placing me at the center of her world.

We coached each other through boyfriends and break-ups. We dried each other's tears of rejection. We made each other laugh in ways no one else understood. We worked together as Subway sandwich artists. We played together in the school marching band. And finally, against the advice of many, we chose to be roommates when we went off to

Clearly, I was the dude in this relationship. And yes, that's a jeandress.

college at Iowa State. You know the rule: *Never* room with your best friend in college, or you will end up bloodied and alone. Well, not only were we both still alive at the end of college, we were devastated when it was time to split up for the first time in eleven years.

I got an internship in Fort Lauderdale, which turned into grad school in Miami and then a job in Chicago. She got a teaching job in Iowa Falls, where she met her future husband, Brad. Being so far away from each other was difficult, but phone calls were like Elmer's glue for our friendship: delicious and necessary. We called each other to share good things, bad things, funny things, and "hey, remember that?" things. It always seemed as if no time had passed. But then one day, I got a different kind of phone call regarding Shelly—the kind that should exist only in nightmares.

I had stood next to her on her wedding day in September of 2004, but just less than half a year later, in January of 2005, I was standing by her again at her hospital bed as she died. A common pregnancy condition called preeclampsia was the villain. Just as instantly as we were brought together, we were tragically torn apart by her sudden death. The same day I said goodbye to Shelly, I said hello to her newborn baby, Hailey.

So yeah, my best friend is dead. But that's not exactly what this story is about. You've already seen that story—it's called *Beaches*. This book is about the beautiful chaos my friendship with Shelly inspired, both while she was alive and while she was not.

Chapter 1:
a different kind of resolution

It's Saturday, January 3, and holiday hangover season is in full effect. While most people are at the gym for the first time in 360 days or at the health food store buying plantlike snacks whose names they can't pronounce, Foxy, Kerry, and I meet up at a local Chicago pub and belly up to the bar (literally, as we all have a serious case of holiday paunch).

I've known Foxy (Ami Fox) since high school. Back then, we were good enough friends to hit up Steak n' Shake together on Friday nights after basketball games, but we weren't close enough to cry on each other's shoulder or anything. (Only Shelly was lucky enough to get my snot stains on her sweaters.) When I first moved to Chicago, Foxy was my savior. She was the only person I knew in the city until I met Christine at work, so our friendship experienced a major rebirth. I had met Kerry more recently through a mutual friend. We had hit it off immediately, thanks to our love of tap shoes and unitards, and we have been friends ever since.

"Anybody decide on a resolution?" Kerry asks. She's practically holding her head up with the beer bottle in front of her.

"I'm not gonna drink pop!" Foxy says, much too eagerly. This is one of Foxy's traits. She likes to do stuff. I'm impressed by her constant can-do attitude—and also a little grossed out.

I give Foxy a halfhearted scoff, offended that she would even try to survive without magic energy juice. This subject quickly devolves into a less than intellectual conversation about things we could *maybe* do for a short period of time, like a week, but definitely not a year. Ironically, "no day drinking" is one of them. It's 2:00 PM.

"You wouldn't have to commit to any one thing, and hopefully you'd feel successful every week!" I say, in an I-just-solved-all-the-problems-of-the-world way. I don't know if it's the beer haze I'm floating in or not, but this notion of a "new week's resolution" makes a lot of sense to me. Why vow to do one thing per year and most likely fail when you can do one different thing *each week* and succeed fifty-two times per year?

We throw out a few more suggestions of things we could probably do for a week, and then we go back to talking about important things, like ham.

Now, usually these kinds of brilliant bar ideas disappear within one visit to the pillow (and thank goodness for that), but this particular concept hijacks my mind all day on Sunday. It makes me think of Shelly and her undeniable crush on life. Maybe it makes me think of her because the fourth anniversary of her death is coming up—or it could just be that she's always on my mind in one way or another. Either way, the thought of trying to accomplish something new and different every week speaks so loudly to everything she was— spontaneous, outgoing, and sometimes batshit crazy. The girl was up for anything at any time, no matter what the consequences. And here I am wasting my days being VH1's bitch. (I'll watch anything they put in front of me.) The more I think about this random idea that was born in a bar just the day before, the more right it feels.

Since Shelly's death, I've been trapped in this weird space of guilt where I feel I'm not doing enough to honor her. Not enough crying, enough talking, enough *grieving*. What is grief, anyway? Who decides how one should go about it? Sure, there are seven stages, but I believe *that* almost as strongly as I believe there were seven chubby dwarfs that whistled whilst doing housework. In other words, *no comprendo*. I tried the traditional method of grief counseling a few months after Shelly passed. It was basically an expensive conversation with someone I would never choose to talk to in real life. At least when I talk to my friends for free, they call me on my bullshit.

Could this half-baked (half-chugged?) weekly resolution thing truly be a way to pay tribute to Shelly?

Would trying to live a little more like her actually make me a better/cooler person like she was?

Shit, why are you asking me?

Good question. Let's go see what's on VH1.

Self-to-self internal conversations continue late into the night; I can't sleep. I decide it's best to unload my thoughts onto someone else's unconscious shoulders, so I hop out of bed and email my older (and much wiser) sister, Courtnee, to see if she thinks I'm crazy for thinking I can accomplish fifty-two resolutions in one year. I get her response first thing Monday morning: "Not crazy. Can I do it with you?"

Shelly was *always* at our house back in the day, so she was somewhat like a second little sister to Court. For the most part, we just bugged the shit out of Court by stealing her flashy outfits and spying on her phone calls, but deep down inside, Court loved Shelly. And although she lost Shelly, too, Court focused on fixing *me* instead of worrying about her own grief. She listened when I cried, she spooned me the night of the funeral, but most important, she made me feel like everything was going to be okay. Court lives in Des Moines with her husband, Eric, and I live solo in Chicago above

"Hey, are there nerds on our backs?" Courtnee, Eric (her now husband), Shelly, and I at a high school basketball game in 1997.

a rib shack, but when it comes to our relationship, we couldn't be closer. If anyone deserves to join me on this adventure, it's Court.

Shelly's "deathiversary" is Friday of next week, January 16. So if we're going to do this, we gotta quit do-si-do-ing around the idea. We've gotta grab it by the arms and swing it around like we're Johnny fucking Castle. Court and I giddily email all day Monday about possible resolutions, from the clichéd (weight loss) to the absurd (farting in public without shame). I make sure it's cool with Foxy and Kerry, since they helped come up with this madness two days ago. They barely remember the conversation, so, needless to say, they're fine with it.

What Court and I ultimately decide is that we'll tackle a new "resolution" each week for a year (to reach our total of fifty-two resolutions). Whether it's by escaping our narrow comfort zones, accomplishing a "daring" feat, or just living life differently than usual, Court and I hope to get off our proverbial (and literal) asses to celebrate the spirit of that popular blonde we miss so much. Of course, we'll keep track of our progress via blog.

Court is a lover of blogs (I loathe them), so she convinces me that keeping a public online "diary" will put more pressure on us to follow through. Hell, maybe other people will even care enough to cheer us on or heckle us if/when we fail. One of my favorite books, Julie Powell's *Julie & Julia* (in which she vows to cook her way through Julia Child's *Mastering the Art of French Cooking*), proved the power of blogging about a personal project, so I'm willing to give it a shot. I write up a rough draft introducing "fifty2resolutions" and email it to Court for approval. Apparently, she likes it, because the response I get from her includes a link to our new blog site she's created, with my chicken-scratched intro front and center. *Whoa. Whoa. Whoa. This is happening.*

We have one thing left to decide: What happens if we chicken out/fail/flee the country? We agree that for each resolution failed, the "faulty" sister must make a $15 donation to the Preeclampsia Foundation (PF) in Shelly's honor. We hope this rule will help to promote preeclampsia awareness, but we also want Shelly to be an active part of this adventure—since, after all, she's the one who inspired it. Well, she and a few beers with friends.

Court and I kick things off by emailing the blog address to everyone we know on Tuesday morning. The intro on the homepage announces that we'll self-assign our first resolution the following Monday. I send a separate email to Shelly's dad, John. He and I keep in touch quite frequently, so he's one of the first people I want to inform about our attempt to live in Shelly-land for a year. John is extremely active with the Preeclampsia Foundation. Some people get angry and want to sue the whole world when tragedy occurs, and some people dedicate their life to trying to prevent that tragedy from happening to others. I am happy to say, Shelly's family chose the latter.

Oh, and just FYI: We're not out to make the world a better place. In some cases, the world might become a scarier place with two introverted basket cases on the loose. We just want to play with life the way Shelly did. She was the biggest basket case of us all and would've done just about anything on any given day.

Chapter 2:
a week to remember

Balls. This is major pressure. What the hell do we do for the first resolution? I imagine this is how a baby must feel when deciding which word to say first. It's imperative that we choose something 100 percent Shelly, since we're starting the project on the four-year anniversary of the week we lost her.

You know where this is going, right?

As previously mentioned, Shelly was a social butterfly. More specifically, she was the kind of girl who would chat up a blood-thirsty mosquito if it would talk back to her (she also might dance with it, high-five it, and give it a nickname). Who has time for this? Who can set aside their own shit to care about the wackjob sitting next to them on the train? Or even the person sitting in the next office cubicle eating Long John Silver's at ten o'clock in the morning? (His name is Lars Larsen, by the way.) Who knows how Shelly did it—she was just that kind of girl.

Court and I are not butterflies. We're the chumps who walk at warp speed and skid to a halt when we spy a casual acquaintance up ahead. The less human interaction, the better. When I score an empty elevator in the office, I chant softly to the door, "Close, close, close" so I won't be forced to indulge in chipper morning conversation. Sometimes I don't even fake an attempt to kick my foot out like most people do when a straggler lunges toward the door as it closes. I just stare, like, *Eh, it's not you, it's me.* I'm not very nice.

The fact that Shelly and I occupied opposite ends of the social ladder only made our friendship stronger. Shelly's acceptance gave me the confidence of someone much cooler than I actually was, and I gave Shelly the freedom to let her inner geek thrive. For instance, I took dance classes from the age of three until I turned fifteen. During my most unfortunate-looking years (approximately ages eight to fifteen), I looked like an Ewok crammed into fishnet tights and sequins. I had zero control over my mullet and wore glasses four times the size of my face. But you know what? I felt pretty up on that stage because the coolest girl in my whole class was there to see *me* shuffle-ball-change my ass off.

How did I pay her back for this sense of confidence? Well, I taught her all my dance moves, of course. I have the videotape to prove it. The very, very embarrassing videotape recorded in my parents' backyard on a sunny day, the summer before we started junior high. It was one of those days you have only when you're a kid: the kind of day where you just look at your friend and say, "What should we do today?" In this case, the answer was "Let's make an exercise video!" We pressed "play" on one of my carefully constructed mix tapes and traded off between being the "instructor" (the one flailing like a jackass) and the "cameraman" (the one struggling to hold the forty-pound camcorder). Here are some things we learned about making a homemade exercise video:

1. Shouting, "Feel the burn!" doesn't sound as motivating
   when you're not Jane Fonda.

2. When the song "Hotel California" plays on your mix
   tape, you should simply press "stop" and find a new jam.
   You should *not* spend the entire six-minute-and-thirty-
   second song swaying to and fro while counting "reps."
   You should also avoid attempting slow-speed tuck jumps.

3. An abdominal workout should not consist of giggling
   like a hyena when a cute boy from school drives by on his
   moped.

4. Breathing heavily when it's your turn to man the camera
   makes your masterpiece feel like a very different kind of
   video. The porno kind.

5. This video will become one of your favorite possessions
   when you become an adult, yet you will refuse to show it
   to anyone.

Court and I know that in order to truly celebrate our favorite
social butterfly, we have to do our best to become one. After we
discuss the pros and cons of facing one of our greatest fears—being
(*gulp*) social—I teeter on the edge of a diving board much too high
for my jumping skills. The only thing to do is exactly what *she*
would've done: "Cannonball!"

To make a true splash, we vow to make five new friends this
week. Saying hello is not good enough. Photographic evidence is
required. Have you ever asked a stranger to take a picture with you?
Yeah, me neither. *Oh boy.*

I plod into my office building Monday morning after an unfriendly
commute on the train. I work at a downtown Chicago advertising
agency located in the Merchandise Mart. I do something called
copywriting. This means I waste my entire day on the information
superhighway and then come up with ideas for commercials when
I'm out with friends. Things at work are off-kilter right now because

I've recently switched ad agencies after four wonderful, friend-filled years. The difference between the old agency and the new agency isn't even night and day; it's more like pajama party and bridge club.

My previous office was like glorified high school. However, in this high school, I finally ran with the popular crowd. We wore the latest fashions, listened to the latest bands, and drank our lunch at the latest restaurants. My new workplace is . . . well, it's *meh.* The people are nice, but they have families and shit. They drive in from the suburbs and wear freshly laundered clothes every day. And to top it all off, I no longer get to be partnered with my close friends Amy and Christine. The art director/copywriter partnership is a lot like a marriage. (I'm lucky to have not one, but *two,* beaus in this scenario, since Amy and Christine are both art directors.) The copywriter focuses more on the words in an ad, and the art director focuses more on the visuals, but really, we do everything together. From brainstorming ideas to jetting off to glamorous locations to shoot those ideas on film, an AD/CW team is practically one person with two bodies. So now, instead of being joined at the hip with Amy or Christine, I'm attached to Lars Larsen. This is not a joke. If you were to shut your eyes and picture what he might look like, you'd be correct. This dude is one thousand feet tall, weighs a ton, and eats big boat-shaped chocolate donuts for breakfast when he's not eating Long John Silver's.

I stop by the FedEx in the Merchandise Mart to buy an envelope. A chance to succeed at the week's resolution falls into my lap. A tightly permed lady stands between the counter and me. She repeatedly turns around to size me up. The Mart is full of beauties, crazies, and everything in between, so I think nothing of it.

Suddenly, she squawks, "Aren't you *freezing?*"

Cue the visuals. She's stuffed into elf-size leggings and a flannel shirt that screams Farm & Fleet. I'm wearing my winter coat and snow boots. As she continues blurting nonsense, I panic. *What do I say? Where's my camera? How do I get her naked?* Wait—not that last one. She's loopy, twitchy, and fantastic, but I just can't close the deal. I'm fully ashamed as I exit with my stupid, newly purchased envelope. *What have I gotten myself into?*

I awake to a blustery Chicago. My bones are cold. If I could feel my skin, it would probably be cold, too. I bundle up like a brightly colored robber and hike to the train. When I arrive at the platform, I spot my target: a young man, even more bundled than I am (less like a robber, more like a snow monster). He's standing alone with a camera. *Bingo!*

I shiver my way over to the snow monster with a teeth-chattering grin on my face.

"Hey, uh, cold out here. Right?" Duh. It's all I had.

"Yep, freezing," he duh'd back to me.

"So, I just moved here from Florida, and I'd love to send a picture to my friends. Would you mind being in it with me? I'm Bree, by the way."

"Sure, no problem. I'm Mark. My parents live in Florida; I was about to do the same thing!"

Maybe I fibbed a skosh. I did, in fact, live in Florida for a couple years. However, I did not "just move," and my friends would judge my sanity if I sent them this picture.

I hold my camera in the air. "Look cold!" I direct, which doesn't explain why I look mental in the photo.

We chat for a moment and the train pulls up, just in the nick of time. A few more minutes, and I'd have to add him to my Christmas card list.

Thanks to my new snow monster friend, glee bursts out of every pore in my body as the train jerks down the tracks. *Do I actually like being social?* Something about the warmth of an unexpected conversation on a frigid day elates me. I can only imagine this is how Shelly felt every day—and also how she made other people feel every day. When I enter my office, the aforementioned glee is vacuumed out of every pore in my body and is spit violently back into my face.

"Morning," Lars Larsen grumbles from his side of our cube wall. "Morning," I mumble back.

Lars is the type of person who gets to the office extremely early, for no reason at all, and wants you to *know* he's been there for hours. I am the type of person who breezes in late, for big sleepy reasons, and doesn't want anyone to know I'm there, at all. Ever.

I call Court to recount the details of my morning victory. She's proud of me, but she hates me a little because she's frustrated by her own failure to make fast friends with a festive department store clerk.

"Just get one and the rest is easy," I assure her.

And then we hang up. I give myself one more hash mark on the fib tally. *Nothing* is easy about this. Nothing. *How did you do it, Shelly?*

I escape to my usual afternoon perch a few hours later. I call it *couch city*. Most people call it *the lobby*. It's a huge open space in the Mart littered with rich-people couches from the nearby home stores. It's my happy place. No one at work ever questions where I am, because I'm now a "senior copywriter." This position comes with the privilege of being dodgy and disappearing for hours. Out of respect, I always alert Lars Larsen as to my whereabouts. He simply cracks a smile, nods his giant Viking head, and goes back to his double cheeseburger with extra burger.

I curl up on one of the couches with my laptop and gawk at the characters milling about, and I begin to hunt for another unsuspecting stranger. My thoughts quickly turn to Shelly. It's three days before her deathiversary. It's also three days before my mother's birthday. Yes, they are one and the same. Life is a fickle bitch like that. My mom has temporarily moved her birthday to the week prior to avoid happy sadness.

I peck away at the keyboard in an emotional flurry. I'm sad she's not sitting next to me right now. I'm sad we can't eat the hell out of chocolate malts at midnight anymore. I'm sad she died while I was still dating someone we called Lazy Eye, instead of my kick-ass current boyfriend, Eric. I miss her, I miss her, I miss her. A tear fights its way out of a perfectly mascara'd duct. I look up and try to blink it away. *Holy shit.* You will not believe what I see midblink.

So, a chicken walks into the Merchandise Mart. There is no punch line; this is actually happening. As I watch the lady-size chicken put on her coat, I know this is a pivotal moment. If I let that chicken walk out the door, I fail at life.

I grab my camera and leap from the couch. *Cannonball!*

"Hi, ma'am? You look awesome. Could I get a picture with you? It's not every day you see a chicken in the Merchandise Mart."

One point for honesty.

She hesitates. I can't help but wonder if she's thinking about her integrity.

"Oh, well, sure. I guess."

"What's your favorite thing about wearing a chicken suit?" I ask, trying to learn more about her (other than the obvious fact that she makes a living imitating poultry).

"It's warm." Okay, then.

There's no denying who was responsible for this bizarre encounter. Shelly never failed to amuse me. She may not have dressed up like a chicken, but she had that same effect on me every day. Her presence alone made me smile. Apparently, she has figured out a way to amuse me once again. I laugh to myself as tears tiptoe down my cheeks. *Thanks, Shelly.*

My boyfriend, Eric, and I are heading to Fish Creek, Wisconsin, to stay with his childhood friends Mike and Nancy for the weekend. I'm secretly hoping to become a fiancée on this trip. Before you roll your eyes, please understand that I am usually *not* that type of girl. In fact, I'm usually the eye roller. Before I met Eric, I was a relationship whore. I was in them all the time, but I never really felt anything particularly deep for anyone. Sure, it was fun, and I definitely *liked* the dudes I dated, maybe even loved them, but the idea of marriage freaked me the hell out. Then Eric entered the picture, and everything just seemed *easy.* I know that's not romantic, and it's not

The only chicken I've ever met who can say, "cheese!" Or any other words.

the word most people would choose to describe their dream relationship, but in the words of the '80s rock group the Cars, I guess he's just what I needed. Eric is artsy (a photographer) and sweet (but not too sweet), and makes sure I eat more than Velveeta cheese dip for dinner. We've been together for almost two years and have recently decided to buy a place together. However, before we start condo shopping, Eric has to sell his loft, so unfortunately, the atrocious housing market is keeping me shackled to my shitbox apartment.

I call Court on the five-hour drive to Fish Creek and learn she's currently kicking my ass on this five friends, five photos thing. She started slow, but thanks to some ice fisherman, a dude on a scavenger hunt, and a lady footballer, she's well on her way to completing resolution number one. Let's hope I can find some friendly Wisconsinites to help me out.

Something feels strange when we arrive at the cabin. I'm in a house full of friends, yet none of them knew Shelly, not even Eric. I don't know Nancy and Mike all that well yet, and I don't want to worry Eric, so as we all sit by the fire and talk about our lives and laugh about ridiculous stories, I keep my sadness hidden. She died four years ago *today*. It feels like yesterday, but it also feels like a million years have passed since I've heard her voice . . . and her laugh. *Oh man, do I miss that snorty laugh.* The last coherent conversation I had with her was the day before she was scheduled for induced labor. At that point, the doctors had already diagnosed her with preeclampsia.

Here's your lesson for the day: Preeclampsia is a pregnancy condition characterized by hypertension and damage to the linings of the blood vessels of the brain, liver, lungs, and kidneys, which can lead to multiple organ failure, convulsions, coma, and death. But we weren't supposed to be concerned. It's common. Everyone seems to know somebody who has had preeclampsia (yet more often than not, none of these people can explain what it is, exactly).

We were in the midst of one of our usual high-energy phone calls, but this one was different. She was going to be a *mother* the next day.

"Ohmygod, I'll be fine," she said. "Wait until next weekend to come home so you can actually spend time with me and the baby."

I believed her—that she'd be fine—because that's what I'd always done. I'd never questioned anything she told me. In hindsight, I wish I had done some research about preeclampsia and what was happening to her. It wouldn't have changed the outcome, but I most definitely wouldn't have disregarded the severity of the situation like I did. We continued to gab, discussing the craziness of her being in charge of another little being for the next eighteen-plus years.

"Hold on a sec, I have to pay the cabbie," I interrupted.

Her response: "Oh, I'm so proud of you! Bree in the big city, paying cabbies!"

All I could do was laugh. "You're having a *baby* tomorrow, Shelly. I'm proud of *you*."

That's who she was. Always thinking about others. She did

indeed give birth to that beautiful baby, Hailey, the next day. However, my visit was much different than we had planned. Shelly held on for a week, in and out of consciousness, and then died due to complications from preeclampsia and HELLP syndrome (hemolytic anemia, elevated liver enzymes, low platelets) at almost the same exact hour she gifted Hailey to the world a week earlier.

I go to bed with Shelly on my mind—and that's just where she stays for the night.

Sunday night, we're wiped out like senior citizens after a trip to the mall. We nestle into pajama mode and sit in front of the fire. It's snowing, and I'm in a cabin surrounded by French onion dip and friends—not a care in the world. Except . . .

Oh shit. I still need one more photogenic friend! I can't fail the first week! Must. Leave. House.

"Uh, anyone want to grab a beer?" I ask. It's pretty clear that no one wants to grab a beer. Eric looks at me like I've just said I keep hamster feet in a jar under the bed.

"I need one more picture," I mouth to him.

After some fake enthusiasm from Eric, we all man up and put on some pants with zippers and pockets and stuff and shuffle down to a nearby pub.

The pub is not hopping (it's limping at best). I try to schmooze with the ponytailed bartender. He doesn't care. Soon, he heads over to the jukebox.

"Hey, whatcha playing?"

He turns and looks at me like, *Really?* Not in the inquisitive sense, but in the I-fucking-hate-you sense.

I quickly recover by complimenting his selection, "18 and Life" by Skid Row. Fortunately, I know the words. Unfortunately, I prove it.

He turns to walk away.

"Wait! Would you mind being in a picture with me? I'm visiting from out of town, and we really love this bar."

His eyes soften from kill to maim. And with that, I get five of

five. I'm exhilarated and exhausted at the same time. I decide to tell
Mike and Nancy the story—or at least the part of it that explains
why I just forced myself into a picture with the ponytailed bartender.
It's always strange to talk about what happened to Shelly. Nobody
knows how to react. I don't want hugs or sympathy. I don't need
people to tell me what a great friend I was to Shelly. (Okay, sometimes that's nice.) I just want people to know that there was once this
girl named Shelly who made everything in life just a bit brighter.

It's been a tough week for those of us who knew Shelly. It's an
anniversary I'd rather not commemorate. However, being a social
butterfly was an eye-opener. Dare I say I enjoyed it? After dedicat-
ing just a week to the way Shelly lived, I learn what she probably
always knew: Life's more fun when you open yourself up to the other
wandering souls out there.

Chapter 3:
going back to childhood

For me, the saddest aspect of my friendship with Shelly is that, like her, it never fully grew up. Yes, we were twenty-five when she died, but our friendship was miles from being fully mature. Most people grow out of the "let's make up a dance" phase around seventh grade. Most people eventually stop screeching songs by Aerosmith at the top of their lungs during car rides. Most people learn that Nutty Bars and Mountain Dew is not an acceptable lunch entrée after the age of twelve. We weren't most people. In fact, one of the last times I saw Shelly, we spent an hour throwing rocks at a giant spider in the middle of the street. It sounds crueler than it was. Neither of us was blessed with the ability to aim properly, so the spider won.

Her death has aged me. I'm not talking about the eye wrinkles or the sun-damaged skin above my upper lip (I like to call it my "summer stache"). It's aged me mentally. I live with more fear, more

pain, more guilt. When I want to return to those good old days, I
can't, because my partner in crime is gone. I want to be that carefree
kid again. Can I do it without a bubbly blonde by my side? We're
about to find out with this week's resolution: revisit activities we
haven't done since we were children.

Suit up, kids, we're going snowmobiling! It's our last full day in
Fish Creek, and Eric, Mike, and Nancy are generous enough to
spend it on gassy-smelling motor vehicles. It's important to note that
I have not mounted my ass on a snowmobile in over two decades.
And even then, the speed at which I drove it was comparable to that
of a legless turtle. Oh, and I think I cried.

Eric and Mike head over to the sketchy snowmobile rental
shack early in the morning to sign all the waivers (i.e., it's not their
fault if we die—or wake up in a bathtub without a spleen). Eric
calls me and describes the transaction by using words like "itchy"
and "tweaked out." Fabulous! Nancy and I roll in an hour later with
bellies full of eggs, bacon, brandy, and fear. *Am I going to die wearing
ill-fitting snow pants?*

I squeeze my head into a dirty rental helmet and jump on the
back of Eric's machine. (When I say "jump," I mean "struggle to
raise my leg above forty-five degrees.") As we start off on our snowy
expedition, I'm hurled three feet into the air with every bump. Helpful tip for the ladies: Snowmobiling might not seem like a sport,
but certain sporty undergarments are surprisingly necessary. I can't
decide whether I'm thrilled or terrified. I lean quite aggressively
toward terrified.

My fear melts away as we dart across the open countryside.
This is amazing. I feel free. I'm like one of the girls in the movies who
spreads her arms out and shuts her eyes and laughs like she's never
laughed before. Except I'm holding on for dear life, my eyes are
bugging out of my head, and I'm screaming a little. Nature makes
the mind work in ways you can't control—ways you don't *want* to
control. *Why haven't I done this since childhood? Why did that squiggly*

stomach excitement of the unknown get replaced with nerves and stress and fear? When did I become a boring adult?

As kids, we never thought we were invincible; we were just oblivious to tragedy. *What if something goes wrong?* didn't exist. It was all about *Can I go higher? Faster? Upside-down and backwards?* Broken bones, bruises, and cuts were merely admission to the fun house of childhood exploration. Shelly and I routinely jumped off the top of the twirly slide, for crissakes! We swung on a tattered rope that was badly tied to a piece of rotting wood! We waded in the town creek without shoes! There were no safety nets, no pads or cushions, no stupid water socks or whatever the hell you call them. Sure, we could've broken a leg or gotten tetanus, but most of the time, it was totally worth it.

I jolt back to the present as I see Nancy fly through the air; she skids across the rough ice of Green Bay. *Oh shit.* We stop and stare. Mike races over to her. No one knows what to do. It takes a little time for her to collect herself.

And then she looks at me through teary eyes and says, "That wasn't even that bad." Spoken like a true knee-scraped child. I can't help but think of one particular night that Shelly and I went Rollerblading in college. I should mention that Shelly was *not* a graceful person—not by a long shot. But that didn't stop her from trying to blade down the steepest hill in the town of Ames. If I remember correctly, there were two ways to stop on Rollerblades: (1) jumping into a patch of grass or (2) spilling onto the cement. Shelly chose option 2. It happened in slow motion. My mouth dropped as I saw her *slide* across the pavement. I quickly dove into a nearby patch of grass and rushed over to her.

"Are you okay?!" I was concerned but was also trying to hold in a bubble of laughter. I mean, seeing her fly down that hill with reckless abandon was kind of hilarious.

"I don't know!" She rolled over onto her side. She looked like a human Nike ad. She had a bloody swoosh-shaped scrape on her upper thigh. My eyes widened.

"Oh man. Is it really bad?" she asked.

"Um. It's not *good.*" And then she broke. She let out a laugh. This gave me permission to giggle. And before we knew it, tears were rolling down our faces.

"Now . . . how do we get you home?"

"Can you just skate a few inches in front of me so no one can see it? I'll hold on to your shoulders."

And that's just what we did. We looked like a humping couple on wheels all the way home. But oh man, did we laugh.

Back to Fish Creek. We slow down after Nancy's spill on the ice. We're all a little tired, a little sore, a little *old*. Eric and I head back to Chicago with new bruises on our bodies the next day, and I'm only minimally annoyed that I'm not wearing anything new and sparkly on my finger.

What's the thing you remember loving most when you were in elementary school? If you said "the Trapper Keeper," you're warm. If you said "all-school skating parties," you're a walking fireball, baby! I believe wholeheartedly that roller-skating is a childhood memory that everyone worth knowing shares. Some of us had fancy Dreamsicle skates; some of us had the medieval-torture-device skates that strapped on over your gym shoes. Some of us could be found cavorting on the rink every Friday night; some of us anxiously waited for that all-school skating party like it was Christmas. Some of us have romantic memories of the "moonlight skate" (Shelly); some of us hid in the video game shaped like a car until it was over (me). In fact, skating parties were a challenge for my friendship with Shelly. She wanted to skate in big lines of five to six people and hold hands and do tricks and shit. I wanted to whiz by those lines of people and ultimately crash into the wall at full speed. Or crash into my other friend, Emily, and chip her two front teeth. It was almost as if I were Shelly's secret boyfriend from across the tracks at skating parties. We'd arrive together and leave together, but we rarely socialized on the rink together. And we were both completely okay with that.

Obviously, the only way to fully revisit childhood is to revisit the skating rink. I decide this will be my second plunge back into childhood. Unsurprisingly, Court has the same exact plan.

"Is it cheating if we both do the same thing?" I ask.

"Um, Bree, this is *our* thing. We make up the rules. So no, it's not cheating. Skating *is* childhood. Duh," Court says. As always, the older sister makes everything seem so easy.

I email a bunch of my friends and invite them to join me. They all know what I'm up to with the project, but I'm still shocked at the number of friends who give up a Saturday night in Chicago to trek out to a roller-skating rink in the dead of winter. I envision myself in sparkly leg warmers and vintage hot pants, circling the rink. Then I realize I don't own any of those things and put on an old Hanson T-shirt.

When we finally arrive around ten o'clock, there's a line out the door. *Ugh, was this a bad idea?* As the door opens and closes, we catch glimpses of our fate.

"It looks like jail," Amy says.

This seems to be a popular opinion amongst my crew. However, as we pay our admission, *another* door opens. Heaven reveals itself. The flashing lights mesmerize us all, and I fully expect a unicorn to deliver our skates.

For the next couple hours, we gracelessly glide in circles. It's just like old times. Only now we're fatter and less agile, and when we fall it takes more than one person to help us up. Oh, and for the first time ever, I go on the moonlight skate with a boy!

After two hours of high-impact roller dancing, we head to a bar near my place. Just as I order the first round of Sex on the Beaches (if kids could drink, that would be their choice), my phone rings. I glance at the caller ID and get butterflies. Not the sexified kind, but the fate kind. It's Shelly's little sister, Kim.

Kim and I weren't close before Shelly died; *she* was the

annoying younger sister that Shelly and I were to Court. However, grief bonded Kim and me for life. No one else felt Shelly's death as sharply as the two of us. At the funeral, I knew I couldn't say anything to make it better, so instead I wrote her a little note that said: *Any time you get the urge to call your sister, call me.* We've emailed a lot since then, and I was honored to attend her extremely intimate wedding, but she'd never actually called me on the phone before tonight.

"Hi, Bree! Are you busy?"

"Kimmy! Not at all! I'm so happy to hear from you! What's up?"

"Well, I'm out at a bar, and I'm drunk."

"Yes, yes, me too. As we should be on a Saturday at one o'clock in the morning," I say.

"They just played 'Come On Eileen'! All I could think about was that time I got to go with you and Shelly to see Mike and Jeff's band play and how that fat Mexican posse circled around you girls on the dance floor!" She's laughing hysterically at this point. So am I. This was back when Shelly and I were both dating "hot" musicians. We were just out of high school and technically too young to get into the bars they played at, but if our moms came along with us, we were admitted. Gah, *so* dorky.

"Ohmygod! We were trapped in a cage of bouncy bellies!"

"And my mom and your mom just sat there laughing. You guys were practically getting molested on the dance floor!"

"I know! Why didn't they rescue us?"

"'Cuz it was too funny!" Kimmy laughs.

"Thank you for that. I appreciate your concern."

"Oh man, I really wish we could call Shelly right now," she says, coming down from her high.

"Me too, Kim. Me too. Have you had any more dreams about her lately?"

"Not lately. You?"

"All the time. It's weird," I confess.

"I wish I dreamed about her more," she says.

"It's a blessing and a curse."

"Okay, I should get back to my friends. Let's get together next time you come home. We can bitch about how unfair life is!"

"Deal," I say. I hang up. I exhale. This call means so much to me. I have the blog to thank for Kim's call. I know she's been following our progress, and just as this project is bringing Shelly back into my everyday life, it's bringing me back into Kim's everyday life.

Unfortunately, due to a nasty cold, Court had to cancel her skating party. Instead, she spent her day watching an old childhood favorite: *The Smurfs*. Even though we've done a pretty good job of reverting to our younger selves, I still feel like there's more fun to be had. I don't want this week to be over yet. Doing things that remind me of the time Shelly and I had together makes me feel like she's with me again. I like being stuck in this world. So on Sunday, I ask Eric to hit the batting cage with me. He's more than excited about this plan. And I'm more than excited that the nearest batting cage happens to be at a bar.

Back in elementary school, Shelly and I were teammates on the ferocious Li'l Demons. We were terrible. "Coach" (my dad) yelled at us constantly. We spent more time running bases as punishment

This was after Shelly's transformation from "Demno" to "Demon." And before my transition from palm tree pant wearing weirdo to spandex pant wearing weirdo.

for screwing around than we spent actually playing. My mom taught us to "dance in the dugout." Apparently, this phrase means to lead off on third base to distract the pitcher. It meant something very different to Shelly and me. Shelly cha-cha-cha'd on third base in the middle of a game. Mom was not amused. (What made this even funnier is that Shelly was the one girl on our team who got a misspelled jersey. Instead of Li'l Demons, her shirt said Li'l Demnos. So meant to be.)

When Eric and I arrive at the batting cage, I'm nervous. I'm a decent athlete, but when it comes to softball, my career ended in sixth grade when the neighboring elementary schools merged and girls who actually owned cleats hit the field. Ducking became my signature move. As I shuffle up to the plate, the first pitch flies at me. I have no time to think. *Crack.* I make contact! I expect to hear cheers and applause. To my dismay, I hear only beer belches. I suppose that's what you get for going to a batting cage in a bar. Regardless, it feels good to swing that bat again.

Eric and I hang around a little longer so he can take a turn at bat. We suck down a few beers, comment on how the place smells like puke, and head out with a renewed sense of childhood victory.

When you can truly strip yourself down to the spastic kid inside, you experience an overwhelming sense of freedom. No pressure, no worries—just pure fun. I can no longer rely on Shelly to bring that part of me to life; it's something I need to do for myself. And now I know I can. Farewell, childhood. It was wonderful to see you again.

Chapter 4:

giving and taking

Shelly was the type of friend who would gladly give you the shirt off her back. Me? Not so much. I'll take your shirt without asking, sell it at a garage sale years later, and keep the money. Yeah, that actually happened.

The summer before college, Shelly, Foxy, and I decided to have a garage sale to raise a little extra cash for school. I would love to sound cool and say we were raising money for our "beer fund," but I was the geek who didn't drink until I turned twenty-one (other than one crazy night with a bottle of Arbor Mist). It was more like a candy, pop, and VHS rental fund.

"Isn't this *mine?*" Shelly asked, holding up a County Seat polo shirt clearly marked with my initials on its $5 price tag. *Busted!* I had borrowed (i.e., taken) it from her four years prior and decided it was finally out of style.

"Uh, I'll give you half?" Of course Shelly just laughed it off, and I was $5 richer at the end of the day.

Much like "Mandy," Shelly gave without taking. I guess that makes me the Barry Manilow of our relationship. (If you don't know the song, look it up. You'll thank me.) Shelly didn't give a shit about her lack of funds. If she had $2 to her name, one of those dollars had my name on it, too. If I had $2, I spent it at Walgreens on Chuckles and a grape soda.

Think about it: When was the last time you treated a friend to lunch for no reason? Not because you owe her money or because you accidentally vomited in her purse, but because you think she's pretty swell. Chances are, it's been a while. So that's what Court and I are doing to celebrate the ladies of our lives this week. It'd be nice to say, "It's on me" at the end of every meal I share with a good friend, but I hover around the income bracket where finding a $5 bill in last season's coat is like winning the lottery, so it's not all that plausible. This resolution totally benefits from the "one week only" time frame. We've set a $15 limit because: (a) we are poor and (b) it will challenge us to give more than we take. If our lunch date orders a $10 burger and a Coke, we'll order the $3 side of tater tots. (Really, not a bad compromise, if you ask me.)

The office has been tolerable lately. Lars Larsen and I still don't see eye to eye (more like eye to giant esophagus), but we are starting to appreciate each other. He knows I don't fit in with the dude-dominated workplace, and I realize he doesn't really fit in anywhere, except at home with his wife and kids. Plus, we *do* agree on two things: Mountain Dew should be renamed "water," and candy is good. We're working on a very glamorous cookie dough project together. This requires us to sit in a tiny room and stare at each other until we come up with something halfway intelligent—*about cookie dough*. It's surprisingly exhausting, so sprinkling in lunch dates with a few of my favorite girls throughout the week is therapeutic. Unfortunately, other than the trashy chicken fingers I treat my friend

Megan to, Court and I both endure massive failure with the $15 spending limit. Our friends enjoy booze and sushi, not burgers and Coke. Between my lunch misadventures and donating $15 to the Preeclampsia Foundation due to a failed resolution, it's been a spendy week. But whatever—I'm sure I owed that money to Shelly anyway.

The weekend arrives, and Eric treats me to dinner in return for treating the ladies to lunch. He makes reservations at Sepia, a swanky restaurant I've been dying to try. This is not a common occurrence for us. In fact, we met each other at a "meatloaf-off" hosted at a mutual friend's house. I was there with my boyfriend at the time (Lazy Eye), and Eric was there on a blind date. I can't say there were explosively romantic sparks, because the timing wasn't quite right, but I had a feeling from the moment I saw him: I wanted to *know* Eric. There was definitely a physical attraction, but the old-school charm he showed his date was what impressed me most. A year later, when Lazy Eye and I crashed and burned, that mutual friend who hosted the party told me that Eric developed a crush that night of the meatloaf-off. Not on his blind date, as everyone had expected, but instead on me. Hello, flattery. He waited patiently for me to get over my breakup (and my make-outs with a few strangers), and our first date was six months later. I chose a Greek BYOB restaurant in my neighborhood. On the exterior, I thought it was a classy establishment, but once we took a step inside, it resembled what I imagine Pizza Hut's Greek brother would look like. Oh, and when Eric presented me with a nice bottle of red wine, we learned that the restaurant was not, in fact, BYOB. Even worse, it didn't have a bar, either. First date and no drinks to calm the jitters? Nightmare! When we walked away laughing after our greasy gyros, fries, and Cokes, I knew this one would be special.

Back to tonight. When we walk through the door at Sepia, we know we're not cool enough to be there—and it's confirmed within a matter of minutes.

"Uh, *how* do you spell that?" The hostess searches the reservation list, eyes darting impatiently.

"Oh. We have you down for *next* Saturday night," she says coldly.

Awesome. This is a case of the have-nots trying to be the haves and failing miserably. We eventually guilt her into seating us in the lounge next to all the fancy people eating their prefood food. Eric seems bothered, but I chalk that up to our less than ideal eating situation. We're sitting on ottomans made for miniature people, with enough table space to fit one fork and *maybe* an oyster cracker.

"Um. Wanna just go back to my place?" Eric says, a little defeated.

"Yes, I think my sweatpants miss me terribly."

I'm mildly disappointed that our faux-swank evening is coming to an early close. It's not often I put on a dress for dinner, so when I do, I expect big things. Like cheesecake. I know it's not Eric's fault, but a piece of me wants to throw a mini–temper tantrum in his direction. Every once in a while, I want to be treated like our relationship is new again. I want flowers (even though I don't like them) and "oh, you look so pretty tonight" and a bottle of wine . . . or two. Tonight I'm getting the "we've been dating for two years" special. No reservation, one cocktail, and a cold walk home.

This dress is cramping my style, so when Eric opens the door to his loft, I intend to hightail it to the corner where I keep all my crap stashed. (This is one of the many inconveniences of not living with the person you stay with every night. Another one? Using Irish Spring instead of fruity lady soaps). But before I can get to my crap stash, something stops me in my tracks. Ya know those flowers I mentioned not getting earlier? Yeah, better late than never. A vase of roses sits on the kitchen counter next to what appears to be a diamond ring–size jewelry box. *Holy. Shit.* Let's just say I would've been less surprised to see a couple pandas playing a game of Hungry Hippos sitting on that counter.

I look back at Eric in shock. I feel shaky all over.

"Go ahead, but read the card first," he says. I head toward the box, thinking to myself, *This just might be better than cheesecake.*

When I open the card, I see words, but my mind is mush. I can't focus until I get to the last line: "which is why I want you to be my wife."

"Will you marry me?" Eric is on his knee.

This is happening. How am I supposed to react? I'm supposed to cry, right? Jump up and down? Scream? I do none of these things.

"Of course. Yes. Yes. Yes." I hug him, still in disbelief. I mean, admittedly, I expected this to happen four other times by now, but that doesn't make it any less surreal. Eric slides the ring onto my finger.

"Eric, I love it! I love *you.*"

"I know you like vintage things; it's an antique."

"It's so gorgeous, so perfect!" Honestly, I haven't even really seen the ring on my finger yet. I'm too busy being crazy in the head. I look down and fall in love with a piece of jewelry for the first time in my life. It *is* so gorgeous. It *is* so perfect.

When I start forming full sentences again, it's time to make the obligatory "I'm engaaaaged!" phone calls. Of course, one of the first calls I'd always imagined myself making was to Shelly. The conversation we had after Brad proposed to her is one I'll never forget. I was living in Florida at the time and had only gotten the opportunity to meet Brad twice. I knew Shelly was smitten, but the girl was boy crazy, possibly even certifiably boy insane, so I didn't see marriage entering the picture quite so quickly.

"*Guess what, Bree!*"

"You're getting married," I joked.

"*Yes!*"

I laughed.

"No, really, I am," Shelly said.

"Stop it! What is it for real?"

"*Bree*, I'm pregnant!"

I believed her after that. "*Oh.* Wow. You *are* getting married!"

"Yes! Can you believe it?"

"Yes and no and I don't know, but ohmygod, Shelly, yay! Congratulations! Tell me everything. Ready, go!"

"Of course, but first, I have a question for you."

"Yeah . . . ?" I braced myself for the question every girl waits for her girlfriend to pop.

"Do you think I'm pretty?"

I burst into laughter. Shelly and I loved asking each other this question at inappropriate times. Usually, it was accompanied with the most hideous facial expression we could muster.

"No, honey. But you're really funny—actually, you're *kinda* funny."

"Okay, for real," Shelly laughed. "Will you be a bridesmaid in my wedding?"

"Absolutely not. I'm getting my nuts waxed that day." We were really not good at being sentimental. Shelly went on to tell me the details. She wasn't freaking out about the unplanned event of being pregnant; she was overflowing with happiness and love. And so was I.

I'm heartbroken that I don't get to return that call to Shelly, but a call to Court is exactly what I need.

"Ohmygod! My little sister is getting married!"

"So, you know you're going to be my maid of honor, right?"

"I'll be whatever you want me to be!"

This night is perfect. Well, except for the part where I flip out like a lunatic. I blame Jason Mraz. He's tonight's musical guest on *Saturday Night Live.* Shortly after my head is retrieved from the clouds, Mraz croons "I'm Yours." That's when it hits me. *This* was it. The proposal. It's over now. Some girls dream about the wedding day or the wedding dress, but not me. It's always been about the proposal, the *story.* I'd imagined so many different scenarios—a beach, a hot-air balloon, even a shitty tent in the middle of nowhere. Not one of my fantasies involved a quiet night at home in the dead of winter. Mraz continues to rub salt in my wounds, and tears start to flow. I want to stop them, but I can't.

I finally have the balls to face Eric. He looks broken. *I'm such an asshole.* I try to explain my feelings rationally, but because they are *irrational,* it's impossible.

"Why didn't you play any music?" I whine.

Do you hate me yet? In my defense, I'm a huge music lover. I think music elevates every situation in life. I also realize I sound like a seventh grader when I say this.

Eric grabs the remote. He should beat me with it. Instead, he rewinds the Jason Mraz performance and hits play.

He holds out his hand. I take it, shamefully. We dance, barefoot and happy, in the living room. *This* is why he's right for me. No. Drama. There are a lot of guys who would've given me my dream proposal, but *this* guy can take my shit and turn it into a romantic slow dance. *Now* this night is perfect.

I spend Sunday relishing my new title: fiancée. I catch myself gazing at the ring on my finger like the clichéd girlie-girls I've always despised. My hand looks like somebody else's hand. Someone with sophistication and class. I like it. The rest of the day is devoted to buying silly bridal magazines, browsing impossible diet plans, and, most important, filling out my bridesmaid roster. A lot of women agonize over this decision, but not me. I know precisely which ladies deserve costarring roles on my big day. I suppose I should discuss my thoughts with Eric first, since he's my partner in this wedding thing.

"So, I'm thinking I'll have seven girls on my side: Court, Amy, Foxy, Emily, Christine, Kerry, and your sister. Who are you thinking for your side?"

"Wait, we have to do this now?"

"Well, *yes,* I can't keep my girls in suspense. They need to know that they're in the wedding so we can start planning."

"Bree, we just got engaged yesterday."

"I *know,* but if we want to have a summer wedding, we have eight months, at the most, to plan."

(Blank stare from Eric.)

"Right? I mean, we can't have a winter wedding, and I don't believe in long engagements. That's like putting each other on layaway."

"Huh. I hadn't thought about that," he says.

Of course he hadn't. Guys never think about timing, right? Women get such a bad rap for rushing men into marriage. It's not that we're in a hurry to get married at all. We're in a hurry to start planning the best party of your life, dude. It's January now, so either we're rushing this shit or we're waiting *a year and a half.* Unacceptable.

"Plus, Kevin and Tara are getting married in October, so we have to space it out far enough that people won't have to travel back to back. So, I'm thinking August?"

"Okay, cool."

"Okay, cool" means *I'll worry about it later.*

"All right, early August it is. One more teeny question, and then I'll let you get back to your regularly scheduled program. What do we do about finding a minister-type person? Churchy people scare me."

"Didn't Kerry say something about being an ordained minister?"

Boom. A million points for Eric.

Kerry worked at a resort in Lake Tahoe a few years ago and got ordained just in case anyone ever needed a last-minute minister. Eric and I aren't exactly religious, and I don't think it's necessary to pretend we are for one of the most important days of our lives. When I'm walking down that aisle, scared shitless, I'd much rather have Kerry at the end of that road than some old dude who is probably silently judging me—and who will probably mispronounce my name. (Court's minister called her husband, Eric, "Erica" during their vows. Funny? Yes. Did the groom think so? Nope. Also, I get called "Brian" a lot.) We call Kerry on the spot, and she's recast from "bridesmaid" to "ordained minister."

I head to work the next day fully expecting to flash my ring and field questions, maybe even get an impromptu champagne party in my honor. And then I remember I work with dudes. Older, *straight* dudes. Uh, yeah, for the first half of the day, no one even notices. *Hmph.* Fortunately, Marie, the human resources woman I pal around with when I'm in need of some fellow ovaries, stops by for an afternoon chat and flips her shit when she sees my ring. Before I know it, we're jumping up and down and hugging and sorta screaming. This makes the surrounding menfolk squirm. All of them except one, that is. Lars Larsen hoists himself up from the other side of our cube wall and gives me a high five. Then he sits back down again. *Aw, Lars Larsen, you do care!*

Thursday night, I buy a bottle of wine and prepare to call my bridesmaids-to-be. I tell Eric that he can take all the time he needs to choose his groomsmen, but that I am far too antsy to wait any longer. I try to compare it to the excitement of a football draft; he doesn't buy it. I call Emily first. I've known her since first grade. She still lives back in my hometown with her husband and their three kids. Growing up, we both had hideous bang perms, we played volleyball, we took dance classes, and we even took French class when everyone else took Spanish. Contrary to the "opposites attract" vibe I had going on with Shelly, Em and I were bonded by everything we had in common. After high school, we lost touch, like a lot of high school friends tend to do. But

Emily and I were like two peas in a dork pod. Sadly, the bags on our heads were an improvement over the situation going on underneath said bags.

whenever we ran into each other, we'd bounce right back again. When Shelly was so taken away so suddenly, I stopped taking Em's friendship for granted, and we've been in touch regularly ever since. She's the only friend I have, other than Court, who can connect me to my childhood memories. It's good to hear her voice and even better to hear her say, "Ohmygod, yes!"

Next up? Eric's younger sister, Holly. I totally lucked out in the future-sister-in-law department. (Actually, I lucked out in the whole entire family-in-law department.) Holly is one of the most delightful people I've ever met. She lives in the South and says things like "y'all." We have a great relationship, and I love her to pieces, but I've never called her on the phone. I breathe a sigh of relief when I get to ask her via voicemail. Is that tacky? Probably. But so am I most of the time.

The rest of the calls will be smooth sailing because I talk to Amy, Foxy, and Christine every day. That's why I'm flabbergasted when Christine says, "Wait, when is it?" It's almost like the joke I played on Shelly, but I can tell Christine is serious, mostly because she doesn't mention a nut wax. *Is she really going to say she's busy?*

"Pretty sure it'll be early August. Will that work for you?"

"Well, I've been waiting for a good time to tell you, but . . . I'm pregnant!"

"What! Oh my g—"

"And I'm due in early August." *Wah-wah.*

"Oh, Christine, I'm so happy for you! I mean, it sucks that you can't carry a bunch of dumb flowers and follow me around all day and wipe sweat off my brow and stuff, but I suppose creating another human being is fun, too."

"Stop it! I'm so sad about the timing. I was afraid this would happen! Can I be an absentee bridesmaid and still do all the stuff leading up to the wedding?"

"Are you kidding? You better be or I'll hate that baby forever."

Even after a few hiccups, everything feels like it's happening exactly the way it should. Well, everything except that one call I didn't get to make. That one friend I didn't get to ask. That one squeal of excitement I didn't get to hear.

I'd give *anything*, including the $5 I earned from selling that County Seat polo shirt, to bring Shelly back. Even if just for that *one* day.

Chapter 5:
flowers from gaylord beans

It's Valentine's week! Okay, okay, I'm aware that this so-called *holiday* is pathetic and commercialized, but I'd be lying if I said it's not a big deal to me. I've come a long way, my friends. Valentine's Day was terrifying for a nerdling like me in junior high. Carnation-grams were to blame. Here's how it worked: You'd sneak up to the intimidating student-council booth before the morning bell rang, and for just a dollar, you got to write a secret love letter to your crush. Said love letter was attached to a carnation and was delivered in the middle of class—in front of *everyone*. I never liked any sort of attention in front of large groups of people, yet I still fantasized about getting a carnation-gram from Jay—or Mike. Even one from crusty-hands Rick would've sufficed. It didn't happen. I did, however, get *one* carnation every year—from an admirer named Gaylord Beans. I always knew it was Shelly, but it made me smile anyway. Sometimes it only takes one person to make you feel special.

With that lesson in mind, Court and I promise to "woo" strangers the same way Gaylord Beans wooed me in junior high. Romance is not the objective; that would be creepy. We just want to go out of our way to make someone else's day a little more special.

Hmmm . . . how exactly do I go about finding my inner Gaylord without the help of the student council? Starbucks, perhaps?

Everyone seems to love the idea of random acts of kindness. We've seen it for years in movies, commercials, and books. But how many of us have actually done it in real life? I think we all have the desire to do nice things for people, whether we know them or not, but sometimes it's just too inconvenient—or in this case, too awkward. I'm not giving myself the option to wimp out today. I shall pounce on a random stranger at Starbucks and pay for his/her coffee, no matter how uncomfortable it makes me.

If everything goes the way I'd like it to go, this will be as easy as whispering to the barista, "I'll pay for mine and for whatever he/she is having." The stranger will then thank me and tell me I'm the prettiest girl in the world, and then we'll both go on with our days feeling lucky to have met each other that morning. But we all know that things rarely go the way I'd like them to go. (See also: engagement.)

When the door squeaks open behind me, I pivot to face my random valentine. This is what my heart does: *thud*. A total suit-douche just walked in. This is the kind of guy who probably kicks ladybugs and shoots finger guns at his grandmother instead of saying hello. I don't want to buy this guy a coffee. Fortunately, there's a second cash register, and a young kid wanders in shortly after Suit-douche. I hover while he orders his drink. *How do I do this without seeming like a creeper? What if he thinks I'm hitting on him? Um . . . uh . . . well . . . cannonball!*

I paw at his elbow. Even I would be scared of me if I were him. "Excuse me. Are you a student?"

"Uh, yeah." I see that familiar *oh shit, it's Greenpeace* look in his eye.

"Your coffee is my treat. I feel like being nice today." I don't sound nearly that suave, of course. I stutter. My voice makes weird inflections. My right hip clenches involuntarily. Regardless of my social shortcomings, his face lights up.

"Thanks so much! I'll totally buy someone else a coffee later."

It worked! I just may have made a stranger's day. And perhaps he'll go make someone else's day. This must be what people mean when they say, "Pay it forward." I just thought it was a crappy Haley Joel Osment movie.

"He can start with me, right now," Suit-douche jokes in that way that's not really a joke at all. *No, Suit-douche, no he can't.* I escape before my high is deflated.

I feel like a million bucks after making someone else feel like a million bucks. (Or an energetic four bucks if we're going to get technical.) I'm reminded of how Shelly treated people to things all the time. She rarely left the school cafeteria without buying some poor sap a boatload of soggy french fries or a burrito if they forgot lunch money. It was *so annoying* to me because I thought they were taking advantage of her. (Only *I* was allowed to do that.) Now I see things in a different light. Giving to others is also giving a gift to yourself. It just feels nice.

Lars Larsen pounces on me like a bucket of fried chicken when I float into the office. (Ouch.) There's an "emergency" on one of our projects, so I have no time to bask in my generous glory. Instead, I'm forced to think of legal ways to say that a product is made with "real chocolate" when real chocolate is, in fact, *not* an actual ingredient. Kill me now.

When my day becomes too intensely futile and Lars Larsen becomes too . . . Lars Larsen-y, I sneak off to CVS for some afternoon beauty-aisle therapy. There's nothing a cheap eye cream or sketchy hair-removal kit can't fix. On my way to obtaining happiness in a jar, something in the seasonal aisle commands my attention. (I usually avoid this aisle because it contains my guiltiest pleasures:

mellowcreme pumpkins at Halloween, Reese's peanut butter eggs at Easter, and amazing gimmicks like the Shake Weight year-round.) I come face-to-face with the most fantastic puppy valentines I've ever laid eyes on. In fact, the puppies have their eyes on me, too, because the valentines are lenticular-3-D style. (In other words, the image moves depending on the angle from which you see it.) Apparently, valentines have become quite advanced since the days of "I choo-choo-choose you." I grab a pack of puppy cards, as well as something made by L'Oréal, and go back to the office ready to change the world, one chocolate fib at a time.

Later that evening, I collapse onto my couch with the box of 3-D cards. It's a variety pack, so I take the time to decide which card to give to whom, just like I did back in elementary school. I always set aside the best one of the bunch to give to my crush. Unlike the other girls in class, who would personally deliver their valentines with a flirty smile, I would wait until the boy wasn't in sight. I'd drop it into the homemade receptacle on the corner of his desk and would skedaddle before he returned. (These receptacles were shoeboxes wrapped in cheap tissue paper and random findings from our moms' emergency sewing kits.) I would then sneak looks in his direction the rest of the day, wondering whether or not the valentine had made him fall madly in love with me.

The giddiness I feel makes me realize there's still something fun about filling out these miniature cards. Especially when you write sentimental things on them like, "Hope you get laid, valentine!" or, "Congrats on another year of no STDs! (except HPV, we all have that)."

After I address one to each of my girlfriends, I make eye contact with the leftover puppies on the cards. They need homes, too! The spirit of Gaylord Beans speaks to me. It takes *one* person to make you feel special. *Well, what am I waiting for? There are a lot of Chicagoans out there who probably need a little love right now.*

I spend the next half hour making my own version of a carnation-gram—sans the carnation. I clip a dollar to each of the remaining fifteen cards and write the message: "Hi, Stranger. Buy a pop on me." I scribble our blog address on the back, just in case anyone wants say hi after his or her midday Shasta.

Saturday marks my last Valentine's Day as a nonwife. *This. Is. Huge.* I'm saying goodbye to an era! Once I entered my twenties (and exited my lengthy awkward stage), Valentine's Day was filled with surprises like pounds of Laffy Taffy on my desk, chocolates by the front door of my apartment, or impromptu drunk nights with the girls when those other surprises were absent. There was always an element of *what might happen?* But when you're a wife? Meh. Everyone knows wives don't get exciting gifts. Wives get heart-shaped pendants from JCPenney or gift certificates to Applebee's. The guy has already won you; unpredictability is over.

I want to make sure my one and only Valentine's Day as a fiancée is special because, let's face it, after my engagement meltdown, I need to take my fantasies into my own hands. (Wow, why do I suddenly sound *super* high maintenance?) I call Kerry and ask her if the hotel she works at has any rooms available. We can't really afford to go on a weekend trip, so why not fake it? Kerry hooks us up, and I start counting down the days to romance. Fortunately, I have the project to keep me occupied until then.

I make four valentine drops on my way to work the next day: one in an ATM slot, one on my train seat, one on a sample table at Argo Tea, and one on a random bench inside the Mart. After sharing the usual morning grumbles with Lars Larsen, I call Court. She's been quiet this week, and I want to make sure she hasn't jumped ship.

"Ugh. I feel like shit. I'm a snot factory," she sniffs.

"Sorry, that sucks. Probably not a good time to ask how this week's resolution is going?"

"Oh geez, sorry for being MIA I'm trying, I swear. I bought a bunch of those boxes of candy hearts and am going to hand them out to strangers, kinda like you're doing with the valentines. I'll write our blog address on them, too. Promise I'll do it soon."

"How cool would it be if we actually hear back from someone who finds one of 'em? I mean, I know that's not what this is about, but it would be awesome."

"Yeah, homeless people love blogs."

"Good point."

Court's grumpiness fades into obscurity after she successfully litters boxes of conversation hearts around the waiting room at the chiropractic office before her appointment. The possibility of bringing a smile to a face we don't even know is strangely intoxicating.

I meet Amy for a celebratory drinking lunch at Hub51 on Wednesday afternoon. It's the first chance we've gotten to have "alone time" since my engagement, and Hub51 serves champagne out of cans, so it's an obvious decision. Within my circle of girlfriends, Amy is the one I'm closest to. I have a sneaking suspicion she was brought into my life to take Shelly's place. I know it's a morbid thought, but I also know Shelly would never have left me stranded without a social blonde by my side.

I met Amy in January of 2002 (my first year living away from Shelly) while we were both studying at Miami Ad School in South Beach. (Yep, *that* South Beach.) I shouldn't even have been at that school. It was for well-to-do kids, not for the girl who had worked since the age of fifteen and still had zero dollars to her name. I was able to enroll only because I was blessed with an aunt and uncle (Georgia and Gary) who believe in me as much as they believe in their own daughter, so they gave me a free place to live and helped me out with finances. It's never easy to accept handouts from loved ones, but sometimes you just gotta say yes when someone offers you a ride—so you're not driving a clunker for the rest of your life.

It took a lot of lady balls to walk through that school's pastel-colored doors. I was already timid about meeting new people in general, especially without Shelly by my side, but the new people I'd meet in this program were international beauties and American fancypants types from the East and West coasts. Being from Iowa,

Amy and I pose for an "engagement photo" wherever we go. This one was taken in Lake Tahoe.

I was not accustomed to this kiss-kiss culture. *Do I kiss one cheek or both? Do I make lip-to-cheek contact? Are kissy noises necessary?* Little did I know there was a girl named Amy from Indiana who felt the same way. After a few quarters of not having any classes together (she was an art director; I was a writer), we were partnered in an advanced-level course. We got stuck with a lazy third wheel whom no one else wanted to work with. On presentation day, Amy and I planned to get to school early so we could practice before class. (I had met my match when it came to obsessive rehearsal before any performance.) We did not include the third wheel in our practice session because she hadn't done a goddamn thing—and we really weren't even expecting her to show up that day. Unfortunately, we spotted her the minute I pulled up to school in my aunt's SUV. Amy dove into the back seat and hid on the floor. "Can we just work from here?" So that's what we did. We practiced our entire presentation on the floor of a Honda Passport on the side of the road in South Beach. This was the moment I knew we'd be friends for life.

My friendship with Amy is similar in many ways to my friendship with Shelly. Her personality is infectious. Her laugh is adorably deafening. And just like Shelly's, her acceptance makes me feel like the coolest chick in town. I find it odd that the two of them never met. When Shelly visited me in Miami, Amy was out of town. When Shelly visited me in Minneapolis, Amy was out of town. Even when Shelly unexpectedly stopped by our place in Chicago while passing through, yep, you guessed it—Amy was out of town. It's almost as if the two of them were never supposed to be part of my life at the same time. Like the earth would implode if I had two of my favorite crazy, blond spazzes in one place.

Okay, so now you know Amy. Back to Hub51. When I arrive, Amy is already waiting. She leaps up from the table.

"Baby!" she cries. Eight people turn in my direction. Her voice carries, to say the least.

"Hi, baby!"

Terms of endearment make me want to vomit, but Amy and I once had a conversation about how it's totally hot when *some* guys call you baby (mostly just rock stars) and totally repulsive when other guys do. So we've been calling each other baby ever since.

As soon as the obligatory engagement updates are out of the way (which aren't many at this point), the upcoming "holiday" inspires us to rehash the Great Valentine's Day Debacle of 2003.

Amy and I had just moved to Minneapolis together for Miami Ad School's "quarter away" program. The flagship school is in Miami, but there are twelve other locations worldwide. Yes, you heard me right: We chose *Minneapolis* over locations like Budapest, London, Berlin, Hamburg, and San Francisco. Have you ever heard of anyone more tragically Midwestern? We probably should've been diagnosed with BCD (Batshit Crazy Disorder). It was four degrees the day we moved in. Amy's boyfriend, Xavier, still lived in Miami, and I was dating David, a classmate who had also moved to Minneapolis that quarter. David was unlike anyone else I had ever dated. He had movie star good looks, he was cocky, and he was *rich*. He appreciated my Midwestern modesty, and I had a hard-on for his pretentious Southern charm. The fact that he had money led Amy and me to ponder various gift scenarios over vodka cranberry cocktails while we sat on our high-class furniture (beanbag chairs and futon).

"Bree, you are dating someone who can buy diamonds and shit. This is going to be huge! What if you get a tennis bracelet?"

"I don't even know what that is, but I can't wait! And you, my dear, will probably get a surprise knock on the door. I can totally see Xavier showing up here with a dozen roses and a box of kinky lovemaking stuff."

When Valentine's Day arrived, our expectations had climbed pathetically high. We were correct about one thing: Amy got that surprise knock on the door. It was Papa John's delivering a heart-shaped sausage pizza. Not the kind of sausage she was expecting. (I apologize if that was kind of gross.)

We still held out hope for my diamond-encrusted future. David arrived that night, impeccably dressed, with a gift and a bottle of wine. The wrapped present was substantially larger than a jewelry box, but from what I'd seen on the hit TV show's Australian special, "The Facts of Life Down Under", opals can get pretty freaking big. When it was time to exchange gifts, we retired to my makeshift bedroom—a storage closet with a flannel sheet strung up for privacy.

"I know you probably aren't expecting this, but I've been dying to give it to you. You're going to love it," he said. He was beaming.

"Aw, *thank you*. Sorry I couldn't afford to get you much," I said as I handed him the gift I had "made" for him. It was dozens of miniature boxes of Nerds candy with a silly haiku about our relationship written on each box. Sure, it took a lot of time, brainpower, and 5-7-5 math, but I knew it would pale in comparison with whatever gloriousness I was about to open.

"This is awesome!" He looked genuinely touched. He had probably never received something so homemade in his life. "Okay, now open mine."

I untied the bow and began undressing the package with care; I didn't want to spill thousands of dollars all over the floor. As the gift revealed itself, I saw my own version of a sausage pizza staring back at me.

"Oh. The *Back to the Future* trilogy. I totally did not expect this!" Well, at least I didn't have to fake my surprise.

"You mentioned how much you love that movie! And I know you like sentimental things, so I just knew it would be perfect."

I had to give him credit. He was right. I had been raised to adore the simpler things in life. A poem, a photo, a mix tape—these are the types of things that melt my heart. But what excited me most about *David* was that he was nothing like me. And to be honest, I was intrigued by the thought of being someone different when I was around him. Receiving a gift that was so totally *Bree* bummed me out, I'm sorry to confess. I wanted to know what it was like to be in his world. I wanted to be the material girl. Dammit, I guess he loved me for who I really was. *Poor me.*

The next day, Amy and I made it a Valentine's Day to remember as we chugged wine, ate cold sausage pizza, and watched *Back to the Future* for six hours straight. We discovered that our love for each other was truly a love worth celebrating.

And as we sip our second round of canned champagne on a Wednesday afternoon, we agree that it still is.

My first friend was a girl named Julie. You know that party-all-the-time mullet I mentioned earlier? She was the only other person (besides Joe Dirt) who had it. Our moms were friends through the Walcott Jaycee-ettes. The Jaycee-ettes is an organization that probably does a lot of nice things for Walcott, but mostly I remember that they made good homemade vegetable soup and cheeseballs. Oh, and they built one helluva haunted house, complete with *actual* rats. Julie and I were friends out of convenience—we were the same age, so our moms signed us up for all the same things: dance classes, gymnastics, French horn lessons, et cetera. I actually saw my first

Little girls' dance class or old timey hookers? Why are the two so similar?
Also, this bang permed mulletry was borderline child abuse.

live penis with Julie when we played a corrupt game of I'll-show-
you-mine-if-you-show-me-yours with one of Julie's brother's friends.
We did not show him ours. Instead, we ran away screaming. Sadly,
that's one of the few crystal-clear memories I've retained from such a
young age. Julie was a year behind me in school, but we were decent
friends all the way through high school. Email was relatively new
when I left for college, so we lost touch.

Why am I telling you all this? Well, because after more than *ten
years* of silence, I get a Facebook message from Julie. It starts like this:

"So I had a chiropractic appointment yesterday . . . "

Holy shit! She found one of Court's boxes of candy with our
blog address written on it. Her curiosity was piqued, so she went to
the site and was delighted to learn that my sister and I were responsible. What are the odds? I'd tell you if I could do math, but I can't.

And the Funfetti frosting on the cake? She knew and loved Shelly to pieces; they were cheerleaders together in high school. Thanks to Court's candy-coated message, I've been reunited with the first girl to see me pee in a sandbox. This is a small, amazing world we live in.

By Saturday night, I'm feeling so much love from this week's resolution that I can't imagine how this holiday could get any better. When Eric and I check into the hotel for our Valentine's Day celebration, I feel like we're indulging in a scandalous rendezvous. I like it. I like it even more when we discover that we've been upgraded to a *suite*, complete with animal-print robes in the closet and rose petals on the bed. Kerry makes sexy magic happen.

"I feel like we're starring in a very white Boyz II Men video," I observe. This is a compliment, by the way. I *love* that shit.

Knock, knock.

I look at Eric, positive we're going to get busted for squatting in someone else's love den. Once you've had a taste of caviar, it's hard to go back to Goldfish.

"Compliments of Kerry Craig," the doorman says as he prances past us with a tray of chocolate-covered strawberries, champagne, and cheese.

"Well, I guess Kerry made it easy on me," Eric says.

My friends always do, I think to myself.

"I did make a dinner reservation for the French restaurant a couple blocks away. We have about twenty minutes before we need to leave."

Aw, he did plan a surprise. "Let's have an appetizer first," I say, picking up one of the strawberries from the tray.

"Champagne, Madame?" Eric presents the bottle to me like a pretentious waiter.

"Eff yeah, Monsieur."

We get to dinner shortly after enjoying our in-room appetizer. The food is deliciously fancy, as is the decor, but knowing what we have waiting for us back at the hotel motivates us to skip dessert. It's not every day that you get to come home to rose petals on the bed. If that *did* happen every day, we probably would've known to remove said rose petals before sexy time. The white sheets are stained with a new "rosy" motif when we get up in the morning.

"Eric, what if Kerry gets in trouble! This is so embarrassing."

"You think this is the first time that's ever happened?"

"Maybe?"

"I doubt people stop in the middle of sex to clean flowers off the bed."

"Okay, but if Kerry asks, I'm telling her you made the mess while I was in the shower."

"That doesn't even make sense."

"I know."

"I love you," he says, ignoring the stupidity of what I've just said.

"*Aw.*" I give Eric and kiss and stop obsessing.

We pack up our stuff and return to our normal Chicago life. All in all, not a bad way to spend my last nonwife Valentine's Day.

On Sunday night, I check the blog one last time to see if we've gotten any late-breaking comments from the people we've accidentally admired.

Oooooh. *One new comment.*

I click on it, bracing myself for spam-filled disappointment. But it's not spam. It's quite the opposite.

Bertha Mason says:

> Well, hello there to you too stranger. I had the pleasure
> of finding your card on the train seat. It made my night.
> I don't drink pop but had a lovely cup of coffee on you. It
> was so sweet and I am glad that lovely people like you are
> out there in the world.

This is the kind of shit that happens in movies, not in real life! I feel ashamed. I don't deserve this compliment. I'm *not* a lovely person. I am simply trying to emulate a lovely person I lost. *Wait. Does that make me lovely?* The phone interrupts my thoughts.

"Ohmygod, how hilarious is Bertha!" Court laughs.

"Bertha rules," I say. I'm slightly confused as to the hilarity of the comment, but whatever.

"Wait, you clicked on her name, right?"

"Um . . . no. Why?"

"Do it, right now," she says.

I click the link. *Oh. Sweet. Jesus.*

Bertha is a man who dresses as a woman, and teaches cooking classes in Chicago. *What?* I know. When a cross-dressing Martha Stewart finds your valentine on a train seat, you know damn well that someone is pulling all the strings to make life as entertaining as possible. More important, though, Bertha's message was straight from the heart, and it touched *my* heart, deeply.

This week is proof that Valentine's Day isn't about candy and cards; it's about reminding people that they're special. Even if you don't know them.

Chapter 6:
breakups and shake-ups

I attempted murder in August of 1997. Hilarious, right? Well, kinda.
This crime of passion occurred the summer before Shelly and I went
off to become grown-ups at Iowa State. We had already purchased
argyle sweaters and had our futon on layaway, but we just couldn't
leave town without one last hurrah. We called up our friend Cindy,
and the three of us came up with a plan. We'd kick the night off
with dinner at Lone Star Steakhouse, and then we'd hit the Mississippi Valley Fair to stalk the boys we liked. There was only one
problem. The boy *I* liked at the time was my ex-boyfriend Mike, and
he had a new flame cooking. This flame was in a different league—
like, if we were playing little league, she was already on varsity, probably giving hand jobs in the dugout. She didn't work in the juniors
department at Younkers; she worked the *perfume counter.* I was still
wearing the wretched teenybopper fragrance Exclamation at the
time. So yeah, I wasn't well versed in sophisticated lady scents. The

three of us knew this chick might throw a wrench into our stalking plans, but we were confident Mike would not miss the fair. *No one* missed the fair! To get an idea of what this sacred event was like to a young Iowan, imagine if everyone you knew, and everyone you ever hoped to meet, went to the mall on the same exact day. But wait, it was even better than that—because *this* mall served corn dogs and people could roam around shirtless!

But shortly before I met the girls at Lone Star, I found out that Mike was indeed skipping the fair to go on an adult date that didn't involve saltwater taffy and the Scrambler. *Oh, the nerve!* Shelly and Cindy listened as I expressed my gut-wrenching pain through slurps of fountain Mountain Dew.

"You guys, I thought we were going to get married! And now he's moved on just like that? What am I gonna do now? I can't go off to college and be *single!*" In hindsight, that last thought is very, very funny.

When I stopped blubbering, we brainstormed ways I could prove my superiority over Perfume Bitch. And then, as the waitress delivered our pre-dinner pail of peanuts, the answer came to us: Mike was allergic to peanuts! Oh yeah, we totally went there. We unanimously agreed that it would be a brilliant idea to dump peanuts all over the front porch of Mike's parents' house so he wouldn't be able to get to the door when he returned home from his date. And if he tried, *he could die!* We each stuffed a pail of peanuts under our shirt, and Shelly chauffeured our crazy asses across town. We slowly pulled up to the curb, gangster style. (Well, as gangster as you can get while blasting Pat Benatar.)

"You guys? What happens if someone's home?" I was still in good standing with Mike's parents. Also, it was light outside. These two factors had not really dawned upon me until the moment I held three pails of peanuts twelve feet from the front door. I was a *nice* girl. I didn't drink or smoke or even cuss (yet), but taking advantage of someone else's life-threatening allergy was something I felt pretty good about. WTF?

"Go! No one will see you. Hurry!" Shelly pushed me out the

This is a wonderful example of Photoshop before Photoshop. My head is literally cut and pasted from another photo . . . onto a hotdog.

door while Cindy crouched down in the back seat. I darted across the lawn as if I were competing for the shuttle run championship title in gym class. (Did anyone actually qualify for the Presidential Fitness Award? That shit was hard! Plus, someone *always* farted during the sit-ups.) I scattered one full pail of peanuts before I panicked. I scrambled back to the car with the other two still in hand, and Shelly sped off (she went thirty-seven mph in a thirty-five-mph zone). We cranked up the tunes, rolled down the windows, and yelled rebellious things like, "Guys suck!" all the way to the fair. I'm not sure this accomplishment proved my superiority over Perfume Bitch, but it did prove that I could be one crazy motherfucker when I had the support of my friends.

    This all went down before cell phones existed, so Mike politely waited until the next day to call and chew me out.

    "Bree, you could've killed me."

    "Oh, whatever. That's what you get for skipping the fair."

    "Seriously, Bree. Like, I could've died. You would've gone to jail."

    That's when it became a *little* less funny. But come on,

people—you would've done the same thing, right? *Right?* Believe it
or not, Mike has since forgiven me, and we laugh about that night
often. That's just the way "love" worked when we were young and
ridiculous. Relationships made us all pint-size felons. We'd call a
crush just to hear his voice, and then hang up. We'd scrawl his name
in heart shapes all over our notebooks, walls, and *skin*. We'd even
drive by his house slowly. Multiple times. While playing Animo-
tion's wonderfully sketchy hit song, "Obsession." And this was when
things were going *well*.

Through all the mad crushes and broken hearts, Shelly and I
had each other's back. If a guy were to break up with me by saying
. . . oh, I don't know . . . something like, "School's out and you're
dismissed!" Shelly was there to call him a jag-off. (That happened.) If
some loser were to break up with Shelly the minute the class crotch
showed interest in his underdeveloped private parts, I was there
to watch *Can't Buy Me Love* with her three nights in a row. (That
happened.) And if another girl swooped in and burgled one of our
boyfriends? Oh, girl . . . you better watch out. That's when things got
serious. And by serious, I mean dirty looks, prank phone calls, and
possibly a rumor or two about said chick's bathing habits. (That *may*
have happened. Okay, yeah, that definitely happened.)

One thing you never imagine you'll have to think about is how
you'll react when your best friend's *widower* starts dating someone
else. When I first heard about Michelle, less than a year after Shelly
died, a prank phone call didn't really seem appropriate. Though
believe me, I considered it. Twenty-two times. I loathed the idea of
this girl as soon as I heard she existed. In the email Shelly's parents
wrote to me to break the news, they had nothing but shiny, happy
things to say about Michelle. Which is why I immediately emailed
Kim to get the real dirt. Kim tried to stay positive, but once I let
my disapproval fly, she joined me in Bitchville. For years, Shelly
and I shut the door on Kim's face whenever she tried to crash our
party of two, but for the first time in our lives, Kim and I banded

together to shut someone *else* out. This cheap Shelly knockoff needed to back the hell up.

Clearly, I was not looking forward to meeting Shelly's stand-in, but I knew I couldn't avoid it forever. I had learned from John that, like Shelly, Michelle was a teacher. Like Shelly, Michelle was friendly and outgoing. And like Shelly, Michelle was madly in love with Brad and Hailey. But all similarities aside, Michelle was most certainly *not* Shelly—and I was determined to make sure she was aware of that the day I met her at a Preeclampsia Foundation fundraiser a little more than a year after Shelly died.

"Bree!" Michelle greeted me. Her radiant smile attacked me without warning. I looked at Court and Kim for support, half scared, half amused. "I'm Michelle. I've been looking forward to meeting you!"

Um, okay. So I guess that was nice, I thought to myself. *Bitch.* "Hi."

"We just loved your last postcard," she gushed.

Wait. What? It took me a minute to register what she was saying, but then I realized Brad must've shown Michelle the postcards I sent to Hailey.

After Shelly died, I wanted so badly to be present in Hailey's life, but I just didn't know how to be. It's a six-hour drive between Chicago and Iowa Falls, so a weekly visit wasn't going to be possible. In addition to the distance, Brad and I were barely more than strangers, *shy* strangers, so I knew phone conversations would be torture for both of us. I should probably mention that even though we weren't close friends, Brad had definitely won me over. After the funeral, he pulled me aside and asked if I was okay, even though he was a man who had just gotten married, had a baby, and lost his wife all within six months. Now *that's* a good guy. After a lot of thought about how to keep in touch with Hailey and Brad, I had a lightbulb moment. During that time, I traveled to commercial shoots all over the world, so I decided to buy a postcard for Hailey wherever I happened to fly. I would fill each one out with a story about Shelly and then would send it to Hailey in the mail. Kids love mail! So I hoped that Hailey would love *me* by association. But even more than that, I hoped that one day she'd have a shoebox full of stories on pretty "paper" to help her understand how freaking rad her mom was.

When I realized that I now had a new pair of eyes on these postcards, *Michelle's* eyes, I felt exposed.

"Oh, great. Thanks," I said. I proceeded to look around like I had somewhere else to be and walked away. This was my attempt at being rude; aggression is not my strong suit. I didn't need her to like me. I knew she was only temporary.

Brad and Michelle married a year later, in 2007. So yeah, I guess you could say Michelle was promoted to full-time. I was not consulted about this decision. Kim had no choice but to support her new "family member." I still kept my distance. I wasn't sure how to feel, but I wasn't thrilled. I didn't blame Brad for moving on; I blamed *her*. She was stealing Shelly's life like it was just another pail of peanuts at Lone Star.

I saw Michelle a few times after that at various fundraisers and holidays, but it wasn't until the time I saw her in 2008 that she bitch-slapped me. Well, not physically, but it was just as shocking. This was the day I heard Hailey's sweet voice chirp, "Mom!" for the first time. The irrational side of my brain expected to turn around and see the ghost of Shelly with her arms outstretched (like that scene in *Ghost* where Molly and Sam finally get to embrace! *Ditto, Sam*). But no, that didn't happen. Hailey was running straight for Michelle. *Fuck.* It was time to admit defeat in the struggle to shut this girl out. When I saw the way they looked at each other—the way they loved each other—I realized that as much as I wanted Shelly's shoes to remain empty forever, Hailey needed a hand to hold on to. She needed that touch. She needed a mom who wasn't buried beneath the ground. The story had been rewritten right before my eyes. Hailey was no longer a girl without a mom; she was a girl with *two* moms.

I still send postcards to Hailey when I visit places, and Michelle still reads them. And now I appreciate her for it. I love that *she* wants to get to know Shelly and in turn will make sure Hailey learns about her, too. Brad and Michelle help Hailey distinguish between her two motherly figures by referring to Michelle as Mom and Shelly as Mommy. Brad told me that after a recent visit to the cemetery, Hailey told her friend "that's where my mommy lives." *Heart. Explosion.* I often wonder how Hailey will feel about Shelly as she grows up. Will she know where her spazzy attitude comes from? Will she give Shelly credit for her adorable chicken legs? Will she remember those few sacred moments she spent in Shelly's arms? I can only hope the answer is yes.

Court and I decide to introduce a new concept on the blog this week: audience participation. The notion itself comes from a blog reader who seems to have a lot more confidence in what we're doing than we ourselves have. Steve Strom, a guy Shelly and I hung out with in high school, suggests that perhaps our blog readers might like to choose a resolution for us to complete. The thought of letting others control our actions is frightening, but it also seems like a good way to raise a few bucks for the Preeclampsia Foundation. We will be *whores* for the project.

We ask for resolution suggestions at $5 a pop. We let everyone know we will select a winner by the end of the week. All proceeds, of course, will go to the Preeclampsia Foundation. *Shit, do we even have an audience?*

We do. We raise $100 in six days. That might sound like small potatoes to some of you go-getters, but to Court and me it's a big-ass yam. Raising money is not our forte. Back in the day, we used our *own* Girl Scout Cookies. People like Sally Sallerson and Walker Winters were our best customers.

When it's time to make the decision, we sort through all kinds of suggestions, from dares to good deeds, but one in particular makes it a no-brainer. It's not the idea; it's the person behind the idea: a woman named Jane who lost her own adult daughter to preeclampsia. Sometimes I forget that there are over seventy thousand Shellys out there each year. More specifically, many of these women are soon-to-be moms who, due to preeclampsia, never actually get to experience motherhood. Jane sends us an email explaining that she found out about our project through a link on the Preeclampsia Foundation message board. *Oh shit, how did our hijinks end up on the Preeclampsia Foundation message board? Does this mean we have to stop being inappropriate? Do I have to stop using the f-word?* Court says no. As always, her permission is all I need to feel like I'm doing the right thing.

Out of curiosity, I click the link Jane referenced to see who pimped our project to the preeclampsia community. Shelly's dad is the culprit. A proud dad will *always* be a proud dad. Jane's suggestion isn't as straightforward as prior resolutions, but who the hell cares? We're doing it. Court and I figure out some logistics and then post the week's winner, along with our new resolution: "Give kids a camera for the day and post his/her favorite photo on the blog. Jump into the mindset of a child and guess the inspiration behind each picture before asking the child the real answer."

At first glance, this photo exploration doesn't exactly fit into what we've set out to do with fifty2resolutions. But if you look deeper, it totally qualifies. Court and I are not kid people. Kids are scary and oftentimes have mysteriously sticky hands. This resolution brings us out of our world and into theirs. More specifically, it brings us into the world of Hailey, our living version of Shelly.

I email Michelle to get her permission to feature Hailey as one of my amateur photographers. She's ecstatic to help. *Bitch.* Okay, not really.

By the end of the week, we learn the following:

1. Children shoot whatever is at eye level.

2. What is at a child's eye level is usually a butt or crotch.

3. We adore the simplicity of a child's imagination.

4. It's fun to raise money for something we care so much about.

And most important:

5. We have an audience of more than just our friends and family. The preeclampsia community is listening.

Chapter 7:
small-town heart

"I love you." This is the most terrifying combination of words in the English language. I've *always* feared those words. Fortunately for me, Shelly didn't. In elementary school, when she said, "I love you!" I gave her my best scratch 'n' sniff sticker out of my sticker book. (*Mmm . . . smells like purple!*) In junior high, when she said, "I love you!" I gave her my last chicken finger. And in high school, when she said, "I love you!" I made her a mix tape, of course, chock-full of Candlebox, Green Day, and Kenny Rogers. That's just how we rolled. But something came over me during that final conversation we had on the phone, the day before her hell began. *I* was the one who blurted out, "I love you!"

"I love you too, B-dawg!" Shelly said. Her voice boomed with joy, yet something felt terribly wrong to me. I wanted to suck those words right back into my mouth. I shuddered as I hung up the phone. *Why did I say that? Something bad is going to happen.* And shortly after, it did.

I know I'm not the only person with an eerie story linked to the sudden admission of love. A dear friend of mine was the driver in a fatal car accident in high school. Just minutes before the car spun out of control on a patch of ice, his best friend (the passenger) looked at him and said, "I love you." The passenger was then thrown violently from the car and was killed instantly. It makes me wonder: Can we subconsciously sense when death is in the air? Is that sudden urge to say "I love you" a curse? I'll never know the answer to these questions, but I do know that I need to get over this fear. It's not healthy to avoid the one expression invented solely for the people we care about most.

Like me (and Paula Abdul), Court is also a cold-hearted snake. Our version of "I love you, man!" is usually something like "You're the cat's pajamas!" or "We're the awesomest-smartest-most-fun-best sisters in the world!" (Depending on how many cocktails we've had.) For sisters who love each other more than anything, we've only said "I love you" to each other a handful of times. Because of this common phobia, it's easy for us to agree that our next resolution should be to speak from the heart. We're going to tell people what they mean to us. And ya know what? We're gonna use the shit out of that "l-word."

After all this bitching and moaning, you might be thinking that Court and I grew up in a frigid, unloving household. Wrong-o. You couldn't be further from the truth. Court and I were constantly shown affection, whether it was with hugs, kisses, or that little lick of the thumb your mom does when you have Pop Rocks all over your face in public. Court and I learned to *show* love; we didn't really pick up the importance of *saying* it. Carrying on this way felt completely normal until boyfriends entered the picture.

"Have you guys said 'I love you' yet?" This was a common conversation topic at the lunch table in the sixth grade. The question was never directed at me, of course, because boys were still repulsed by whatever wild animal may've been living in my mullet at the time. But secretly, I couldn't wait to exchange those words

The adult velour shirts and adorable match-y dresses screamed love, so we didn't have to.

with a boy one day. Shelly had already experienced her first kiss, at the top of the twirly slide, and had been "in love" multiple times before my chance came.

Finally, when I was in the seventh grade, Alex Milton took pity on me and asked if I'd "go" with him. And *go* we did. We strolled to science together; I escorted him to his bus stop after school; we even went to the mall together . . . once. And then he dumped me. I can still recall the way that brace-faced stallion cruised up to my locker that morning, sans eye contact. "Bree, I don't think this is working. We just don't get to talk on the phone as much as I'd like to." My ears already burned from the bitter air I'd trekked through to get to school that day, but those two sentences made them sting in a way they'd never stung before. My forced smile quivered. "Okay. Um. That's fine. Boy, it sure is cold out there." I tried my best to act like it wasn't a big deal. But inside, I felt cartoon javelins puncturing my heart. (I was a big Nintendo fan.) Shelly made me feel better by calling Alex a "butt-munch." She was determined to coach me into a new boy's skinny, prepubescent arms as quickly as possible.

"How about Nick Bolten?" she asked.

"He's going out with that eighth grader who looks like Kelly Kapowski from *Saved by the Bell*. She has boobs and everything," I replied.

"Hank's cute," she said, trying to move her eyebrows up and down in a suggestive way, but really just looking crazy.

"He smells weird. Like bacon," I said.

"You're right. He totally does. Ummmm. Sam?"

"He calls me fuzzy."

"What!" Shelly's brainstorm came to a screeching (literally) halt.

"Because of my hairy arms," I explained. In his defense, they really were hairy. I often performed a trick where I'd rub my arms and magically create tons of tiny arm-hair knots in a matter of seconds. Wow, why didn't boys like me?

"He's dumb anyway," Shelly said, trying to make me feel better. "Have you noticed he wears pink jeans? He says his mom washed 'em with a load of reds. But he wears them *every day*. It's gross. So let's see . . . who else is there?"

"Forget it, Shelly. I don't even want a boyfriend. I want to focus on school right now," I said. I had heard that on TV once, and it seemed completely respectable.

"Cool. But I'll think of someone. Just give me some time," she said.

I wanted to share Shelly's enthusiasm, but I couldn't. For Shelly, this stuff came easy. She could just smile at a boy and he'd be carrying her Trapper Keeper to U.S. History faster than you can say "Appomattox Court House." It took me *twelve years* to snag some positive male attention. Alex Milton really did a number on me. In the two blissful weeks we spent together, I never got a kiss. We never had a song (though we did consider FireHouse's "Love of a Lifetime"). And I definitely never heard *the* three words. The fact that I actually loved Skittles more than I loved Alex was beside the point. I was destroyed. I didn't know it then, but it shaped the way I'd handle boys and men for the rest of my life. From that day on, I shut down emotionally when it came to relationships. I wasn't about to get my heart crushed again. Even now, Eric gets my hugs, my kisses, and an occasional saliva-thumb face swipe, but I rarely voice my affection.

I always hoped that the right guy would be able to change my ways, but now I know better than that. I need to change myself.

Monday night, I walk over to Amy's apartment to play the *Bachelor* drinking game. You know the rules, right? Just put on your favorite pair of sweatpants and mock the desperate women vying for love on TV by taking a swig of vodka infused with whatever you have in the fridge whenever one of the women says words from a predetermined list of clichés. You're guaranteed to get a buzz within the first twenty minutes. In between gulps, I can't help but notice that in *Bachelor*-speak, "I love you" seems to have the same meaning as "I like your belt" or "maybe there's something here, but I'd like to bang you first to find out." Watching two hours of this insanity makes me thankful that the Sisters Housley aren't so quick with the schmoopy love stuff. But alas, I must proceed with the resolution. I make a call on my walk home from Amy's. Who's the lucky recipient, you ask? Well, the voice that greets me is eerily similar to my own.

"Hello?"

"Um, Courtnee?"

"Yeeeeah?" I can sense that she already knows exactly why I'm calling. And maybe it's a cop-out, since she's privy to this week's resolution, but whatever—it feels absolutely right.

"This is totally gonna be weird, and maybe I'm cheating, but um—"

"*Dammit!* I wanted to call you for my first one!" she interrupts.

I laugh but shift quickly (yet not smoothly) back into serious mode. "Ahem. You're . . . uh . . . important to me because I don't know what I'd do without you. Like, I can't even believe you're doing this resolution thing with me. For real. You're the best. I love you." *Phew. I said it.* I feel like a whiter, more clothed Toni Braxton. *("You mean the woooorld to me. . . . You are my eeeeverything. . . .")* In an effort to dial down the cheese, I switch gears. "So, you know how I won the essay contest in the Miss Walcott Day Queen Pageant back in high school?"

Court laughs. "Of course! That was major."

"Well . . . I won because they asked who my hero was, and I said it was you."

"No way! That's so sweet and kind of hilarious."

(Pause due to the fact that this kind of conversation is foreign to us.)

"Well . . . aaanyhoo. Glad I got to tell you that," I say. "I always wanted to."

"I'm still pissed you beat me to it! I was going to call *you* tonight, but I wanted to wait until *The Bachelor* was over." Court wouldn't be caught dead watching that filth, but she knows I'm a passionate viewer/mocker of the show.

"Well, no rules. Right?" I ask.

"Good point. Let's at least pretend I called you. Or should I actually hang up and call you back right now for authenticity's sake?"

"No, I think we're good."

"Um . . . okay." As Court begins, her tone morphs into a valley girl's. It's a strange and highly entertaining vocal transformation that tells me she's just as uncomfortable expressing these feelings to me as I was expressing them to her. "I love you because you're Bree and you've always been Bree. No matter what."

I'm speechless. Not a good reaction to have on the phone, so I force myself to say something. Anything. "Wow. Thanks." Not exactly profound, or keeping with the spirit of speaking from the heart, so I force myself to try again. "That really might be the nicest thing anyone has ever said to me."

"Oh, and I also love you because you referenced the Miss Walcott Day Queen Pageant," she adds.

After we hang up, her words sit with me. There were a lot of years when "being Bree" meant being weird or nerdy—a bit of an outcast, if you will. Court was always the cool sister. She wore floral bodysuits and Guess jeans. I wore penny loafers—with athletic socks. Finding out that Court approved of me during all those years makes me proud of that odd little lunatic I was—and proud of the lunatic I still am.

Later, as I blog about everything that occurred between me and Court, I question whether or not it's pathetic that she and I need something like a silly resolution to open up to each other. Is there something wrong with us? Are we a dysfunctional family? Should we be more like Stephanie and D.J. Tanner? (They hugged at the end of almost every episode of *Full House*.) But the more I think about it, the more those overly sweet sister relationships seem fabricated. I'm much happier being a Housley sister. We're the real deal. And now, thanks to this project, I feel closer to Court than I've ever felt before.

As a copywriter, I spend most of my days writing commercial scripts that are later picked apart and criticized—mercilessly—when I present them. Currently, all my coworkers in the creative department are men. They're nice and all, but still, they are *men*. After a bad meeting where I get raked, reraked, and set aflame over the proverbial coals, these guys would never think to offer support in the form of a sarcastic eye roll or a sassy one-liner like my old workmate Jeanine used to do.

I met Jeanine at my first *real* job in advertising. It was in the fall of 2003 (soon after I finished Miami Ad School) and I was, once again, living with Georgia and Gary in Fort Lauderdale. It wasn't my dream job yet, but I was getting paid a nickel more than I made as a sandwich artist at Subway during high school. (That nickel was sooo worth not having to ask truck drivers, "Foot-long or six-inch?")

I was treated *horribly* at that job and worked with a lot of grumpy hacks. I was already a fish out of water, but these people made sure I felt like a guppy. A guppy with learning disabilities. Oh, and the devil? He was my boss. Enter Jeanine. She was the devil's hot secretary. For the first month I worked there, I watched her bust through the door every morning with her cocky attitude. She didn't seem like someone who would care about the quiet copywriter in the corner. But one fateful day, after the devil had taken a massive dump on my work, Jeanine approached my desk, where I was whimpering all over my carefully constructed PB&J.

"Girl, you just gotta act like you don't give a shit. He'll respect you more," Jeanine said. If there truly were a sassy black friend in every woman's life, Jeanine would be mine (even though she isn't black). Our friendship was born. She helped me find my inner bitch, and the rest of my days at that agency were much less infuriating. We've both moved on, and our lives are quite different, but she affected me in a way few people have. And that's exactly what I tell her the night I call her on the phone to let her know how she saved me. By the time I hang up, I'm beaming. This talking-to-people-about-my-feelings thing is really panning out.

Can you imagine dreading the thought of attending a fundraiser created in honor of your dead best friend? Welcome to my reality. This Saturday is the annual Trivia Night that Shelly's family organizes in my hometown. I know it's wrong to dread it, but I do. I dread every one of them, even though I love the cause that brings everyone together.

I've survived four years of these events. On top of my naturally high level of social anxiety, I can't shake the self-conscious worry that sucker-punches my ass right before each one. People stare at me. They see *her* when they look at me. We were rarely seen without each other in this town for such a long time, it's almost as if we were a two-for-one deal. I never walked alone to the town grocery (which also sold snow tires and adult OshKosh B'Gosh overalls) to charge Tombstone pizza and Big League Chew to my mom's account. Shelly was always my accomplice. And that was the most *normal* thing we did in that town.

Please take a minute to envision a marching band of two strutting down your sidewalk at 3:00 PM on a Saturday. That was us. While other thirteen-year-old girls were probably braiding each other's hair or riding ponies, Shelly pranced with her piccolo (the pretty-girl instrument) and I galumphed along next to her with my tuba (the fat-boy instrument). This musical combination worked out surprisingly well because the piccolo usually got the melody line and I would just *ooompa ooompa* along next to her. I think it's safe to say we were the only piccolo-tuba duo in the entire country. Eat your heart out, John Philip Sousa.

But I digress. Back to Trivia Night . . .

This Trivia Fundraiser, which should be a celebration of my best friend's life, just makes me uncomfortable. Does that make me selfish? Perhaps. But while being Shelly's best friend was an honor, I never asked for the attention she craved, and to get it now, after her death—*because* of her death—feels wrong. After the first fundraising event, four years ago, Court felt my pain without my even saying a word. "I hate the way everyone looks at you," she said. "I wish I could protect you from it all." That's something only a sister can say—something only a sister can understand.

On top of all the anxiety about the upcoming fundraiser, we've got a wedding to plan! Eric and I will be looking at two possible venues while we're in Iowa: (1) the fantastically well-worn ballroom I've always dreamed of getting married in and (2) the other one. These two venues are drastically different. It's like comparing apples to . . . Cheetos.

Option 1, the Walcott Coliseum, is a mere two blocks from my childhood home. I've fantasized about Electric Sliding the night away with my future husband there since I was a little girl. However, on the off chance that Eric isn't impressed with a location that also offers weekly bingo and the town fish fry, I ask Court for other suggestions. Ya know, *just in case.* She finds option 2, the Renwick Mansion, online. From the pictures on the website, it looks like the classiest, most romantic place ever. Gross.

The Trivia Night Fundraiser will be taking place at the Coliseum, so we check out the Renwick Mansion on Saturday morning, prior to the event. Within minutes of our arrival, Eric's in love—with more than just me, unfortunately. Yes, the view of the Mississippi River is picturesque. Yes, the antique architecture is brilliant. Yes, the cost of renting the entire building is ridiculously low. But where's the beer-drenched dance floor? Where are the metal chairs and card tables? Where's the freaking *stage?* They're at the Coliseum, that's where. As we drive away from the mansion, I see a twinkle in Eric's eye.

That twinkle is extinguished the moment Eric, Court, Court's Eric, and I set foot in the Coliseum for Trivia Night. Yes, Court and I both chose men named Eric. We call them E1 (Court's Eric) and E2 (mine) to avoid confusion.

"Isn't this just so perfect?" I ask dreamily as we head to our assigned table.

"Um, sure, yeah. It's nice." Eric says, trying to convince himself. Shelly's dad interrupts Eric's faux enthusiasm by giving me a giant bear hug.

"Bree! Hi, sweetie!"

"Hi, John! How are ya?" I say, genuinely happy to see him. He pulls away and smiles warmly, and just for a moment, I know he sees his daughter in me.

"We've been reading the blog. What a fun idea," John says to Court and me.

"Aw, thanks. That really means a lot to us," I reply.

"So, is this the lucky guy?" he asks, extending his hand to Eric.

"It's great to meet you," Eric says.

Shelly's mom, Brenda, approaches. She has tears in her eyes. She always seems to have tears in her eyes. Her hug is cold but friendly.

"Shelly sure would've loved to meet you," Brenda says to Eric.

Eric pauses for a moment, unsure of how to respond. "I would've loved to meet her, too," he says.

(Silence.)

I smile awkwardly.

Court pipes up, "Brenda, did Bree tell you Eric is a photographer?"

I offer a thank-you to Court with my eyes as the conversation shifts to a lighter, less death-y subject. Shortly after, the guys walk ahead and Court stays right by my side as I say hi to the people I know I have to say hi to. Amid all the small talk and laughter, the unspoken sadness is deafening. The only person that would ever bring me into a room with all of these friends and acquaintances is no longer able to make the party.

"So, what do you think of this place? Pretty great, right?" I say as I sit next to Eric. "I mean, the mansion is nice, but *this* is where you have a balls-out, crazy-ass, once-in-a-lifetime party."

"Yes, I can see that sort of ambience here. But I do still think we should consider the mansion. Was there anything you didn't like about it?"

"The only thing I didn't like about it is that it's not the Coliseum." I'm sorta joking, sorta not. I have to admit, the Renwick Mansion is gorgeous, but the charmingly unrefined ambience of the Coliseum owns my heart. I'm a small-town girl. I like Crock-Pot dinners and hope to wear jeans with an elastic waistband by the time I'm forty. That's what the Coliseum is about. Dad's company Christmas parties were held here. Court's wedding reception was here. Shelly's wedding reception was here. There's so much history in these shabby-non-chic walls.

"All right, let's think about it some more tonight, and if you still feel this way tomorrow morning, we'll book the Coliseum."

"Okay, deal." I was hoping that once Eric saw the Coliseum, it would be an easy decision. Clearly, that's not the case.

The trivia questions start flowing, so we drop the subject. Just as our team slides into first place, Brenda taps me on the shoulder. She crouches down behind my chair and whispers, "Ya know, I just remembered that day we moved you girls up to college. What a disaster!" I'm fairly sure Brenda did not "just remember" this story; she wants to reminisce with me about her daughter. I quickly get over my ridiculous insecurities. I realize at this moment that perhaps I need these events and conversations just as much as Shelly's family does. It's a way for us all to hold on to her for a little bit longer.

"Ohmygod, yes!" I laugh. "That's when the nickname Stupid John was born," I say. Shelly's dad, John, made a few small mistakes while trying to loft the beds in our dorm room. Shelly and I got a kick out of shaking our heads with fake disappointment while saying, "Oh, *stupid John.*" It was one of those moments where parents started to seem like real people—like friends you can tease and laugh with, instead of authority figures you fear. Much to John's dismay, the nickname Stupid John stuck. I still call him that to this day. (Don't worry; he gets a kick out of it. I promise.)

"Oh, that was too funny," Brenda says. "And then when we came to move you guys out, you and Shelly had practically glued that Berber rug to the floor. Your mom and I were on our knees scraping for four hours."

"The pube rug!" I yell, as if I have a mild case of Tourette's. "That's what we called it, because whenever someone got up from sitting on the floor, they'd have questionable-looking hairs on their pants."

"You girls. You were trouble," she says, with a smile on her face.

"Only when I was with Shelly. Otherwise, I was an angel."

Brenda and I spend the rest of the evening sharing "Shelly stories," just the two of us.

Oh, and we win second place in trivia . . . no thanks to me. We donate our winnings back to the Preeclampsia Foundation and say our goodbyes to Shelly's family. On our way out the door, I make one final attempt at selling Eric on the Coliseum.

"We've never won anything at the mansion. This is probably a sign."

"A sign that the Coliseum means *second place?*"

Touché.

Eric and I pack up the car to drive back to Chicago Sunday morning, still undecided as to where our wedding will take place. We have a three-hour drive in front of us, during which we'll get to discuss our decision in more detail.

On our way out of town, I ask Eric to stop at the cemetery. I usually sneak down there alone so nobody worries about my mental health, but I was so busy this weekend, I didn't have time.

"Do you mind staying in the car?" I ask.

Eric nods. "Go ahead."

I dart across the snow, stopping abruptly when I see her name. After four years, it still shocks me to see SHELLY BRIDGEWATER on a headstone. My knees hit the cold, wet ground. I dig them in farther to make it hurt just a little more. My voice shakes as I whisper, "Hi, Shelly. I miss you." I notice an Iowa State University flag waving proudly in the wind next to some fresh flowers; a banner with the word FRIEND decorates them. I brought her nothing, but I don't feel bad about it. That's how our friendship always worked. Other people brought her stuff. Other people tried to win her love. I gave her only myself—and *maybe* a chicken finger—and that was more than enough. Tears fill my eyes. There's something I want to say to her. Something I haven't said to her since the last time I got to hear her bubbly voice.

"I owe so much of who I am to you. I love you. I love you so much. I wish I had told you that more."

Tears spill down my cheeks.

"I just hope you knew. You knew, right?" I sit quietly as if I expect an answer. "Well, it's true. And I miss you every single day." I kiss my fingertips and touch her ice-cold headstone. I don't want to leave her yet. I close my eyes and silently wait until I'm ready to say goodbye.

I slump back to the car, tears smeared down my face. Eric says nothing. He asks no questions. He doesn't even give me sympathetic eyes. He just treats me like a normal girl who has lost her best friend, and squeezes my knee.

We drive slowly out of the cemetery. As I see her gravesite drifting farther and farther away in the rearview mirror, I'm reminded of why this week's resolution is so crucial. Time may separate you. Time may change you. Time may run out. If someone makes you happy, tell them. Say. The. Words.

"I love you, Eric," I say, rather suddenly. It's liberating to say those three words so freely. It's as if I'm finally letting go of all those years of insecurity and fear that someone wouldn't love me back.

"I love you, too."

By opening my heart, I opened my eyes. The decision seems much clearer now. It's not about having the wedding I always dreamed of as a little girl. It's about marrying the guy of my dreams and having a wedding that is uniquely ours.

"Let's get married at the mansion," I say. "It's perfect."

And I mean that from the bottom of my outspoken heart.

Chapter 8:
dress shopping

Well, with just five months left until the wedding day, it's time to think about the dress. *The* dress. Ugh. While I excel at the crucial things in life, like jaywalking and candy consumption, fashion is not my forte. I've always depended on others to help dress me. In fact, Christine isn't just one of my favorite advertising art director partners of all time; she also art-directs *me*. I met Christine when I interviewed for my first job in Chicago. I sent my portfolio to the agency on a whim after one of my hellish days of working with the devil in Fort Lauderdale. It was the only portfolio I sent, and I made it by hand, so it was one of a kind. It was also a bit sloppy and was mailed in the middle of a meltdown, so I was shocked when I got a call from them—and even more shocked when they offered to fly me in for an interview. I was freaking ecstatic when I met Christine, the partner I'd be working with if I got the gig. I moved to Chicago for the job a few months later, and Christine and I became insta-friends. What she lacks in spelling skills, she makes up for in fashion sense—which makes us the perfect art director/copywriter team.

I've only known Christine for five years, but she can point to something completely ridiculous in a store window and say, "That looks like you." And after a quick trip to the dressing room, she's always right. Why don't I know what looks like me?

In the days of high school dances and college dating, Shelly played that role. I'm not sure she had Christine's artful eye, but she definitely had the enthusiasm.

Shelly and I double-dated to almost every school dance from ninth grade all the way to senior prom. Remember your very first boy-girl dance? I'm not talking about the un–sexually charged "mixers" that the elementary schools hosted. Those were child's play. I'm talking about the first time you wore baby's breath in your hair and received a corsage made of withered carnations. (If you're a guy, it was the first time you got pricked in the chest with a boutonniere and told the other guys you were going to "get some.")

The theme of our first dance was "Unforgettable," and it totally lived up to its name. Ninth grade was a good year for me personally. Doctor Allard had gained control of my wonky dental situation, and I was no longer under the impression that it was normal to shower biweekly. Boys even called me on the phone that year. Plus, I had a pair of Girbaud jeans. (I'm pretty sure these two statements are not independent of each other.) Shelly had been going with an eighth grader all year but abruptly broke up with him just days before the big event, probably because eighth graders were not allowed to come to this dance. Most of the girls bought poufy getups at Maurice's or Gigi. Or if you were kinda slutty, you bought your dress at Wet Seal. I bought *mine* in the women's department at Montgomery Ward. I was much more sophisticated than everyone else. Our wardrobe selections were so important that Shelly and I held a dress rehearsal in her bedroom a week before

Shelly, Emily and I pre-partying at the truckstop. Luckily, we didn't get mistaken for Lot Lizards. (See also: truckstop hookers.)

the big night. I wouldn't have dreamed of showing up in a gown she hadn't approved. And she needed my approval on her latest dance moves. Both were, of course, slam dunks. Home runs? No, no . . . quadruple jump-spins with jazz hands!

Shelly, Emily, and I met at the truck stop restaurant and feasted on fine foods like taco pizza and fried cauliflower dipped in cheese before the dance. (What's funny about this is that we were absolutely not doing this to be funny.) Our dates, Chris, Randy, and Hank, met us at the dance. In hindsight, they were terrible dates. No free dinner? WTF? These guys were NOT gonna "get some." As we stepped into the community center, Pepsi-fueled butterflies slam-danced in our bellies. It was a wonderland of shiny burgundy and sea foam.

"Hi, you look nice," Hank (my date) said.

"Thanks, I like your silk shirt," I replied.

"Thanks."

Then we both just stood there, stiffly looking around at anything except each other. *Oh god, do I have pizza stuck in my braces? Is he going to ask me to dance? Do I smell bacon?* Before I could answer any of the questions in my head, he walked away. Those were the only words we said to each other all night. You might think my night was ruined by this dude's lack of attention, but au contraire! Before I knew it, Shelly grabbed my hand and led me to a wild pack of adolescent animals. Boys, girls, friends, enemies, all of us jumped up and down in unison to Cypress Hill's "Insane in the Membrane." It was a night of pure fun and innocence. We enjoyed just being kids—on the verge of becoming adults. Shelly spent the night at my house that evening. We stayed up until 2:00 AM and gabbed nonstop about the whole night. "Did you see Tammy's slutty dress?" "How cute is Nick?" "I think Heather and Tim might've frenched in the coat closet." "Hank never danced with me." "Randy farted during 'Unchained Melody.'" "I think I like Rob." "I think I like Tim. Or Mike. Or Nick." "Ohmygod, that was so much fun."

There was another celebration—maybe even *more* important than school dances—that Shelly and I dressed our best for every year. What was this magical event? Well, Walcott Day, of course! It was sorta like the Mississippi Valley Fair, but without the carnies, corn dogs, and award-winning farm animals. To a young Walcottian, it was the biggest social event of the year. People (boys) came from as far away as Bettendorf, a neighboring city that actually had stoplights! Plus, there were sno-cones.

Can you imagine our excitement when we were finally eligible to reign over this fabulous day? Shelly and I entered the Miss Walcott Day Queen Pageant in the summer of 1995, when we were sixteen years old. Court competed in the pageant a few years earlier, and our pal Missy actually *won* it the year before. It was a very prestigious honor. Well, if you consider wearing a crown whilst sitting on a pile of hay on a parade float an honor. And we *totally* did.

Finding the perfect dress for a school dance was challenging, but selecting a dress fit for a queen? Whoa. In situations of this magnitude, you walked right past Montgomery Ward and splurged at Younkers (but *not* at the perfume counter).

There were five girls in the running, and we competed against each other in four categories: (1) the interview; (2) the essay; (3) congeniality; and (4) button sales. Even though we were competitors, Shelly and I went door-to-door together to sell our crappy buttons. If someone actually answered the door, Shelly gabbed with him or her for what seemed like hours while I ate whatever food they offered to us. At the end of a grueling six-hour shift, we walked away having sold three buttons between the two of us. I think we raised $7 total.

Finally, the day arrived. We got ready at my house a few hours before the pageant. We tried our best to look fashionable yet sophisticated. As I cracked open my white L'eggs nylons, I complimented Shelly on her tan librarian-style flats. We appeared as if we'd just stepped out of the pages of *Small Town Pageant Weekly*. If that magazine existed. (Thank god it doesn't.)

Shelly and I were nervous, but, as with most things in our lives, we had each other. Our dads proudly escorted us up onto that fateful plywood stage, where Shelly and I stood in front of tens of people. (The population of Walcott was just over 1,500; 1,475 of them were already at the beer tent.)

First, they announced the winner of the interview portion: "Bree Housley."

Then they announced the winner of Miss Congeniality: "Shelly Warner."

Then they announced the winner of the essay portion: "Bree Housley."

And the winner is: "Amanda Keppy."

SCANDAL! OUTRAGE! OTHER DRAMATIC WORDS! Amanda Keppy had sold the most buttons, so Amanda Keppy got the coveted crown. She wasn't even *from* Walcott. Talk about needing to tighten up on immigration laws. We learned an important lesson that day: You don't have to be nice or smart to win, you just have to make more

When you're a celebrity in Walcott, you get to sit on a throne . . . made of a hay bail and/or cardboard. (Shelly, me, the Walcott imposter, and Missy in the parade.)

money than everyone else. My mom told me they changed the rules after that year, but she probably just said that to make me feel better.

Shelly and I had been rejected in front of the whole town (*plus* the boys from Bettendorf). As Amanda marched across the stage to claim her victory, Shelly nudged me in the ribs. I turned to see her making the most ridiculous cross-eyed, doubled-chinned face. She winked and I laughed. That day was proof that rejection doesn't hurt as badly when you have a lovable nutcase by your side.

Shelly won't be able to help me pick out my dress for the ultimate boy-girl dance, but Christine and Court offer to step in and help. I'm extremely grateful that Court is making the trip, because I know she despises shopping as much as I do. We both embrace online shopping so we don't have to put ourselves through the torture of staring at our badly lit selves in a mirror while some perky stranger with a headset asks, "How's that workin' for ya?" Very rarely is it "workin'" for me, but like everyone else, I holler, "Great!" and then avoid eye contact when I make a run for the door, empty-handed.

Since we'll both be in Chicago this weekend, Court and I choose a resolution we can complete together: bring back game night. While living in Ames for school, Shelly and I made frequent road trips to visit Court in Des Moines. (It's a forty-five minute drive—thirty if Shelly was driving.) The purpose? Game night, of course. Court, E1, Shelly, and I would spend hours playing Trivial Pursuit, Taboo, Shit On Your Neighbor, *whatever.* Those visits became some of our favorite nights in college. (Yeah, Nickel Night at the Dean's List was fun, but that's not the kind of fun you remember for the rest of your life. Or even the next day.)

I happen to own the original Nintendo Entertainment System, so we set a goal to pass Super Mario Bros. by the time she leaves on Sunday. Court and I *loved* that game as children. We played it until our thumbs got sore. We can't wait to pick up a controller and bring back the magic this weekend.

I'm pretty jazzed about bringing back game night because I get to pack my Ouija board in my overnight bag for Eric's house. (Yes, we're *still* playing slumber party. *Stupid housing market.*) It's somewhat embarrassing to admit, but I haven't yet given up the belief that it truly *is* a mystifying oracle, just like it says on the box. When Court and I were kids, we played Ouija all summer long at our friend Tonya's house. She was a latchkey kid, which meant that the minute her parents left for work, we gathered at her place to do scandalous things, like watch HBO. (The first pair of naked lady boobs I ever saw appeared at her house during an afternoon screening of *National Lampoon's European Vacation.* I'll never forget it.) We turned off all the lights, sat in a circle, and summoned the spirits with childlike impatience.

"Spirit? Are you there? Are you there, Spirit? *Spir-it!*"

It would take only a few rounds of questioning before the plastic heart game piece (a.k.a. the planchette) jumped into action. We looked at each other with *holy shit* eyes as it circled maniacally all over the board. It was terrifying yet exhilarating. We communicated with all kinds of famous dead people during these sessions. And no matter who we were talking to—Elvis, Ryan White (the AIDS kid), the local girl who died from choking on a peanut—they always seemed to know what boys liked us. I knew I didn't move the game piece, and I trusted that Court didn't either, so that left Tonya. Could she have been *that* creative? Could she really have made up story after story and gotten away with it? Most likely, yes. But I'm ready to find out the truth. Before leaving the house, I call Eric.

"Hey, guess what I'm bringing," I say.

"Funyuns?"

"Good guess, but no. Ouija!"

(Silence.)

"Ouija!" I repeat.

(Silence.)

"Uh, last time I played that game, it told me I'd never get married," he says.

I slowly place my friend Ouija back in the closet. I don't wanna die in the next five months. We opt for a less risky, less gamey night.

Kerry, Foxy, and Amy make up for the Ouija fail. We all show up at Amy's studio apartment amped up to play *Dirty Dancing* Trivia (a very thoughtful gift I received earlier this year) and Girl Talk (thank you, eBay).

The four of us had the extreme displeasure of attending a stage version of *Dirty Dancing* a few months ago. I know what you're thinking—dream come true. Well, turns out, the casting people overlooked a few tiny details. Stage-style Johnny Castle (every woman's flexible, pointy-toed, tight-panted, gyrating, wiiiiiiild fantasy) was super gay. Somewhat acceptable. But even less acceptable? He was *an Aussie!* An Aussie who couldn't hide his accent. And I believe they added in the line "I'm from the streets, Baby!" We stifled giggles throughout the entire production.

Dirty Dancing Trivia is far more suggestive than we anticipate.

Instead of testing our knowledge with questions like "What song was playing during one of the hottest scenes of any movie ever?" the game tests our knowledge of smutty dance moves. (The answer to that question is "Cry to Me" by Solomon Burke, by the way.) The cards we draw have instructions like "hold hands" and "grind lightly," followed by "roll your upper body until you're folded over your partner." I am not kidding. *Who was this game made for?* Good thing we're toasted, thanks to Amy's special drink concoction, the Swayze-tini.

Next up: Girl Talk! Do me a favor: Play this tomorrow. You'll only be cheating yourself if you don't. Here are a few highlights: Kerry jumped like a frog for a minute, Foxy called a boy and told a dirty joke, I called a friend and disguised my voice, and Amy was punished with a face full of adhesive zits for not doing any of the above. I'm not sure I've ever laughed so hard. The game is even more fun when you're way too old to play it. (Though, once again, we probably have the Swayze-tini to thank for that.)

At the end of the night, we agree to do this every week. We won't. But we should.

Court arrives for our weekend shopping adventure after hustling her husband on the video bowling lanes. He's one of the only people under the age of forty who owns a bowling ball, so it's a pretty big win for Court. I inform her that we have three dress shops to check out and that Christine, the Shopping Goddess of Chicago, will be joining us for the third stop. (Christine offered to schedule a *second* day of dress shopping next weekend if we don't find anything. I am determined to make sure that doesn't happen.)

We enter the first store on my list Saturday morning. The splotchy carpet welcomes us with a skeevy Kmart vibe. There is one particular dress I have seen online that seems to be available at this story *only*. I'm beginning to think that it's sold solely at this store because the owners murdered whomever it was originally made to fit. A Ukrainian woman shoves her way into my dressing room and yanks my clothes off. She doesn't say a word. It's an odd feeling to bare my breasts in front of a stranger without so much as a hello. Admittedly, I've had fantasies about this sort of thing, but said fantasies never involved a two-hundred-pound Ukrainian lady with borscht breath. The dress is an overwhelming disappointment, so Court and I mosey on outta that store faster than you can say "blue-light disaster."

We head to the next store on my list, feeling prematurely defeated. If this were a game, we'd forfeit. Fortunately, this shop serves champagne! It does not, however, serve anything that doesn't make me look like a stumpy fairy princess.

We stop and pick up Christine for the last appointment, in the suburbs. By this time, I'm considering taking my prom dress out of retirement, so it's good to have a shopping enthusiast in tow. A storm rolls in just in time to give my hopelessness the appropriate backdrop. After an hour of rainy driving, we sprint into the tiny store just before one o'clock, drenched and marginally pissy.

"Your appointment was an hour ago," Bitchy McBitcherson, the receptionist, snaps.

"I'm sorry? I'm pretty sure it's at one o'clock," I say confidently. The tears welling up in my eyes tell a different story.

"Your appointment was an hour ago," she repeats.

"I'm sorry, I guess I wrote it down wrong," I say. The customer is *always* right—unless that customer is me.

Her nostrils flare in response.

A wizard-esque woman breezes into the room. "Oh, goodness! No worries, honey!"

I'm immediately drawn to her lazy eye. History has proven that there's just something about a lazy eye that makes me tick. While my ex-boyfriend had the kind of eye that just wanders off a bit without warning, this woman has the brand of lazy that intrigues me most. It's like she's not even looking at you, yet she's looking right into your soul.

The Wizard creates a makeshift dressing room for me—in the *middle* of the store—because of the scheduling snafu. Sweet. I try on dress after dress, stripping naked in front of a room full of spectators. Court and Christine try their hardest not to laugh as I awkwardly maneuver my body to expose the least amount of my lady parts as possible. *Damn, I should've worn better underwear.* Bare-assed humiliation aside, I do find two dresses I adore. As Court, Christine, and I focus on crowning a winner, the Wizard floats back into the room.

"Bring down that one dress," she purrs to her assistant. "You know, that plain one with the T-back."

T-back? *Oh, brother.* I politely wait for the girl to return and then mentally roll my eyes when she presents the dress to us. It's all wrong. It's satin and boring, and yes—it has a racerback, like a sports bra. I slip it on quickly to appease the Wizard and—*ohmygod,* I've found my dress.

The Wizard leans in close and whispers, "You looked too *cute* in those other dresses. You look like a *woman* in this dress." She turns into a raven and flies away. Okay, not really, but I wouldn't have been surprised if that had happened.

When it's time to pay, I get out the envelope of cash my mother gave me to help with wedding expenses. I'm not proud of this, by the way. I was hoping Eric and I could pay for most of the wedding ourselves, but I crunched some preliminary numbers and realized my bank account was lacking a few thousand dollars. The resulting panic forced me to come clean with my parents about the credit card debt I'd accumulated since moving to Chicago. My pride ached upon the admission that I wasn't as well off as I'd pretended to be over the last five years. I only pretended because I wanted them to be proud. I wanted them to think I was a fancy career girl and that all the money that they, and Georgia and Gary, had invested in me was worth it. When they came to the city for the first time, I surprised them with tickets to the Blue Man Group. When I visited home, I brought all kinds of Chicago goodies with me. And at holidays, I splurged on things I knew they wanted but wouldn't buy themselves. MasterCard generously paid for the majority of it. And now MasterCard was being a royal bitch and demanded to be paid back, with interest—*lots* of interest. My recent switch in advertising agencies advanced my career to a place where my paycheck is no longer a joke, but I consider the income boost to be a lot like finally earning my first Band-Aid after getting shot in the head long ago. Sure, it helps, but it's gonna take a shitload of Band-Aids. So anyway, after a mildly disappointed sigh from my dad, my parents gave me an envelope containing a chunk of their hard-earned cash to help with the wedding.

I hand the money over to Bitchy McBitcherson.

"Oh, uh, I'm not sure anyone has ever paid in cash," she judges.

Court and I look at each other and laugh. It's one of those "it's awesome to be a Housley girl" kind of moments.

"My parents believe cash is the only true form of money. If you don't have it, you don't spend it."

"That's the cutest thing I've ever heard," Christine says. McBitcherson's stink-eye becomes a little less stinky. We leave the building with the dress I'll be wearing for one of the most important days of my life. I only wish I could hold a dress rehearsal at Shelly's house to make sure I made the right decision.

Court and I drop Christine off at her house and stop at the nearest bar to detox. It takes three beers to get rid of the shopping stench.

"Thanks for making the trip. This really would've been horrible without you."

"I owed you! Don't you remember picking out mine?"

"Of course I do! It was the first time you ever let me pick out an outfit for you—I bragged about it for months."

We both sit in happy silence, probably thinking about Court's dress, or my wedding, or Shelly's absence, or all of the above.

"All right, let's get out of here. We've got a princess to save!"

We head back to my apartment and suit up in our uniforms—gnome flannel pj's for me, sock monkeys for her—and we reenter 1985. We pass Super Mario Bros. in two hours flat. Bring Back Game Night is a success!

Chapter 9:
call me!

When you share the majority of your childhood—your laughs, your tears, your ups, and your downs—with just one girl, you're kinda screwed once that girl is gone.

I constantly fear that all the memories I shared with Shelly will vanish. If I can't recall even the slightest detail, that detail is erased from the universe forever—as if it never happened. For instance, the second week I had my license, I took Shelly for a joyride and accidentally hopped the curb with my Dodge Shadow. We both screamed as I screeched to a stop on the front lawn of McDonald's, just a few yards away from a terrified Egg McMuffin lover. (I bet he reassessed his life that day after his near-death experience.) Don't worry, I had a good excuse for my careless driving—a good song was on the radio. We had to belt it out and incorporate dance moves! Unfortunately, I have no recollection of what that song was. And now, I can't call Shelly to find out.

The upside of this predicament is that Shelly kept a *very* detailed diary, so while I can't make that call I'd love to make, I can consult her pile of journals.

Kim showed up on my parents' doorstep with a box full of old journals shortly after Shelly died. I didn't feel I deserved such a treasure, but as Kim explained, "Most of it is about you anyway." I flipped through the bubbly letters on the pages and felt as if I were getting to hear her voice again. She didn't just document the interesting parts of her day, she documented every waking minute—right down to the pork chops she ate for dinner and the list of people she called on the phone each night. Her phone log proved that if anyone were ever destined to be a great telemarketer, it was Shelly. She even took the time to introduce herself—to herself.

Excerpt from the inside cover of Shelly's diary:

The Diary of Shelly Warner,
    Her life consists of her best friend Brianne Housley and her good friend from Texas Ashley Kurtenbach. She has other friends that are not listed on this list. She likes exercising, boys, shopping (with money), eating, friends, the phone, and boys. She likes volleyball and other sports. She has 1 sister, 2 dogs, 6 cats, and a mom and dad . . . ~~Young and the Restless~~ Days of Our Lives is her favorite soap opera.

Our phone fetish began in seventh grade when we stopped obsessing over Ken (Barbie's smug boyfriend) and started obsessing over Mike, Matt, Ryan, Joe, Ben, Aaron, Jason, Charlie, all five New Kids on the Block, Chad Allen, Danny Pintauro, and Lou Diamond Phillips. Shelly had her own bedroom (I shared with Court), so instead of spending all our time at my house, we relocated to the Warners' farmhouse.

The moment my mom dropped me off, we headed up to our "call center" and never came back downstairs—except to make chocolate malts at midnight. Shelly's room was smothered with horse posters and pinups torn from the pages of *Teen Beat* and *Bop!*. We followed protocol as we navigated through our multipage phone list. First, we called our top two crushes and demanded to know who they "liked." Then we called the rest of the cute guys from class and demanded to know who they "liked." Then we just called anyone who answered and, you guessed it, demanded to know who they "liked." And when I say "we," I mean Shelly. How the girl had the balls to pick up the phone and call anyone and everyone is beyond me. But it always worked because people liked talking to Shelly.

Phone etiquette has changed dramatically since we were in seventh grade. Cell phones, voicemail, text messages, and caller ID hadn't been born yet. (The select few cell phones that hatched early were the size of a small airliner.) We had to leave messages on family answering machines. We had to answer the phone politely without having the slightest idea who might be on the other end. And when we called our friends, we had to do crazy things like ask, "Is so-and-so there?" because so-and-so could be literally anywhere and she didn't have a pocket-size tracking device.

There was one particular phone call I made to Shelly that I'll always remember, no matter how much time passes. It was a chilly November morning in 1996, our senior year of high school. It was the time of year when football season was just ending and basketball season was just beginning. During this time, Shelly and I were multitalented athletic supporters. Wait—that sounds dirty. We supported athletes. Yeah, that's what I meant. We played in the marching band for football season (insert band camp joke here). Then for basketball season, Shelly was a cheerleader and I was a pom-pom girl. Yeah, yeah, I know . . . what's the difference?

Well, the cheerleaders were known as the prettier, more *friendly* (wink, wink) girls who bounced around spastically on the sidelines during the basketball games. Pom-pom girls were the smarter, more respectable girls who Roger Rabbited to classic hits such as "Rumpshaker" during the halftime show. It was a game

Why don't telemarketers hire fourteen year olds? I would've purchased eight of whatever this girl was selling.

day, so Shelly and I both got the privilege of wearing our border-line slut-tastic uniforms to school. In other words, we both wore skirts that intentionally did *not* cover our asses. Did I mention that it was a balmy thirty degrees outside?

At approximately 6:05 AM, I scurried out of the house in my nonexistent skirt and hopped into my car. I was eager to get to "early-bird marching band" *early*. (I think I've just written the defi-nition of "super-nerd".) If everything happened according to plan, I'd get to school with just enough time to shake out my Conair hot rollers before marching onto the field with my sousaphone (march-ing version of a tuba). Unfortunately, everything did *not* happen according to plan. A block from home, the ole Dodge Shadow went into early retirement. I executed a quick high-school-girl meltdown (high-pitched squeal, pouty face, gentle punch on the steering wheel) and then left my wounded Dodge behind. I raced back home as fast as my Kaepa dance shoes would allow (not very fast) and made an ungraceful leap up the front-porch stairs. My toe caught the last step, and I took a magnificent spill onto the frozen cement. There was no time for another hissy fit, so I brushed off my bloody knee and kept going. I felt a lot like an Olympic athlete.

It was 6:20 AM by the time I frantically dialed Shelly's phone number. She should've already left her house by this time—she lived ten minutes farther away from school than I did—but she was habitually late. For everything.

"Hello?" (She answered even though she had no idea who was calling at the crack of dawn. How *weird* is that?)

"Shelly, help! My car broke down!" I wailed into the phone.

"Okay, I'm on my way! Be there in five."

I stood, shivering and bloody, on the front porch and waited patiently. Then less patiently. Then not patiently at all. My lip had just begun the pre-cry quiver when Shelly's red Cavalier screeched around the corner.

"Uh, sorry I'm late. There was a bit of an *incident,*" she said.

I wanted to be mad at her for being late, but I could tell by her sheepish expression that she had gotten in trouble for something. I was correct. Apparently, Shelly had been in such a big hurry to rescue her best friend that she had neglected to open the garage door before peeling out in reverse. *Crash.*

"My dad had to take the garage door off the hinges so I could get out. Now I'm grounded from the phone for *two weeks!*" Shelly was *always* grounded from the phone. Her parents knew it was the only punishment that would shake her right down to her social-butterfly core.

I tried to hold in the laughter, but I couldn't. I let it all out. Soon after, Shelly unleashed her signature snort laugh, and her sheepish guilt vanished in an instant.

Fifteen minutes later, we tiptoed onto the practice football field, hoping to go unnoticed. This is not easy to do when the instrument you play weighs fifteen pounds and is almost as tall as you are. Our band teacher, Mr. Mott, was notorious for making kids run laps, *with their band instruments in hand,* for being late. It never failed; the jocks arrived at school just in time to witness the shmuck puttering around the track with a trombone. (Come on, aren't band geeks teased enough?) Just when I thought we'd successfully dodged Mr. Mott's watchful eye, his voice boomed over the loudspeaker.

"Welcome, Shelly and Bree! Glad you could make it this morning."

My ears burned with the heat of a million Atomic Fireball jawbreakers. *Oh god. Oh god. Oh god. I cannot run around the track in a skirt with my sousaphone.*

"As you all know, punctuality is very important," he continued. *Oh boy, here we go.*

"But sometimes, there's a good enough excuse to let it slide. I just hope the garage door Shelly drove into is all right." The entire marching band broke into giggles and guffaws. I turned a shameful color of red, but Shelly shrieked with laughter.

Shelly and I loved retelling that story. To us, it never got old. But now I have to tell it on my own; Shelly will never again interject with her spastic side of the crazy caper. And I know that if I dial her number for a refresher on a forgotten detail, I'll just hear static. (Believe me, in a few moments of weakness, I've tried.)

Think about the freedom you have to pick up the phone and call a friend whenever you want—when a certain song comes on the radio, when you're reminded of an inside joke, when you just wanna laugh. Now imagine if that freedom were taken away from you without notice. Perhaps you'd watch one fewer episode of *The Housewives of Whatever County* and call that friend instead? Maybe not. It's a hard lesson to learn hypothetically, and even now, I'm not sure I practice what I preach. Who am I kidding? I know I don't practice what I preach. I screen 75 percent of my calls for one reason or another. It can be something as mindless as "I'm too cold to move my hands" or as intentional as "Eh . . . I don't like you."

The joy of the telephone is gone. We don't talk to each other anymore. We don't get excited when the phone rings.

"So, I'm thinking we should do something involving the phone," I say to Court during a rare Sunday afternoon chat. (Court despises talking on the phone as much as I do.)

"Yuck." Pause. "But yes. What are you thinking?"

"Well, I know we're both gonna hate me, but how about no screening calls or texting? We'll actually have to call our friends if we want to say something—*and* answer every call no matter who it is, just like in the olden days."

"Oh, lord, that sounds terrifying. And I will absolutely do it."

Growing up in a household with only one phone line and no call waiting instigated a lot of wars between Court and me. The most violent era was when she was in junior high and I was in elementary school. While I wanted to talk to my friends about *He-Man* and *Sweet Valley Twins*, Court wanted to talk to *her* friends about *90210* and boys. Mom and Dad tried to solve the conflict rationally by giving us a schedule: I had odd hours and Court had even. But what if Shelly's line was busy during the odd hours? (There was no "what if" about it; her line was *always* busy.) In that case, melodramatic screaming matches ensued. It wasn't pretty.

When boys started calling the house for Court, my role as the little sister from hell became much more established. Anytime the phone rang, I *raced* to the kitchen like a chubby four-eyed cheetah so I could answer it before her. (Cordless phones weren't even all that prevalent yet.)

Boy: Uh, is Courtnee there?

Me: (Giggle, burp.) Maybe, who is this?

Boy: (Insert name of terrified young man.)

Me: Ooooooh. Hang on. *Cooourrrtneee!* It's a boy!

Once that part was over, I did one of the following activities: (1) pretended to hang up the downstairs phone when she picked up the upstairs phone, but actually listened to the entire conversation; (2) spun around on the kitchen floor in front of her while she talked; (3) returned to the living room and finished watching *227*.

When Court left for college, our behavior changed. I anxiously awaited her Sunday night calls and jumped up from *227* as if it were Jackée herself calling to invite me to go hat shopping. The conversations we had during those years turned bickering sisters into friends. (Aw, cue the *Full House* music.)

On an average day, Amy and I entertain each other with textual rubbish at least three times. It's torturous riding the train without alerting her that I'm sitting across from an adult sporting one of those winter hats with animal ears that babies wear. *What company in downtown Chicago employs fox imposters?* I don't want to keep this disbelief to myself, but alas, I just stare at the fox-eared lady helplessly and make a mental note to call Amy later.
So bummed.

I fall even further from joy when I arrive at my desk and see that Lars Larsen has already set printouts of our ads on my chair. A word to the wise: I require a little office-style foreplay to function professionally. I need *at least* twenty minutes to get "in the mood" with a cup of coffee and some online gossip.

Lars rises slowly from his side of the cube wall. "Hey, um, we need to send these to the client ASAP. So . . . can you take a look at the layouts real quick?"

I look at him blankly. It's too early for facial expressions.

"Okay, how about I give you a minute to get settled." He lowers himself back down, out of sight. *Wow, you're learning, Lars Larsen.* I exhale deeply, then inhale my coffee and glance at the ads.

"These are awesome, Lars. Let's send 'em through to the client."

"Are you sure? Do you like the font okay? I played around with it for a while. [Insert a shitload of font-speak here.]"

"Lars, for real. I think it looks nice."

He's not satisfied with my answer. When I first started this job, a coworker told me that Lars *loves* problems. I'm finding this personality assessment to be annoyingly accurate.

"Wait, hmm. Can I see a few of the other options you tried?" I guess I'll play along.

Lars presents somewhere around thirty font options to me. The difference between them is invisible to the non–Lars Larsen eye.

"Oh, I like the simplicity of this one. It speaks to the tone of the campaign." *Totally talking out of my ass right now.* When I worked with Amy or Christine as my art director, we discussed these types of things for two minutes, agreed on the best option, and then moved on to a quick game of Marry, Fuck, Kill. (If you aren't familiar with this game, simply pick three people and then assign each one of them to one of the words above. For instance, if the choices were Joey, Chandler, and Ross. I'd marry Chandler, fuck Ross, and kill Joey. See, isn't that fun?)

Lars smiles. "Yeah, I like that one, too." *Phew, crisis averted.*

Just when I think I'm safe, he pops up again.

"Oh, hey—one more thing."

Please, no more fonts. Please, no more fonts.

"How's the wedding planning going?" *Oh man, I'm such an asshole.*

"It's great! We're going to do the registry this week. Any suggestions?"

"Case of Mountain Dew?"

I play in a four-on-four volleyball league at the elementary school gym across the street from my apartment on Monday nights. My team, the Badass Cowboys, consists of Eric, Kerry, and another good friend, Jon. We get pummeled every week. We aren't *bad;* we just aren't as good as the former collegiate athletes we play against. We step onto the court for our last game of the season. (Sweaty volleyball montage goes here—we are not wearing jeans, but "Playing with the Boys" is definitely the soundtrack.) We get eaten alive in record time.

"Good game, guys! Wanna stick around and play another just for fun?" *Okay, Team Masochist, why the hell not?*

Crack. Kerry is writhing around in pain two minutes later. *Oh, that's why the hell not.* Game over. We do what any good friends would do and convince her that she's fine and that we should all go home. It's already nine thirty on a school night and we've got showers to take and Skittles to eat.

I enjoy a long shower post-annihilation. I relish having a night to myself for the first time in what feels like decades. I even put lotion on my legs. Then I check my phone: one missed call. *Dammit!* It rings again.

I stare at the caller ID before picking up: KERRY CRAIG. *Oh shit, my night of nothingness is about to explode.*

"You're supposed to answer every call for the resolution!" Kerry bellows.

"I was in the shower!" I halfheartedly bellow back.

"I think I need to go to the ER."

(Silence.) The voice in my head is *not* silent. It's cursing profusely. I want to cry. The last time I took a friend to the ER was in college when Shelly sliced her thumb while trying to cut a lime for her beer. We were there for six hours, and she left with a couple stitches and a Band-Aid. "I guess that wasn't *totally* necessary," she said on the way home. *No shit.* I've avoided the ER ever since.

"Well, are you sure? Maybe just ice it and see how it feels tomorrow?"

"I'm pretty sure my foot is broken."

"Okay. Uh, where do we even go for something like this? I don't know how hospitals work in Chicago." This is a true statement. Going to the grocery store in Chicago is stressful enough; I can't even imagine what a hospital would be like.

"Good question. Ya know what, on second thought, I'll be fine. No worries."

"Seriously? No. Let me take you."

"It's not even my pedal foot, so I can drive. I'll let you know if I have any problems." This is not okay. Yet at the time, it seems okay.

I sit on my recliner and eat Skittles off my belly. (It doubles as a plate when I don't feel like doing dishes.) Oh, this is the life . . . except for the part where my friend *might* be out driving her car with a broken foot.

This is confirmed the following morning. *I'm such a dick.*

The guilt I feel after talking to Kerry makes me realize that it's not just about picking up the phone; it's about being a good friend to whoever is on the other line. It's about backing your car into a garage door to come to that friend's rescue.

I may not have failed at the resolution, but what I did was much worse—I failed as a friend. *Have I learned nothing?*

It's wedding registry day! Running rampant through a store with the magic gun that makes all your domestic dreams come true has always been my fantasy. Apparently, it's Eric's nightmare.

"Let's just do it online. Amazon.com?"

"Um, okay, that's fine." I'm disappointed by this suggestion, but that's not the only reason registering for our wedding isn't the *Supermarket Sweep* extravaganza I expected it to be. Eric's loft hasn't sold yet, so we have no idea what kind of space we'll be furnishing. It's not easy to agree on items for a home you don't yet have. By the time we click on the fourth page of potato peelers, we're over it. I volunteer to finish the registry later.

When I get home from Eric's, I suit up in my ugly bachelorette clothes (giant green grandpa pants and a vintage sweatshirt that has probably lived through some stuff I would rather not know about). I scroll through pages of grown-up stuff, only to realize that I'm not grown up at all. I'm nervous for the first time since Eric and I got engaged. Am I responsible enough to get married when I can't even pick out a blender?

Hmmm . . . maybe it will help to look at someone else's registry. Lazy Eye got engaged recently, too. In fact, he's marrying the woman he started dating shortly after we broke up. Obviously, I'm over him, but it still stings. He was special to me. I had been dating him only a month when Shelly died, so things progressed pretty quickly. We were together for a year and a half, and then, during one of our infamous rocky phases, he got a job offer in California. I told him his career was a "sure thing" and I was not.

(I didn't know if I believed that, but it sounded good.) One of the last things he said to me before he moved across the country was, "It's going to take a long time to get over you." It was like a movie moment where we both walked away feeling good about each other. Those good feelings stabbed me in the heart when I learned he was dating a woman he met the day he interviewed for that job. And that he was probably over me before he even left. *Anyhoo,* from what I can tell on Facebook, his fiancée seems respectable—and more mature than I'll ever be. Surely *she* knows how to fill out a wedding registry.

It's not until an hour later, when I disagree with their choice of pillow shams, that I realize what I'm doing is absurd.

I call Amy to confess. (Just like Shelly, she *always* answers the phone when I call.)

"I don't deserve to get married!"

"What? What happened?"

"I just cheated off Lazy Eye's wedding registry."

"You did *what?*" I can barely understand her through the laughter. "Oh god, Bree. That is all kinds of awesome."

"Did you know you're supposed to register for napkin holders? What the hell? When will I ever need something to hold my napkins? Fuck, when do I ever *have* napkins?"

"Marry *me,* baby. Marry *me!*" Interestingly enough, this is not the first time Amy has proposed to me.

"I think this is a sign that I need to go to Bed Bath & Beyond tomorrow to use the shit out of that gun."

"You have my full support, baby. Let me know if there are any emergencies."

I erase the items I pillaged. (Well, I keep a few things on there. Who knew cheese gets its own special knife?) The next morning, I make a solo visit to Bed Bath & Beyond. I get a few concerned looks from other shoppers when I register for the Bra Baby, but I'm too busy enjoying the magic gun to care.

As difficult as this week was for me, telephonically speaking, I must admit it's nice to hear a warm voice on the line rather than a one-sided voicemail, to hear laughter instead of seeing "LOL" (ugh), and to say, "Talk to you later" and actually mean it.

Oh, and do me a favor. Call an old friend and have a "Remember that time . . . " chat right now. Or you can call him/her tomorrow. Just do it soon . . . while you still can.

Chapter 10:
our songs

Shelly and I officially went from being friends to being *best* friends right after we butchered *Gershwin Greatest Hits* at our fourth-grade chorus concert. Before that night, we'd chatted in class, maybe even swapped a sticker or two out of our sticker books, but we hadn't bonded yet because Shelly's gaggle was always nearby. I was more of a lone wolf (or maybe a lone muskrat, thanks to my unfortunate grooming/bang perm situation). After the concert, Shelly's cool friends left and my co-dorks skittered away. However, our dads, John and Craig, kept the party going because they recognized each other from a job they'd both worked years ago. This left the popular girl with a heart of gold and the nerdy girl with a heart of tinfoil standing there, all hopped up on Gershwin and jazz squares. Within moments, Shelly grabbed my hand. We ran to the drinking fountain, singing all the way: "We're going to get a drink, a drink, a drink. We're going to get a drink and we hope you like this song." (You probably wouldn't like that song.)

Music continued to play a role in my friendship with Shelly for years to come, and it still plays a role even after her death. Court and I decide to pay tribute to tunage by seeing as many live shows as possible this week.

Music is powerful. It can awaken the past in a way nothing else can. In fact, I read online that Petr Janata, a cognitive neuroscientist at the University of California, Davis, explained, "What seems to happen is that a piece of familiar music serves as a soundtrack for a mental movie that starts playing in our heads. . . . It calls back memories of a particular person or place, and you might all of a sudden see that person's face in your mind's eye."

There are roughly 267 songs that can make me an emotional mess in ten seconds or less. Certain songs make me so happy I could burst Lisa Frank–style hearts and rainbows, and others make me ill with pain and regret. For instance, whenever I hear "You Really Got Me," by Van Halen (originally by the Kinks), the jubilation of young love bum-rushes my heart. The first guy who ever really liked me (like, *liked me* liked me) made me a mix tape, and that song was the first track. Other girls got mix tapes with cheesy pop ballads and R&B sex tunes, but I got the mix tape featuring one of the greatest songs ever written about raw obsession. It made my innocent teenage libido explode. (It also made me discover I actually *had* a libido.) On the other hand, whenever I hear "It's So Hard to Say Goodbye to Yesterday," by Boyz II Men, I want to ball up into the fetal position and cry for days like I did when Charlie died. We were only sophomores in high school the morning my mom woke Shelly and me up from our slumber on the hide-a-bed to tell us the news that Charlie had been killed in a car accident. I had crushed on him hardcore in junior high (he was a regular recipient of our late-night phone calls), and I didn't know how to process the fact that he was suddenly dead at fifteen. I went up to my bedroom after Shelly left and listened to that Boyz II Men song on repeat for hours. It consoled me in a way that no person could.

This brings me to our songs. I can rarely go a week without hearing something that makes me say, "Oh, this reminds me of the time Shelly and I [fill in the blank with wacky hijinks]." The importance of these songs, and the memories they evoke, are impossible to explain with words, but I'm going to find my inner Casey Kasem and try. Here are some of my favorites:

Any NKOTB song. If you're a lady around my age (give or take ten years), you probably busted a nut in your Z. Cavaricci jeans over these guys somewhere around 1987. They were like the Beatles, only less talented and less British. By the time we were seniors in high school, NKOTB had disappeared from the face of the earth, but the enormous lapel pins and VHS videotapes we coveted had not. Shelly, Foxy, and I, along with two other female classmates, decided to pay tribute to the gone-but-never-forgotten quintet by lip-synching a six-minute routine to a medley of their hits in the school talent show. How lip-synching qualified as a talent, I'll never know. (But thank goodness it did.) We stayed up all night and studied the old VHS tapes, trying to peg the mannerisms of our assigned New Kid. I got

Ami (Joe), Sarah (Jon), Me (Jordan), Shelly (Donnie), and Kristine (Danny) showing we've got the right stuff. Or maybe just the okay stuff.

to be Jordan, the most talented one of the five. And of course Shelly was Donnie, the most outspoken one. Three minutes before we went onstage in front of hundreds of people, Shelly ran up to me frantically. "Donnie's jeans were always ripped! I couldn't find any ripped jeans!" I sprang into action and grabbed a stray pair of scissors. I vigorously slashed at Shelly's legs. There was probably a much safer way of getting Donnie's bad-boy look, but we chose to do it spontaneously with reckless abandon. Because *that's* the way Shelly and I always did things. Our performance was a hit—and of course I have the VHS to prove it.

"Got Your Money," by Ol' Dirty Bastard. As previously mentioned, I rarely drank alcohol before I turned twenty-one. It's not that I was a goody-goody; I was just notorious for getting caught anytime I tried to do something even remotely scandalous. (Who gets a ticket for not wearing a seat belt to drive two blocks? Me, that's who.) Shelly wasn't one to turn down a party, so she had experienced a kegger or twenty by the time I was ready to see what this boozy hubbub was all about. I told her things started to "look fuzzy" after my second amaretto sour, and by the fourth, I was getting rowdy on the dance floor—by myself. I have Ol' Dirty Bastard to thank for that. I just couldn't fight the urge to shake my hips to those brilliant lyrics. It was only 6:30 PM and everyone in the bar was watching in amusement, but Shelly joined me anyway. Don't worry, we didn't hoochie-dance like most college girls. We danced like sixty-year-old women in Jazzercise. From that point on, the DJ played "Got Your Money" whenever Shelly and I entered the bar. We were total celebs.

"We Are the Champions," by Queen. Remember Jump Rope for Heart? I do, and it's mostly because of this song. In grades four through six, our whole school packed into the gym after seventh period and jumped rope for three hours to raise money for the American Heart Association. For the first two hours and fifty-seven minutes, Shelly and I hopped around like amateurs while flirting with the boy team next to us. (For me, staring = flirting.) But when "We Are the Champions" blared through the shoddy speakers, we knew it was our *final* three minutes to shine. We pushed into high gear: one-legged jumps, double jumps, side straddles, crisscross, and other flashy moves we had invented. When the song ended, we celebrated like we'd just found the cure for childhood acne. I'm always catapulted right back to that moment when I hear that tune on the radio.

"Invisible," by Clay Aiken. First of all, let's discuss the chorus to this song: "If I was invisible, then I could just watch you in your room." Really, Clay? Creepy much? Shelly and I first heard this ditty when I was in town for the holidays in 2003; we found it *wildly* entertaining. In fact, we sat in the car after we'd arrived at our destination just so we could hear the whole thing. A month later, when I was back in Florida, I got a voicemail from Shelly. I expected to hear her usual chipper voice, but instead I heard an odd, whispery growl. She got through the first verse before breaking into a fit of giggles. "Hey, I'm in a bathroom stall at Applebee's. That creepy Clay song just played, so I had to call you. Miss you!" When I tried to prank her back from the office the next day, I crashed my computer while looking up the next verse to the song. I lost a lot of respect from the IT department that day. But Shelly loved me for it.

"Tiny Dancer," by Elton John. Singing in the car was one of my favorite things to do with Shelly. (Yeah, we were easily entertained.) Nowadays, I don't sing in the car unless I'm by myself—and even then, it's more of a self-conscious hum. I miss yell-singing at the top of my lungs. Especially when I hear Elton John. This is a classic tale of mistaken lyrics. I don't know where we were going or when exactly this occurred, but I know it was during a long road trip and we were slaphappy. When Elton hit that famous chorus from "Tiny Dancer," I learned that Shelly had her own version of the song.

"Hold me dancer, kinda closer . . . " she belted out.

"Wait, what did you just say?" I couldn't keep a straight face.

"I don't know. What *did* I just say?"

When I repeated the mistake to her and then told her what the lyrics actually were, she had no shame. I've been singing her version ever since.

There's another song that reminds me of Shelly. One that belongs in its own category. I was first introduced to the Bright Eyes song "This Is the First Day of My Life" at a family friend's wedding. The bride's brother sang it during the ceremony. Indie birds wearing handkerchiefs and skinny jeans fluttered around my heart. I bawled my eyes out and then bought the album as soon as I got home. I was obsessed with the tune for weeks and then, like 95 percent of my music library, it got lost in the shuffle.

I was unexpectedly reacquainted with this song a few months later. This time, love wasn't in the air; it was buried deep beneath the ground. It was my first visit to the cemetery since Shelly's funeral six months prior. I had only visited the graves of old people up until this point. That's what cemeteries are supposed to be full of—*old* people. When other young friends had died prematurely, I had said my final goodbye at the funeral. I refused to chat up a rock in the ground—no matter who had supposedly taken up residence underneath it. But with Shelly, it was different. I needed her. I needed to talk to her. I needed to *feel* her. And I would try just about anything to make that happen.

I walked down to the cemetery alone, listening to my iPod as if I were headed out to meet any other friend. I hit "stop" on my favorite Cory Branan song when I saw all the paraphernalia from Shelly's fan club. I walked the rest of the way in silence. When I reached the headstone, a shiver ran down my spine. SHELLY BRIDGEWATER AUG. 3, 1979 – JAN. 16, 2005. Her death felt painfully real. I didn't know what to do next. *Do I talk to her? Can she hear my thoughts? Is she laughing at me?* I started by telling her hello and that I missed her, the same way I had told her that same thing every time I'd seen her since I moved away. Then I lowered down to my knees and tried my hardest to talk to her like she was standing there, listening to every word. I apologized profusely for boring her with things she might already know. I mean, if spirits exist, they probably know everything going on in our lives, right? What's the correct way to address someone who may know *everything*, but at the same time could know *nothing?* One thing was certain—talking to her made me feel normal again for the first time in months.

When it was time to walk away, I hit "play" again on my iPod. It should have started where it left off—with Cory Branan. But it didn't. Instead, I heard Bright Eyes:

This is the first day of my life.

I'm glad I didn't die before I met you.

But now I don't care—I could go anywhere with you,

And I'd probably be happy.

And once again, I cried. And cried. And cried. And felt so damn glad I didn't die before I met her. Those were the first tears that had fallen since Shelly's death.

Tuesday morning, I awake to sunlight. This is a big deal. We haven't seen the sun in almost four months. I pop into the office and pop back out just a few hours later. Days like this are made for playing hooky—even Lars Larsen agrees. (He *agrees,* but his ass stays planted firmly in his chair.)

I forge out into the great wide clusterfuck of Michigan Avenue in search of live music for the project. At the very least, you can usually spot a drunkish guy playing a battered saxophone at any given time in downtown Chicago. This is one advantage I have over Court. Iowa's music scene is decent, but it's less of an impromptu thing and more of a buy-tickets-four-months-in-advance thing. Except for the lady who plays department store piano. She's a sure thing, 365 days a year. Court takes in an afternoon show with all the bored husbands carrying their wives' shopping bags while I fight my way through aggressive crowds of window-shoppers.

I want to murder no fewer than twenty-seven people within the first few blocks of my mission. The tourists are out in packs of eleventy billion today. *What the hell is going on?* I lose my patience rather quickly. The only thing that can remedy this level of annoyance is an afternoon cocktail. The odds that Amy can meet me in the middle of a workday are pretty slim, but I call her anyway.

She trots over and meets me across from the Wrigley Building in five hot minutes.

"Happy Saint Paddy's!" she sings.

"Oh, duh. So . . . Mexican?"

"Absolutely. It's the new Irish."

Halfway to Mi Casa, we come across the battered saxophone man I was hoping to run into. Amy politely stands next to him so I can get proof of my first live music show via iPhone video. When we get to the restaurant, I realize that I'm seventy-five years old and don't actually know how to work the iPhone. I recorded everything *except* the part where the man serenaded Amy with "Isn't She Lovely." By our second round of margaritas, I'm laughing about it.

"So. We're drunk. Right?" I need confirmation.

"In. Deed." Amy trails off into laughter.

"I love us," I confess.

"*I* love us," Amy replies.

I notice the pedestrian traffic is picking up, so I glance at my watch. It's five o'clock already. "Oh, shit. I have my first personal training session at Bally's in an hour!" I jump up dramatically. Then I sit back down lazily and laugh. "No, no. But really, I do."

An hour later, I'm at the gym, nervously waiting to meet the man I'm paying to kick my ass repeatedly for the next four months. Most people do research for this kind of decision. But not me. This guy was on sale!

"Hey. I'm Pete." A five-foot-four powerhouse appears in front of me, and he's not smiling. I search for kindness in his face and come up blank. He leads me into the personal-training room, high-fiving douchebags and making grunty animal noises at them. *Oh boy.*

"Stand on one foot for as long as you can."

"Really? Um, why?" *Shit, does he know I'm not sober?*

"I want to test your balance."

Is this guy an undercover cop? Is it illegal to pump iron under the influence? Am I going to be handcuffed at the gym? I want to laugh and tell him I warmed up with Jose Cuervo, but I know he won't find it funny. I bet he thinks homicide is funny.

After the balance/sobriety test, he fires health questions at me. I keep the fact that I ate Girl Scout cookies for dinner a secret. "Ya know, by the look of your physique and your muscle tone, you'd probably be a good bodybuilder."

I go from wanting to laugh to wanting to cry. This guy sucks.

"Our goal is to make me look skinny in my wedding dress. Let's stick with that," I say. He murders me with his eyes. This is going to be a loooong four months.

The office is hellish on Thursday. Lars and I sold our campaign, but we have a long way to go before we get to produce the work. Here's how the process usually works: Once we finally sell a campaign to the client, they say something like, "Oh, we love it! We just have a few small changes we'd like to make." What they really mean is, *That campaign will be perfect once you take out all the humor and fun stuff and replace it with product-speak.* It's always an uphill battle, but this one seems especially steep. Between the resolutions, the wedding, and this job, I'm exhausted both mentally and physically. I decide to combat this overwhelming fatigue with a big fat messy Potbelly sandwich.

Potbelly is my favorite lunch place to nourish my gut. Not just because they have *giardiniera* that tastes like angry angels made it. Or because the oatmeal-chocolate chip cookies drip with buttery cookie grease. It's those things *plus* the tiny hippie who plays guitar in the corner.

I sit my sore ass down at a table for one and get ready to annihilate my sandwich. Court calls before I go in for the kill.

"I hadn't heard from you all day, so figured I'd make sure everything is okay."

Court and I usually email each other seventeen times by 10:30 AM, especially since we started doing the fifty2resolutions project. But today I was busy fielding horrible suggestions by businesspeople who love to say, "I'm not the writer here, but you should probably write exactly what I tell you to write."

"Yeah, I'm fine. Just a little overwhelmed."

"Wedding stuff?"

"Yeah, work, wedding, blah blah blah."

"Well, I was talking to Denise, and she offered to help you with the wedding planning if you need it. I know how much you hate calling strangers on the phone." Denise is Court's closest friend in Des Moines. She is one of the single nicest people I've ever met in my life. "Also, I can send you Sarah's email address. She's super crafty and could probably help you with decorating ideas."

"Aw, this maid of honor thing is totally working out. You're the best. Now I feel bad for being twenty-one and stupid when I was *your* maid of honor." I had never even been in a wedding before getting to be the maid of honor in Court's. I thought my only responsibility was writing a speech for the reception. Fortunately, her matron of honor picked up my slack and planned the shower and bachelorette party. Seriously, there should be lessons on this shit.

After we hang up, I resume annihilation. One bite into my turkey club, my heart stops. (Don't worry, it's not a heart attack.) I hear these words:

This is the first day of my life.

I'm glad I didn't die before I met you.

But now I don't care—I could go anywhere with you,

And I'd probably be happy.

No. Way. I don't even know if *I'd* believe me if I told myself this was happening. I look up at the musical hippie in the corner. He is singing directly to me. No one else in the room seems to hear him. *She's with me.*

I'm happy to find out that one of my favorite college bands, Hello Dave (*not* a Dave Matthews cover band), is playing at a local bar tonight. Whenever they played at Iowa State, Shelly and I got to the show super early so we could be in the front row. I was *such* a fangirl. When I moved to Chicago, I found out they lived here and befriended them after frequenting a few of their more intimate shows. I couldn't wait for Shelly to come visit so I could introduce her to the band. In this case, *I* felt like the popular girl with the cool friends. If only I'd known I had such a small window of time to do so. Unfortunately, it never happened.

Before I head out to the concert and check off my last live music show of the week, I hunt down the mix tape Shelly made for me when I left for Florida. Like any good significant other, she came to the airport with me that day. And like any good significant other, she shielded my mother's eyes when airport security dug through my suitcases, the contents of which included a Hawaiian-print vibrator I'd gotten as a "joke." (It was only three months after 9/11, so I hadn't been brought up to speed yet on just how thorough airport security had gotten.) When it was time for me to head through the gate, she handed me a CD titled *A Musical Tribute to Our Friendship*. If that isn't romantic, I don't know what is.

Music speaks to us in ways people can't, takes us back to places we can no longer go, and brings out emotions we can't control. When you open your ears, you open your soul.

Chapter 11:
for keeps?

I live my life not unlike a needy person. I don't have a dishwasher. I don't have "pay channels." And in the winter, I keep my thermostat at fifty-five degrees and carry a space heater with me wherever I go. My frugal ways are a direct result of having been raised by parents who compromised when it came to the finer things in life so that we could enjoy the *funner* things in life.

   Court and I didn't grow up with money. But here's the thing: We didn't *know* we didn't grow up with money until we were grown up. Our parents were *that* good. Court and I weren't jealous of the kids who flew to exotic destinations, like Branson, Missouri, on airplanes. We felt *lucky* that our family drove across the country in our two-door Dodge Colt Spitzer and camped the entire way to the Grand Canyon. We thought nothing of it when our family van (complete with shag carpeting and wood-paneled walls) habitually broke down while going to and from dance classes, sports camps, and music lessons. As long as we got there, we were happy as mildly talented clams. When UPS delivered hand-me-downs from my cousin in Florida, it was like winning a shopping spree in a box. I could never have too many B.U.M. Equipment sweatshirts, even if they were from ten years earlier.

The only disadvantage to being raised in such a frugal fashion (other than cuddling with a homemade Care Bear instead of an authentic one) is that you never learn to let go of things. I'm a full-bred pack rat. If it's not moldy, broken, or bloody, I keep it. (Broken is negotiable. I wore a pair of sunglasses with only one arm for almost a year before replacing them.) This is all well and good until you have a closet full of outdated, ill-fitting clothes you wouldn't be caught dead wearing and storage bins full of VHS tapes you can't watch anymore because no one has a VHS player. This week we shall trash our stash. Court and I make a promise to purge clutter by donating to charity. Everybody wins!

Easier said than done. This is the first time I've been debt-free in almost a decade. Is it really time to start being wasteful? I don't want to be too frivolous with my generosity, so I begin making a pile of things I can definitely part with. So far, it consists of:

- Pitted-out T-shirts. I always tell myself I should save these to wear to the gym. But will I really wear a pre-sweated shirt to go to a place where I'll sweat even more? Negative. That's disgusting. It'll be hard to ditch the unicorn shirt I found for $2.50 at a flea market in Orlando, but alas, it must be done.

- Old books. Some people keep books as trophies. (*Look how smart I am!*) I don't even keep trophies as trophies. I buy books, I read them, and then either I give them to my friends to read or they become dust collectors. I love you, *Bridget Jones,* but you have to go. That goes for you, too, *Owen Meany.*

- VHS tapes. Yes, it's time. This is going to hurt. While I don't think books are a status symbol (even if they're leather bound), movies are definitely a *social* symbol that I greatly respect. I will judge the hell out of someone based on his/her movie collection, and I expect him/her to do the same to me. Movies are immediate. If I'm at your house and I see that you own *Clueless,* you better bet your ass we're going to sit right down and roll with the homies. My DVD collection isn't nearly as impressive as the VHS tapes I hoard, but why keep something around that you can't even enjoy? They *all* go in a box, even my very favorites: *Harold and Maude, Punch-Drunk Love, The Newsies, Strictly Ballroom, The Jerk,* and *The Goonies.*

I'm exhausted after handpicking the above items. When I see the measly result of my labor, I know there's a good chance I'll get a "thanks, but no thanks" from the bum down the street. It's all crap.

Then I ask myself, *What would Shelly do?* She did nothing halfway. In fact, she was more likely to *overdo* everything. During the school food drive, she filled her Cavalier with freshly purchased canned goods from Aldi. I showed up with a can of garbanzo beans my mom had purchased for that night's dinner. Of course, rather than letting me look like the hack I was, Shelly always let me take credit for half of what she brought.

Inspired by this new mantra, I ransack my apartment. Everything goes! Well, *almost* everything. Clothes aren't clutter, they're *memories!* We all keep certain shirts, skirts, dresses, and costumes in the back of the closet with the irrational intention of wearing them again—even though we know damn well we won't. That college sweatshirt with the giant hole in the armpit? I'll wear it to wash the car someday. (I don't have a hose, a bucket, or any possible way to wash my car other than the automatic car wash across town.) Oh, that dress I bought in South Africa? That would be the perfect outfit for an outdoor BBQ between the months of October and Never. (It fits me more like a mitten than a glove—big, bulky, and oddly tight in all the wrong places.) And those palazzo pants I bought on my first trip to L.A. when I was ten pounds thinner? I'll wear them around the house when I paint. (I don't paint. Ever. Especially in tight knickers.)

Court has a similar experience when trying to clean out her closet. We decide to test the "I might wear that again one day" excuse. We extend "purging" week and focus solely on our closets this time around. The challenge: Wear at least one article of clothing per day that you've kept in the closet, even though you haven't worn it in years. If you feel even a little self-conscious, *get rid of it.* We promise our blog readers that we'll post pictures online daily as proof. Goodbye, dignity.

I have a stalker in my closet. It ogles me every morning, but I do nothing to rid myself of the harassment because I fear I'll miss it when it's gone.

I don't remember much about Shelly's funeral, but I know exactly what I wore. I still recall buying that lovely black sweater at Anthropologie. I had gone back to Chicago for a few days in between her death and the funeral. I needed to distance myself from what had happened. Sitting around Walcott, Iowa, *our* town, would only make things worse. Also, Lazy Eye had driven me to Iowa so I could be with her while she was struggling to live, and while *my* world stopped after she died, his didn't. He had to get back to work.

"Shopping for anything in particular?" the store clerk chirped. *Oh, just an outfit for my best friend's funeral,* I thought.

"No," I said. The sweater was much too expensive and didn't even fit me that well, but it was black, and it was sad, and I didn't have the energy or brainpower to keep looking.

As Court walked me up to the church that gloomy day in January, the scene felt far too familiar. I had just walked that same exact path four months prior for Shelly's wedding. I don't remember whom I spoke to when we got to the funeral or what thoughts were going through my head; I just know that I avoided that open casket for as long as possible. I understand why some people yearn to see a deceased loved one just one more time before the burial, but when you've witnessed that loved one in the process of dying, it just feels redundant. The only way I wanted to see Shelly again was alive and laughing. It was impossible to enter the service without walking by the casket, so eventually Court took my hand, as she had so many times when we were children, and guided me forward. I paused next to the casket ever so briefly because I knew that's what people expected me to do. Shelly looked like a mannequin corpse. She wore a wig, she was pale, and she was bloated, but what upset me most was that her lips were sealed shut. Forever.

When it came time for the burial, I tried to stand in the back. I didn't need a front-row seat to see her descend. But little by little, layers of people were effortlessly stripped away. Just as I'd found myself at the front and center of Shelly's life, I found myself at the front and center of her death. As the coffin lowered, I didn't think of myself as a woman losing her rock. I thought of myself as a fourth-grade girl afraid of how she would survive without her best friend.

So that sweater, the one I was *not* buying for anything in particular, stares at me every morning when I open my closet. It begs to be part of my life again. I tell myself that the invisible stain of sorrow will eventually fade. But right now, pain is all I see. Will I really ever wear that sweater again?

Not today.

You know how some people can get away with wearing just about anything? Even if the ensemble looks less than fabulous, you still respect them for taking the risk. Well, I'm not one of those people. But I seem to think I am when I'm traveling abroad (i.e., going on commercial shoots on the company dollar). When my feet return to U.S. soil and I put on whatever "authentic" garb I spent too much money on, I realize I just look authentically mental.

The flowery-shirty-dress thing that I bought on my trip to South Africa fits into this category perfectly. I had never stepped foot outside of the United States when I found out that Christine and I were going to be producing a commercial in Cape Town. So yeah, I went from "never even been to Canada" to "I'm flying first class with one of my best friends to *South Africa*." It remains one of the best experiences of my life. We had a few days to explore while we were there, so our producer showed us all the local shopping gems. Because I couldn't do the currency conversions in my head, I pretended everything was cheap. That's how I ended up with the outfit I'm wearing right now, the flowery-shirty-dress thing that fits like a mitten. I glance at my reflection in a store window on the way to work. *When did my elbow get fat? Shit, did I grow a third boob last night?* The jeans I'm rocking aren't any better. They are the cut you see only on trashy butts in stores like Menards or KFC. By the time I get to the office, I've received two judgmental "up-down" looks. I also receive a compliment that I look "springy." Isn't that like telling an ugly person they're funny?

The fact that I don't have any close friends at work makes this challenge even more terrifying. Court's coworkers are totally in on the joke. When she walks into her office wearing a velvet blazer made for a senior citizen with pizzazz, her friends all give her knowing smiles and a thumbs-up. When I walk into my office wearing a vest that could easily be mistaken for Grandma's afghan (which I do on day two), Lars Larsen is my only confidant. And he wears skull T-shirts every day. My productivity is at an all-time low. I feel too unattractive to get anything done.

Friday is the ugliest day of all. I wear a T-shirt that I've neglected for all the right reasons. It's blue, with a *painted-on* belt and police badge. I bought it when vintage T-shirts were hard to find. Nowadays, any slacker hipster can find a reproduction at Urban Outfitters. (*I shake my fist at you, hipsters!*) What does one pair with such an exquisite piece of eye candy? Well, sparkly tweed pants from the Gap's 2002 collection, of course!

I hope to go unnoticed as I scurry through the fashionable halls of the Merchandise Mart. For the first time ever, I'm relieved to enter my dowdy office. Lars Larsen is already perched behind our cube wall, per usual.

"Are you ready for this?" I ask.

"It can't be worse than yesterday," he laughs.

I take off my coat, preparing for mockery.

"Those pants are sweet!"
*Oh, Lars Larsen, the world needs
more of you.* "I mean, they probably aren't stylish, but they seem
kinda rave or somethin'."

"And the shirt?"

His face contorts into
laughter. "No comment."

I slowly sit down, blocking
his view of my faux police badge.
We yak over the wall about our
campaign until a cryptic email
lands in our inboxes: "ALL
AGENCY MANDATORY
MEETING AT 1 PM." *Oh shit.*

At my former office, "all

Stop or I'll . . . put some Dutch shoes on
my hands.

agency mandatory meeting" meant we needed a good old-fashioned
pep talk. Or maybe some snacks. I know that's not the case here.
There is barely a culture to begin with, so no one ever really tries to
preserve it. Whispers about layoffs start swirling, but I block them
out with my "office-style jams" playlist on iTunes.

Shortly before noon, we see stuffy executives from the New
York office milling about. *This can't be good.* Marie, my friend with
ovaries in the HR department, walks by and gives me a nod. This
nod generally means, *You. Me. Coffee. Now.* Like cheating lovers,
we leave at separate times so nobody knows we're cavorting. I find
her at our usual place in the magazine aisle of the convenience store
downstairs—too many witnesses at the fancy coffee places.

"What's going on? Should I be looking for a job?" I don't fuck
around.

She doesn't smile. Marie *always* smiles. "The agency is closing
in two months. They are going to announce it at the meeting, so
keep it on the down-low until then." She doesn't fuck around either,
and I'm thankful for that.

"Oh, neat."

"Bree, I'm really sorry," she says. Marie was part of the team who poached me from my former agency seven months ago. I hadn't been looking for a new job, but it felt good to be wooed. I had been running in place for four years and knew that if I stayed, I would never get the jump in salary I needed to afford the lifestyle I was pretending I could already afford. I almost doubled my salary by jumping ship. But who knew I was jumping into a leaky ship?

"Don't apologize. I needed to leave. I needed a change." And even though I'm scared shitless right now, I really mean that. When we get too set in our ways, it's easy to mistake effortlessness and comfort for happiness. It wasn't until I deserted my familiar sur-roundings that I realized my heart had not yet healed from the emptiness Shelly's death caused. Shortly after her funeral, I jumped right back into work and filled the void she'd left like you'd fill a hole in the wall with spackle. Sure, it covers up the damage on the outside, but the inside is still hollow and broken. When I suddenly faced a job I didn't love and people who didn't really get me, the emptiness revealed itself; the spackle began to crack. That's why the bar conversation about resolutions with Foxy and Kerry stuck with me when it usually would've disappeared. That's why I felt the urge to start something new to improve myself. And that's why I feel like I might actually be healing for the first time since Shelly's death. So maybe I do feel a little cheated for being laid off seven months after starting, but I'm glad I took the chance. Because really, is coasting along on a plateau ever as fun as riding uphill and back down again?

"So . . . can we hang out down here and read *Us Weekly* until the storm hits?"

"Please." Marie hugs me, and then we spend some quality time gawking at George Clooney.

When I return to the office and see Lars at his desk, my heart breaks. I can't tell him what I know, out of respect for Marie, so I do the selfish thing instead.

"I'm gonna work from home for the rest of the day. If we're fired, we're fired. I don't need to be told by a bunch of New York bigwigs. Cool with you?"

"Yep. No worries."

"Be safe. I've got crime to fight," I say, pointing to my fake cop badge.

Lars gives me finger guns. "See ya Monday. If we're still here."

I stop by my boss's desk on the way out the door. He's a cool guy, and we've always communicated openly. In fact, if anyone were to judge my fashion choices, it'd be him. But clearly his mind is elsewhere today.

"Hey, Bill. Do you mind if I head out? I've got a lot of scripts to write, and I can't get anything done here."

He gives me that same guilty smile Marie gave me. "Yeah, go ahead. I'll let you know if anything goes down this afternoon."

I know I'm getting the free pass to skip the mandatory meeting because I'm the newbie. Almost everyone else, including Lars Larsen, has been working here for a decade or more. It'd be like talking about divorce in front of the kid.

On the way to the train, I call Eric and get his voicemail. "Hi. So, I just found out I'll be losing my job in two months. Plus, I'm wearing sparkly tweed pants. Do you still like me?" Tears well up in my eyes. Saying it out loud always makes things so much worse.

At the stroke of 1:00 PM, the Internet is ablaze with news of the closing. Someone had already tipped off AgencySpy.com, a popular advertising blog, so while my coworkers were sitting in a lifeless boardroom being told they were no longer needed, everyone in the outside world already knew. *Fucking Internet gossip.*

My boss calls shortly after one thirty and leaves a voicemail: "So, I'm sure you've already heard. We are—uh. We're closing. We'll talk Monday, but stop working on those scripts and go have a drink!"

Good idea, boss.

I text Amy: "Agency closing in 2 months. Happy hour at Tilli's?"

"Congratulations!" Amy sings, setting down two shots of Jäger-meister on the table.

"Um, thanks?"

"Here's to getting time off work while planning your wedding!"

"Right, except for that no-more-paychecks thing."

"You'll be fine, baby. You always are. Remember when you were gonna drop out of ad school because you felt guilty about borrowing money, but then we got the Chicago internship that *everyone* else wanted?" We had beaten out a lot of art director/copywriter teams for this prestigious gig—including my filthy-rich boyfriend at the time. (He's a fantastic writer.) When we got the call informing us that we'd been chosen, we rolled around on the floor and screamed for twenty minutes. We also went to church the following Sunday. Amy is a loyal churchgoer, but it was my first time in twenty years. And I almost missed it because I was naked with my boyfriend. I heard the front door to our apartment shut around 9:45 AM. "Shit, I told Amy I'd go to church!" I sprang out of bed, put on a dress and heels, and sprinted four blocks in negative-four-degree Minneapolis weather to get there on time. I'll never forget Amy's face when I slid into the pew next to her. My hair was matted to my face, my skin was frozen purple, but I was *there.* Amy grabbed my hand and smiled at me with tears in her eyes.

"Yeah, that was pretty awesome."

"Right? And the rest is history. Things work out for you, Bree. I'm not even a little bit worried."

For some reason, hearing Amy say she's not worried about me helps *me* not worry about me quite so much. Or maybe it's just the Jäger. Either way, I leave the bar in a much better mood than I was in when I got there. I talk to Eric when I get home and assure him that I'm fine and that everything will be okay, even though I don't know if either one of those things I'm saying is true.

I'm getting married in four months. I'm turning thirty in one month. I'm hoping to buy a condo in the near future. And now, I'm basically unemployed. But I've still got my friends, my family, and a man who wants to marry me. It could be worse, right?

I call my parents on Saturday to tell them the news. I would prolong the dropping of the loser bomb until I figure out what my next step is, but my agency is a legend in the advertising world, and I fear the news might make the local paper back home.

Telling your parents you're going to be laid off is like telling them you got "cut from the team." There's an element of "I'm just not good enough" that you know will hurt your parents even more than it hurts you. I fake as much confidence as I can muster.

"We have two months before the doors close in June, and then I'll get a month of severance, so I'll be fine. A lot of agencies are hiring right now." *Not true.*

"Well . . . okay, sweetie. Are you sure? Do you need us to send some money?"

"No, no, you guys have helped enough."

"Have you and Eric talked about maybe postponing the wedding?"

"No. It's all good, Mom." I almost believe myself when I say it.

After a few (or seventy-five) more questions, we say goodbye, and I curl up on the couch like the women in Lifetime movies do when they are sad.

Layoffs are supposed to happen to old, washed-up people. Or people who are bad at their jobs. Layoffs aren't supposed to happen to young, hardworking people like me. I've never been fired from a job in my life. Not even when I should've been, like when Shelly and I worked at Subway and attempted juggling tricks with the mayo and mustard bottles like Tom Cruise did with liquor bottles in *Cocktail*. It wasn't just any Subway, by the way—no, *this* Subway was inside a gas station—at the World's Largest Truckstop. It was not at all unusual to hear, "Bart, your shower is ready," over the intercom halfway through the construction of Bart's Cold Cut Trio. We also had access to the intercom that the gas attendants used to announce when the gas pumps were on. So every once in a while (i.e., during the shifts Shelly and I worked together without a manager), in the

A true Subway Sandwich Artist at work. "Would you like to make it a meal deal?"

middle of "Driver one, your pump is on," or "Driver two, your pump is on," you might hear, "Tuna, tuna, tuna," or, "Meeeeeatbaaaaalls." We were positive this subliminal messaging would boost sales. It didn't. Our clientele was a mix of traveling families, dirty truckers, and Greyhound Bus drifters, but Shelly and I loved every minute of it. Oh, except for the time a trucker chucked a foot-long meatball sub in Shelly's face because he said it was too sloppy—she didn't love that. (I secretly thought it was hilarious.) Man, that was the best job ever. *Can I go back?*

On Sunday, I rummage through the bag of clothes I've collected to take to the Salvation Army. Now that my paychecks are endangered, perhaps I shouldn't be so quick to trash the stuff that makes me look just a *little* fat or just a *tad* deranged. I come across that black sweater and pluck it from the sea of misfits.

Letting go of the past can be as easy as giving up your VHS copy of *Xanadu* and the pile of one-size-fits-none tees that you got as "proof of participation." But sometimes, despite what other people say, it's okay to hold on to a little baggage. Perhaps one day I'll be able to let that sweater go, but it's the last thing I wore in Shelly's presence, and I'm not ready to give that up just yet.

Chapter 12:

moving on ~~up~~ over

"Unemployed." Think about that word. "Not useful." If there were a picture next to the definition in the dictionary, it would be someone wearing stained sweatpants with pockets, lackadaisically scratching his/her crotch while watching *Maury Povich*. Soon, that will be me. Until then, I must continue to report to an office that no one cares about anymore. We were given two months to tie up loose ends before handing the work over to the New York office. (The whole company didn't close, just the Chicago office.) This means Lars and I have to do all the legwork for our campaign and then someone else will get the glory of shooting it. *Not cool*.

"Good news," Lars says when I slug into work. I haven't seen him since my escape before the announcement of the closing on Friday. *Did he somehow miss the memo?*

"The New York office took pity on us, so we get to stay around until we're done shooting our campaign," he says.

Court and I are avoiding caffeine this week, so I skipped my sketchy pal, 5-hour ENERGY, this morning. Without it, my brain limps at the speed of an elderly snail with polio. (I was hoping the magic energy potion contained something other than caffeine to make you feel like a million wacked-out bucks, but this is what I found out: "Unfortunately, the manufacturers of 5-Hour ENERGY are not willing to disclose the levels of caffeine in their product. Caffeine levels are concealed within a Proprietary Blend of amino acids." Great. That only makes me want it more.)

Lars senses the deadness in my eyes. "We'll be shooting in New York, mid-July. So, with two weeks severance after that, you're employed right up until wedding time!"

"Dude, that's amazing!" We almost hug, but we've never hugged before—so we high-five instead. I think I love Lars Larsen.

There's a reason wedding planner has never been on my list of dream jobs. This shit is hard. I can barely organize my pencils, let alone a once-in-a-lifetime event.

I've had a few phone conversations with Ken, the owner of the mansion where we'll be hosting both our wedding and the reception, and I've learned he's a tad nutso. The last time I called, he answered the phone during a dog surgery. Yes, he's a veterinarian, but still, he was talking to me on the phone with one hand and *cutting into a dog* with the other. Plus, I had to jog his memory as to who I was, so it's not like he picked up the call for "business" reasons. *Poor Fido.* When I asked Ken if we should hire bartenders, he said, "No, no. That won't be necessary. My girlfriend and I like to bartend. I play the accordion sometimes, too." *Wow. What have we gotten ourselves into?* I asked Court for backup, just in case, and she said E1 and his friend Nate would be happy to jump behind the bar if necessary. We're having an open bar, so I can only assume it will be extremely necessary.

After a conference call with the New York office to figure out how we're going to proceed with the campaign, I call catering companies back in Iowa and learn that we can afford to feed each of our guests a carrot stick before we go over budget. (Did I mention Eric and I never even talked about a budget?) I'm starting to wonder if the Coliseum, with its buffet-style dinner, was the way to go. Too late now.

The only thing that has been easy so far is ordering the cake. I copied Shelly for that decision. It was at her wedding that I first tasted the Ho Ho cake. It's exactly what it sounds like—the gourmet version of every kid's favorite Hostess snack. Where do you find such a novelty? A classy bakery in Chicago? No. The local grocery

Proof that Lars Larsen really does exist! (Not pictured: big, boat-shaped chocolate donuts.)

store in Walcott? No. The lady who lives down the gravel road from Shelly's parents? Why, yes, yes indeed. She said she'd bake some sample cupcakes for us to try when we're home in a few weeks for the Preeclampsia Foundation Promise Walk. "Just call and let me know when you want to come get them. I work the drive-through window at McDonald's, so you can pick them up there. I don't do email or any of that stuff, so make sure you call first." Aw, *so* wonderfully small-town. I agree to send her a down payment without even sampling the cupcakes because I sampled the hell out of them at Shelly's wedding. It was one of the first things she said to me when we got to the reception: "Make *sure* you get one of the pieces of Ho Ho cake before it's gone." Wiser words were never spoken.

To prevent myself from experiencing a premature bridal breakdown, I decide to call Sarah and Denise, the two girls Court recommended to help me with the planning and decorating. Denise agrees to be in charge of staying in touch with Ken so he doesn't forget we exist, and Sarah takes on the role of "wedding designer/ decorator." After I talk to both of them, my head is spinning. *Color scheme? Flowers? Centerpieces? Trash receptacles? Porta-potties? So overwhelming!* I scour websites for "budget bride." Who knew party favors were so expensive? The only favor our guests will be getting is *not* having to do the chicken dance.

"So, my loft sold," Eric tells me on the phone that night.

"Wait, what? Like, *sold* sold?" We've been waiting to hear this news for months. And it happens *now?* My future has never felt so wonky. Timing is a massive bitch.

"Yeah, they have to do some inspections, but if the sale goes through, we'll have until July to find a place."

(Silence.)

"Bree, we'll finally get to live together. That's a good thing, right?"

"Yes—yes. I'm sorry. I just don't know how we're going to buy a place right now."

"We'll figure it out. Maybe we just rent for a while?"

"Yeah. I think that's our only option."

Humph. So there it is. I suppose I shall wallow in the world of landlords and Berber carpeting for another year or two. But at least I'm acquiring a "roommate." Better yet, he's a roommate who likes to cook and clean. He's my very own Tony Danza! I'll miss sitting around wearing giant, snagged lady panties, peeing with the door wide open, and watching eight hours of *Little House on the Prairie* without shame, but there's something pretty thrilling about the thought of living in sin with my fiancé. Plus, I need to make sure we won't murder each other when there's no option to "go home and be by myself."

"While we're on the subject of slumming, how 'bout we serve pizza for the wedding?"

Eric laughs.

"No, for real. Wedding food usually sucks, and it's, like, a million dollars. Pizza is affordable and *everyone* loves it."

"Sure. I think that's an awesome idea. Happy Joe's?" (Happy Joe's is my favorite pizza in the universe.)

"Hell. Yes. I'll call tomorrow. Also, I talked to the cake lady and sent her a down payment the other day."

"Okay, cool. Thanks for doing that!"

"And the check I wrote for the mansion just cleared, too. Plus, I agreed to an estimate with the girl who will be helping us decorate." This is my subtle way of hinting that I've been planning/paying for all wedding-related things thus far. (Other than the lovely ring, of course.)

"Sounds good! So, do you wanna start looking at apartments this week?"

Huh, maybe *too* subtle? I don't want to be a nag about money just yet, because we have a long way to go before August, but the bridezilla inside me is screaming.

"Yeah, that's cool. I'll start looking on Craigslist. How do you feel about a studio apartment?"

Eric laughs. I don't know if I'm kidding.

With all the decisions I need to make about my life, the last thing I want to do is come up with another resolution. *Will anyone notice if we take a week off?* The project has become like a second job, and I'm barely hanging on to the first. *Eh, I'll figure it out later. I should probably go get a lip wax.*

Much like the beauty aisle at CVS, a trip to any sort of salon usually brightens up my day. Well, except for the time I almost paid for sex in Prague. I was shooting a commercial there and decided to make a massage appointment on our day off. I had been frequenting the hotel's gym and was surprised to find that the same young dude who checked me in and out of the facility was also the guy who would be giving me my full-body massage. I was skeptical because he didn't seem old enough to be looking at naked lady bodies online, let alone touching them in person, but we were staying in a nice hotel, so what could go wrong? He led me into a brightly lit room the size of a shoebox and said, "Take off clothes." He hit "play" on the stereo, and a marching-band version of "Eleanor Rigby" filled the air. I shit you not. I scurried my chubby naked ass onto the table as quickly as possible, wondering if I'd made a mistake. There wasn't even a blanket or sheet to hide under. Perhaps "massage" meant something different in Czech? *No, no, no, I'm being a prudish American,* I assured myself. And then he leaned down and whispered into my ear. "You have rubber?" *Oh fuuuuuck. What do I do now? Should I run? Running naked in public would probably be worse than just having sex with this dude. He's pretty cute. Oh shit. Oh shit. Oh shit.* And then he continued, "For your hair. Rubber? Hold hair back?" *Riiiiight.* So yeah, that's the one time a trip to a salon did not brighten my day.

Sorry to derail. Off to the waxing boutique I go!

Regina is probably a nice girl when she isn't yanking hot wax off my face. But right now she is doing just that. She's also talking to me and asking questions while she does it. How do I answer her when my mouth is covered in sticky, thick goo? It almost seems as if this is her first time waxing, but, as expected, I do feel shiny and new once all the pain subsides. Now I'm ready to face the day with more positivity (and less facial hair).

On my walk home, I wrack my brain for next week's resolution. I think about what is truly at the heart of this impromptu project Court and I created. It's not just about wacky antics—it's about living life a little more like an extraordinarily vibrant girl who no longer gets to live. We *get* to live. Breathing and walking and talking are not chores, they're gifts.

The first movie I saw after Shelly died was *Million Dollar Baby.* I remember it vividly because I cried like a seven-dollar baby (price of admission). It wasn't the heartbreaking film that got to me; it was the act of watching a film. Shelly would never get to do that again. She would never get to slouch down in a cushy seat with a Cherry ICEE and Junior Mints in her lap. She would never get to escape to a fantastical world where men say things like, "You make me wanna be a better man." She would never get to feel that rush after witnessing brilliance or that bellyache after laughing for two hours straight. She would never get to feel *anything*—ever again.

As these thoughts tumble through my mind, I breathe in my surroundings. Chicago seems more beautiful than usual. This, right here, is our next resolution. We need to slow down and take time to notice all the beauty that surrounds us every day. I know it's not groundbreaking, but the best things in life usually aren't.

I smile to myself and continue on my way. (I would whistle a happy tune, but I wasn't blessed with whistling powers.) I look in the mirror when I get home, and my smile fades. Due to my lip wax, I now look like a burn victim. *Oh, Regina.*

"Hi Bree, sorry to tell you this, but your personal trainer has quit. Take this week off, and we'll set you up with a new trainer next week."

"Oh, that's too bad." *That's not too bad at all. Pete was a douche.* "Would it be possible to a request a female trainer?"

"No problem. Yeah, Pete is a little . . . intense. Sorry about that."

Well, now that I have the week off from the gym, I decide I might as well try that lemonade cleanse so many people (mostly anorexic starlets) rave about. I had planned to do it closer to the wedding, but this will be like a dress rehearsal in case anything goes wrong. I do some quick online research and am psyched to become pocket-size in three days, though I have to admit, the suggestion to have "lots of toilet paper on hand" and to "consider using adult diapers" is rather frightening. Oh, and also this: "Don't ever fart during this process. It's probably not a fart."

The cleanse consists of drinking lemon juice, maple syrup, and cayenne pepper at least six times a day—and to eat nothing else. Sounds gross, but my first serving isn't too shabby. What *is* shabby (and by shabby, I mean fucking disgusting) is the Salt Water Flush.

The Salt Water Flush is an important step in the cleanse. The instructions tell me to simply dissolve one teaspoon of sea salt in a quart of water and chug. Easy enough, right? Maybe if your name

is Madison and you are a mermaid in love with Tom Hanks. It feels
like warm snot trickling down my throat. I gag. I've never chugged a
quart of anything. When I've finally choked it all down, I keel over
on the couch. For the next hour, I skip to the loo multiple times.
I give up on the cleanse two hours later. I'd rather keep the five
pounds on my ass than poop it out in liquid form. (Sorry, but you
deserve the truth.)

Eric and I look at apartments the following evening. Nothing
seems right. Everything is too small, too generic, too expensive, or
too anti-dog. Yeah, did I forget to mention that? Not only will I
inherit a Tony Danza—I'll also inherit a dog almost as big as me.
I've never owned a dog. I've never *wanted* to own a dog. I've only
had the two types of pets women get mocked for owning: cats
and hamsters. And while we're on the subject, women with cats
and hamsters are *not* creepy or sad, like the stereotype suggests. It
comes down to shit. Women like cats and hamsters (and rabbits,
fish, etc.) because we have small hands that don't enjoy scooping up
turds bigger than our heads.

We give up on the apartment search for the night and go back
to Eric's loft. He cooks a lovely dinner, and we relax in front of the
TV with a bottle of wine. Well, *he* relaxes. I let my mind run at one
thousand miles per hour. This never ends well.

"So, should we make some more appointments for tomorrow
night?" he asks.

This innocent question sets me off in a way that I'm not proud
of. "Yeah, why not? I'll fit it in with the forty-hundred other appointments I have tomorrow."

"Uh. Okay. Do you have a busy day at work?"

"Probably, but I don't even know anymore because I'm too
busy playing wedding planner all day."

"Bree, if you need help, just ask."

And here it is. The most embarrassingly clichéd yet honest
thing a woman can say. "I don't want to *have* to ask!" I hate myself

for saying it, but I keep going. "I want you to *want* to help plan this wedding. I'm not the kind of girl that *likes* doing this shit. If we would've chosen the Coliseum, we wouldn't have to make these decisions, but we didn't. *Everything* is our responsibility. I don't know how much we should pay for aisle runners, tents, lights, silverware, flowers—I don't even know what a fucking topiary *is!*"

"I had no idea you were doing this stuff, Bree. Why didn't you say anything?"

"I told you! I *told* you I was writing checks and making calls! We have four months to figure this out—most people need an entire year."

"Okay, I'm sorry. I didn't know. Please, let me help."

"Just understand how hard this is, okay? I don't know what I'm doing. And pretty soon, I won't have a job. And on top of all that, I can't stop thinking about how Shelly won't be here for any of this!"

I'm a blubbering mess. Eric hugs me, and the drama slowly dissipates.

"I'm really sorry. I promise to be more attentive. I didn't mean to make you feel like you need to do everything. This wedding will be awesome no matter what. Even if nothing goes right except for being married to each other at the end of the day."

"That's a nice thought, but I'd rather have a good party—and *then* be married to each other at the end of the day."

Eric laughs. "We will have the best party. I know it."

In the search for everyday beauty, Court and I both discover everyday absurdity. But it's just as rewarding, if not more. In fact, Shelly probably would've appreciated weird stuff more anyway.

While I'm out shooting pictures of colorful bike baskets and chalk drawings (not the murdery kind) all over Chicago, Court simply drives down the street and captures pictures of lawn ornaments. I'm not talking about your average lawn ornaments—the cutout that looks like an old lady bending over, or the shiny ball on the podium—I'm talking about evil cat statues, dinosaur skeletons, and a green torso protruding from the ground. This setup would be completely normal if it were Halloween, or even *close* to Halloween, but it's not—it's April. Court's post on the blog makes me laugh so hard that I'm motivated to explore my own neighborhood.

I should probably explain a little bit about my neighborhood. It's full of multimillion-dollar homes. These homes have heated sidewalks and garage doors that cost more than my entire self-worth. Barack Obama ate dinner two houses down from me. I, of course, live in a run-down apartment above the rib shack that the rich people think is "kitschy."

As I make my way around the block, it's difficult not to peer into windows like some sort of peeping Bree, so I try to keep my focus down toward the sidewalk. And that's how I discover the most appallingly awesome yard I've ever laid eyes on. This particular yard lies below street level, which is why I never noticed it before. I see some very recognizable cartoon eyes peeking up at me from between the slats in the stairs that lead down to a garden apartment below. Scooby-Doo lives in my neighborhood? Who knew? He looks scared. I crouch down to get a better look.

Whoa. Whoa. Whoa. WTF? My eyes widen as the most obscene yard decor in history is revealed to me. Scooby is *not* alone.

Please note that the large Scooby on the right is wearing a Six Flags hoodie. He killed someone for it.

There's an entire yard display of crusty stuffed animals posed in strange positions. Some are driving in plastic cars, some are hunched over in a very intentional way, and some are *hung on stakes*. I'm enamored, yet terrified. *There's no way these stuffed animals don't come alive when no one is looking.* I'm freaked the fuck out, but I know I'm meant to relish this lunacy. It's not every day you come across a stuffed garden-party hell. (If you do come across this kind of thing daily, seek help immediately.) I shoot some pictures, post them on the blog, and marvel at how much this discovery added to my day. It made my heart beat faster. We should all do at least one thing a day that makes our heart beat faster. Or at the very least, we should do something that just reminds us that our heart is still beating at all.

Don't be afraid to look down every now and then—shit is waiting to be discovered.

Chapter 13:
keep dreaming

Shelly entered my dreams immediately after she died. In these dreams, we sat on my bed and shared memories, talked about boys, and made stupid faces at each other. I would wake up and feel lucky that I got to have another conversation with her. The only problem was that it felt too real. And it started to freak me out.

I emailed Kim and asked if she was seeing Shelly in her dreams. She replied: "I wish."

After months of this, I began to wonder: *Is it a blessing or a curse?* I loved our nightly chats, but falling asleep started to become next to impossible. I lived alone and was scared by the thought of a ghost hanging out in my bedroom—even if it was my best friend's ghost. When drowsiness started to affect my work and I got one too many "Wow, you look tired today" comments (seriously, when is it ever okay to say that?), I researched cures for insomnia. I tried the usual methods—less coffee, more exercise, sleepy music—but those methods are bullshit when you're dealing with ghosts. It was time to go holistic on insomnia's ass.

I made appointments for Court and me at Shen Shen Health & Harmony on a weekend she'd be in town for a Barenaked Ladies concert.

We walked into the new age spa like two teenage girls walking into a gynecologist's office for the first time. We knew someone would be poking around our bodies, and had no idea if we'd make it out alive. Unfortunately, the waivers we had to sign, which absolved the spa of any permanent damage (i.e., death), solidified that fear. I decided to try acupuncture and cupping. Court opted for cupping only. In case you don't know what cupping is, it's an ancient treatment that is supposed to promote healing by mobilizing blood flow. This is done by heating a cup *with fire* and then placing said cup onto the skin to create airtight suction. Once the cups are stuck tightly to your back, they are then shifted around on your body to alleviate internal congestion. I had learned from paparazzi pictures taken of Gwyneth Paltrow that it oftentimes results in circular, alienlike bruises up and down the back. Wait, why had we decided to do this again?

After I filled out the scary paperwork, the cupping/acupuncture practitioner led me to a small, dimly lit room. "Is there a particular reason you decided to come in today?"

"I've been having trouble sleeping," I said.

"Any reason you know of?"

"Um. Well . . . my best friend, Shelly, died recently—and I feel like she's in my room at night."

"Okay, let's talk about that. Why do you think she's in your room?"

"My dreams about her are super vivid and always occur in my bedroom, it's as if I never even fall asleep."

"This is actually pretty common, so you shouldn't feel weird about it."

Hey, who said I felt weird? Okay, yeah—I felt totally weird.

"We'll do the cupping and acupuncture, but I'd love to give you a few tips, if you don't mind."

"Sure, why not." I was impressed that, unlike my "grief counselor," this woman was ready to give me answers.

"Many people believe in clearing out spirits by waving sage around the room. Is that something you might consider doing?"

"Uh, to tell you the truth, no. That's not likely." People in horror movies do that—before getting bludgeoned to death by whatever spirit they're saging away.

"That's okay, it's a bit extreme. Another way to break up the spirits is to clap loudly when you feel a presence." That sounded slightly more doable, but still cuckoo.

"Lastly—and this is important—you need to tell her to leave."

I looked at her like she'd just told me to kick a kitten in the nuts.

"I know it sounds harsh, but spirits don't know that you don't want them around. You need to say, 'Thank you for visiting me, Shelly. I love you, but you need to leave now.'"

Who the fuck do you think you are? I thought.

"Okay, I'll try that," I said.

We moved forward with the acupuncture. I wish I could tell you I experienced an emotional release of epic proportions like Addison on *Private Practice*. But alas, I felt nothing. Cupping, however, made a lasting impression on me. Literally. It was torture. I had the aforementioned alienlike bruises all over my back by the time we left.

Court and I followed up our sessions with lattes at a nearby café. Sure, the therapists told us to drink water, but water is for wimps. We needed a highly caffeinated reward after the voluntary abuse we had just endured.

"I guess we're just not the cupping type," Court declared.

"First of all, that sounds pervy. Second of all, my lady was a total wackjob."

"What do you mean?"

"Well, I've been having sleeping problems. I told her that I think Shelly is in my room at night—"

"Really? Why didn't you tell *me* that?"

"Because I feel like a basket case. Anyway, she told me to tell Shelly to *leave,*" I said. I paused to give Court time to protest before I further mocked the lady's advice. But to my surprise, she didn't.

"I've informed you to leave," she said.

"Huh? I don't get it."

"The Barenaked Ladies song. Ed wrote 'Leave' about his brother who died in a motorcycle crash. He felt haunted by him and couldn't sleep, so he was 'informing' his brother to leave."

"Wow. So asking dead people to leave is a real thing?"

"Yep."

We continued nursing our lattes, but all I could think about was that song. I had always thought it was about a polite breakup. I tried to replay the lyrics I'd heard a million times in my head, but it wasn't until that night at the concert that I really understood them for the first time. As I listened to Ed sing, the very concept that had seemed so disrespectful suddenly sounded beautiful—and normal. When the song was over, tears filled my eyes and I smiled at Court. "Thank you."

These are the moments that make life so special. Moments where you realize that even though you feel so alone and so helpless, you are *not* the only person going through something painful. You are not alone. You are not crazy. You just have to open your eyes, ears, mouth, whatever—just *open up*. And chances are, the world will be ready to help you heal.

I never told Shelly to leave, but I did ask politely if she'd consider letting me sleep. She still pops into my dreams quite often, and I still have the sleeping habits of an owl, but I no longer feel haunted by her.

Court and I have always been intrigued by dream interpretations. We are both vivid dreamers and even share some of the same types of recurring dreams/nightmares. Any of these sound familiar?

- Your teeth fall out. (Everyone has this one at some point, right?) Sometimes they all collapse in your mouth; other times you pull them out one at a time. No matter what, it's terrifying. I've read this has something to do with feeling self-conscious, which explains why I have the dream at least once a month.

- You lose your locker combination. You try and try, but the numbers will not cooperate. *Ohmygod, I'm going to be late for class!* Why, as adults, do we still have this dream? Here's what the Dream Moods Dictionary (DreamMoods.com) tells me: "To dream that you cannot open a locker or that your forgot the combination suggests that you are unsure of where you stand in a particular situation. You feel you have lost some aspect of yourself. In other words, you are on shaky ground." So yeah. . . .

- You are naked. You're chugging along, having a great day, and then you look down and see your junk staring back at you. Yep, you're buck-naked in public. This is yet another dream linked to feeling self-conscious or emotionally exposed. If you haven't had this dream, we probably shouldn't be friends.

- Holy shit, I'm shitting! This is the newest member of my family of recurring dreams. And it's freaking disgusting. It involves my pooping in random places and not being able to stop. (You're welcome.) I've interpreted this one myself: I'm sharing too much shit with strangers.

And it's only going to get worse this week. Court and I decide to dig deeper into our dreams by treating the blog as a dream journal. (Oh man. *What if I have another sex dream about Steve from* Blue's Clues?) Maybe we'll learn a bit about ourselves; maybe we won't. But one thing is for sure: We'll expose ourselves in a way we never have before. Let's just hope I don't have reason to share any poop dreams.

The annual Preeclampsia Promise Walk is Saturday. Shelly's parents, along with a planning committee that my parents are part of, organize this event on Mother's Day weekend every year. Everyone attends—Shelly's old friends from elementary school, high school, and college; preeclampsia survivors; families of preeclampsia victims; the entire Warner clan; and anyone else who ever knew her.

The purpose of this walk-a-thon is simple. We walk to bring awareness to a disease that's one of the oldest on record but that still has no definitive cure. We walk because the only way to soften the sting of what happened to Shelly is to make noise. In fact, we want to make enough noise that every pregnant woman is aware that sometimes puffy ankles aren't just puffy ankles. Sometimes puffy ankles can kill you. Knowing the symptoms and having the guts to speak up to your doctor is half the battle.

Participating every year is rewarding, but I can't say I look forward to it. I feel the same way about it that I felt about going to sporting events in high school. All the popular people will be there. I'm still the four-eyed reject in class when I'm around them. Shelly never made me socialize with her other groups of friends because she knew I was a nervous wreck around people who intimidated me. So why would I want to socialize with them now?

I call Court and whine about my insecurities. She promises she'll be there to ward off evil bitches and then suggests I relax and have a "Bree night" before heading to Iowa for the weekend. Don't mind if I do.

My nights of watching pathetic chick flicks in my big panties are limited, so I go for the worst one I can think of: *Bride Wars*. It's about two BFFs whose wedding plans get botched, and the weddings end up being scheduled on the same day. Through a ridiculous turn of events, the less annoying girl calls off her wedding in the middle of her ceremony and walks across the hall to show up at her BFF's wedding. Thanks a lot, Anne Hathaway—now I'm a sobbing disaster. There's no chance of *my* BFF busting through the door on my wedding day. We won't share a secret glance during the ceremony. She won't do a toast that embarrasses me. I won't get to hear her laugh. I won't get to see her dance. She won't be there at all.

Or will she? It occurs to me that there *is* a way Shelly can be part of my wedding day. There's a tiny replica of her running around in Iowa Falls right now. Without a second thought (or a call to my fiancé), I email Brad and Michelle and ask permission to cast Hailey as the flower girl in our wedding. Michelle replies immediately "We were hoping you'd ask!"

"Hi, I'm Lisa."

This is my second attempt at hiring a personal trainer. I'm not tipsy this time, and Lisa isn't wearing a puka shell necklace, so it's already going better than the first time.

"What are your goals?" she asks.

"Sexy arms in my wedding dress?"

She shoots me a disgusted look.

"Any *measurable* goals? Like, do you want to be able to do a pull-up or try some new machines?"

"No, not really. Back muscles would be nice." I feel my voice getting ditzier by the minute.

"Okay. What's your diet like?"

"Bad."

She's not entertained.

"Okay, we'll work on that. Do you drink alcohol at all?"

"Yes."

"Okay. Would you say you're a casual drinker?"

I have no idea what this means, but I oftentimes enjoy cocktails while wearing sweatpants, so . . .

"Yes, I'm a casual drinker."

"How much would you say you drink per weekend?"

After a bunch of mumbling and stuttering, I settle on "I don't black out *every* weekend or anything." I'm not sure if that's better or worse than saying I have an average of nine cocktails per weekend.

It's a rocky start, but I leave the gym excited about my new trainer. Skinny arms, here I come! I finish off the night with a screening of *The Wrestler* and hit the sack.

Unfortunately, *The Wrestler* creeps into my subconscious. I'm forced to blog about the dream I have where I'm dating Evan Rachel Wood. *So not cool.* Court's dreams suffer a severe case of stage fright, so she is spared public embarrassment. She donates to the Preeclampsia Foundation to make up for it. Small price to pay, in my opinion.

Eric and I drive to Iowa Friday night in preparation for the Promise Walk. We meet my parents for dinner at Happy Joe's Pizza and discuss our wedding menu with the manager. She admits they've never done a wedding before, and she's beaming like a B-team kid who has just been told she gets to play with the A-team tonight. She's more than helpful and even offers us a 10 percent discount for our "bulk" order. I let out a huge sigh of relief on our way back to my parents' house.

"It's *so* good to have that decision out of the way."

"Totally," Eric says. "There is one small detail I've been meaning to mention, though. When I told my mom we were going to serve pizza, she wondered if we could maybe do a steak option as well."

"A *steak* option?" This is less of a question and more of a *are you freaking kidding me?*

"Um. Yeah?"

"We can't afford to invite half the people we want to invite. If we add steak to the menu, we'll have to cut another fifty, unless you have a secret pile of money hidden somewhere." Our guest list currently includes around 120 people. This is after cutting anyone we haven't spoken to in the last two years and also after asking my mom to shorten her list by about 75 percent. It wasn't easy to break it to her that the ladies who work at the nail salon she frequents (who also give her moonshine) were not going to make the cut. They really are lovely ladies, but you have to draw the line somewhere.

Eric notes the tears welling up in my eyes and responds accordingly. "Okay, that makes sense. I'll just let my mom know."

"Thanks. Sorry if I'm being a bitch. But if it were socially acceptable, I'd be fine with serving *no* food and inviting everyone we've ever met."

"Why not do that?"

"Because people bitch about weddings when they aren't properly fed. It's not pretty." I'll never understand why people judge other people's weddings so harshly. You've been invited to a *free party* in celebration of two people in love, and you're going to bitch about the chicken cordon bleu? Assholes.

"So, they'll be fine with pizza?"

"No, probably not."

Eric and I meet Court and E1 in the stadium parking lot fifteen minutes before the Promise Walk begins. I give Court a big hug hello. This gesture is relatively new for us. Casual hugging wigs me out. I don't understand the instinct to say hi by pressing your body up against someone else's body. However, Shelly's death taught us to embrace the people we love in every way possible. So while I'll never go belly-to-belly with a casual acquaintance at happy hour, I'm okay with a sisterly hug. It's nowhere near the hug on steroids that Shelly would give us if she was here right now, but it's still nice.

"How's about a tailgate?" Court says in an old-timey accent as she reveals a jug of Bloody Mary mix.

Forget hugs—I almost open-mouth-*kiss* her. "Best idea ever."

The four of us fill some travel mugs, cheers each other, and head toward the stadium. Don't even think for a minute that this is disrespectful. Shelly was the queen of tailgating and would've been the first in line for a prewalk Bloody Mary. She also would've worn a foam hat and painted her face.

As we near the entrance to the stadium, Popular Girl #1 pops up out of nowhere.

"Hey, Bree, how are you?"

"Um. Yes. Not much. Uh—" *Shit, why can't I speak in sentences?* Court knows I'm not good in front of an audience, so she grabs the two Erics and they keep moving.

"I've been reading the blog. It's awesome," she says.

"Oh?"

"Yeah, Shelly's dad emailed it to a bunch of us."

"And you *like* it?"

"Yeah, the stories you tell about Shelly are so funny. I love reading them."

"Thanks. Wow. Thanks. Yeah." *Use your words, Bree.* "That's so nice of you."

"Can't wait to see what you guys do next. I'll let you go, but it was great running into you." She goes in for a hug. I tense up and smack her on the back like a robot. I take a gulp of my Bloody Mary and continue on my way. I replay the conversation in my head, wishing I'd said something bitchy like, "Oh, you like my stories? Well, maybe I'd write stories about you if you weren't so mean to me in high school." Yeah, that definitely would've been a cool thing to say.

"Bree!"

I turn and see Hailey running toward me with a big smile on her face. Michelle is trailing just a few steps behind.

"Hi, Hailey!"

"Tell Bree how excited you are to be in her wedding, Hailey." Michelle winks at me and whispers, "She has been talking about it all day. She wants to wear her Spider-Man costume, but I told her no."

"You know what, Hailey? You are going to be the best flower girl in the world no matter what you wear."

"Thank you." She blushes.

"Well, we've gotta get in there," Michelle says. "The whole family is waiting to see this little one." She grabs Hailey's hand, and they walk away. Hailey turns and waves at me three more times before they're out of sight. Tears well up in my eyes, but before they have a chance to fall, Popular Girl #2 accosts me.

"Hey, Bree!"

Getting ready to take a walk with my two rocks, Court and Emily (and Em's son).

"Hi, Claire."

I fear the worst, but, just like Popular Girl #1, she tells me how much she likes the blog. Geez, maybe *I'm* the asshole. I escape before saying anything too idiotic and find a seat on the bleachers next to my clan. Instead of replaying the conversation in my head and coming up with bitchy zingers, I replay the conversation in my head and realize that Shelly's "popular" friends are not the fame-whoring beasts I thought they were. They loved her, too. I'm not the only one who lost her. This is yet another reminder of how grief can connect us to the most unexpected people. I should also mention that they were never actually mean to me. I was just scared of pretty people.

Emily (my hometown bridesmaid) breezes in late and plops down next to me. "What's with all the spandex? Make it *stop,*" she whispers. I can always count on Em to bring me back to the bitter dork I truly am.

"Seriously. You couldn't pay me to wear spandex. Actually, I take that back—when I'm unemployed in two months, you can totally pay me to wear spandex."

Before the actual walking begins, there are a couple speakers who tell their personal stories about preeclampsia. It's hard to listen to these real-life nightmares without becoming a weepy mess, so I zone out in an effort to keep it together. I scan the bleachers, looking for familiar faces. I spot one looking right back at me. It's Hailey. She's turned around in her seat, staring at me from a few rows ahead. She smiles.

Oh, little girl, you are a miracle.

The walk commences, and I spend most of the time catching up with Emily. She feels like home to me. While I have a fantastic group of girlfriends in Chicago, Emily is the one friend who has attended this walk with me every year since it began. I know she does it to support the cause, but I also know she does it to support *me*. I'm so lucky to have this friendship of twenty-two years in my life.

On our way out of town Sunday morning, Eric and I stop at AAA Rentals with my mom and Court. The squirrely woman behind the counter rattles off a laundry list of things she thinks we need to rent for the wedding. I see panic in Eric's eyes. He finally understands why I've been such a nutcase. We agree on the basics, like tables and chairs, and Eric puts his credit card down for the ginormous bill. But only after my mom tries to sneak some cash to Miss Squirrely.

To get the icky taste of debt out of our mouths, we stop by the mansion on our way to the highway. We stand on the hill that overlooks the river. Eric grabs my hand. And we feel excited all over again.

Chapter 14:
thirty

When I was a young buck (young doe?), I thought I'd be married by the age of twenty-one. I thought I'd be a mother by the age of twenty-three. I thought I'd be *ancient* by thirty.

Thank goodness I was wrong.

I'm unmarried and kid-free, and my upcoming thirtieth birthday is sounding pretty awesome right now. If my initial calculations had been correct, I wouldn't be the wonderful mess I am today. I wouldn't have had the freedom to move all over the country whenever an opportunity arose (from Ames to Miami to Minneapolis to Chicago to Fort Lauderdale to Chicago). I wouldn't have met Amy or the other kindred spirits I fell in love with at Miami Ad School. I wouldn't have been hired at one of the coolest advertising agencies in Chicago. I wouldn't have gotten to live in an apartment that was all mine. I wouldn't have met Eric. I could go on and on, but the point is, most of my favorite things in life wouldn't exist if everything happened the way I expected. (I don't mean any disrespect to people who got married and had kids earlier in life, but oh man, have I loved my selfish twenties.)

Through a pretty amazing twist of fate, Kerry, Amy, and I turn thirty within days of each other. We've planned an aggressive celebration schedule for this weekend. It will start Friday morning with brunch followed by an afternoon of spa treatments, and then the three of us will check into a hotel downtown and eat pizza, watch Pay-per-view, and get spray tans from someone who calls herself the Golden Girl. (Shady? Probably.) We'll return to our respective abodes Saturday morning and then meet up again that evening for the *real* party. Court and E1 are making the trip to celebrate with us on Saturday, so I'll be surrounded by almost everyone I love. *Almost.*

Milestones without Shelly always feel a bit empty and usually lead to drama. Birthdays (mine and hers) were difficult the year she died, but New Year's Eve broke me. I hated that Shelly would never see 2006. I felt that by celebrating the new year, I was leaving her behind. It killed me to think that I would have no memories with her from 2006, or any year after. I warned my then-boyfriend, Lazy Eye, ahead of time. "Please take care of me tonight. This is going to be tough." (I never say that kind of shit, so it wasn't easy to admit.)

We went out to a club with a huge group of friends that night. The drinks were flowing, the music was pumping, and Lazy Eye was face-deep in conversation with a girl he'd hooked up with in the past. I tried to ignore it; I'm not usually the jealous-raging-bitch type. But my emotions were already confused, and this fucked them up even more. I charged over to him and grabbed his arm. "I'm leaving," I hissed. I shook with anger. (I'm not sure I'd ever shaken with anger before this moment.) He tried to stop me, but you can't stop a freight train in cheap heels after it leaves the station. I stepped out into the bitter cold air, hailed a cab, and rang in the new year alone, missing my best friend.

I hope this thirtieth-birthday milestone is drama-free, but

I'm already thinking about how the girl who chipped in with Court to buy me my first shot when I turned twenty-one can't be here to buy me a cocktail when I turn thirty. She's not just too busy. She's too *dead*.

Court and I choose a resolution that will hopefully lift my spirits: Musical Awareness Week. We each agree to watch/review at least three musicals.

Shelly and I had an unhealthy obsession with *The Newsies*. In case you're one of the 97.2 percent of Americans who didn't waste your time with this gem, it's a Disney movie starring sexy beggar boys who do jaunty heel-clicks while slinging newspapers at "a penny a pape." We mastered the dance routines with the play/pause/rewind/play/pause/rewind VCR method. Because I own the DVD and I know Shelly would expect nothing less, I make it my first review.

This musical is like a teenage girl's wet dream—if that actually exists. It features your run-of-the-mill crippled guy, your racially ambiguous guy, your dirty-sexy cowboy, and your obligatory eye patch guy. And finally, there's Spot, from Brooklyn. We are supposed to fear Spot and his dangerous ways (he uses a slingshot and spits on his hand before shaking!), but instead I want to *do* him. There seems to be a plot, but I've never paid attention to it—and even at twenty-nine and five-sixths, I still don't.

Much like the whole Third Reich section in *The Sound of Music*, Shelly and I always fast-forwarded through the historically significant scenes starring Pulitzer and Hearst. *Snooze.* I resume normal speed toward the end when Christian Bale straddle-jumps onto a horse. I laugh out loud. Not because of Bale's horse-dancing, but because I see flashbacks of Shelly's famous flail. It involved a lot of elbow pumps combined with foot spasms and ungraceful leaps. I couldn't re-create it if I tried.

I want to call her right now. We need to laugh about this together. But instead of dialing Shelly's old number—which is a constant temptation—I call Court. Her voice cheers me up. Her story about watching Cab Calloway in *Stormy Weather* cheers me up. Knowing that someone loves me the most of all the girls in the world cheers me up.

The wedding finally feels like it's coming together. Sarah, the girl helping with decor, has hooked me up with a floral genius, Maya. (She dropped the f-bomb out of excitement at least three times during our first correspondence. Love her already!) Denise is keeping the owner of the mansion in line (i.e., constantly reminding him that there *will* be a wedding taking place on his property). Plus, Court and the girls have planned my bachelorette party to take place in lovely Lake Geneva, Wisconsin, and the date is rapidly approaching. We considered something glamorous, like Dollywood, or Kellerman's Mountain Lake in Virginia for "Dirty Dancing Camp" (yes, you can actually stay at the resort featured in the hit movie and take dance classes), but Christine and another good friend, Megan, are with child, so we choose to keep it somewhat local. Location, location, location, my ass. Friends, friends, friends is what it's all about.

Eric and I continue to check out apartments—and we continue to be disappointed. The only one we've liked so far is a loft in Bucktown. Keyword: *loft*. As in: no privacy. I'm barely okay peeing when Eric is within earshot, so doors and floor-to-ceiling walls are absolutely necessary. (While we're on the subject, why must all sitcoms about married people insist on showing couples on the toilet in front of each other? Perhaps I've still got lovey-dovey stars in my eyes, but I don't see that happening. Ever.)

During one of the bajillion conference calls with Lars Larsen about our upcoming commercial shoot, I find an online listing that looks too good to be true. It's a two-bedroom, two-bathroom unit in a brand-new building. It includes a huge deck, a garage space, and, best of all, a private elevator that opens right into the apartment. I don't know about you, but ever since watching *My Two Dads,* I've prayed for my own private elevator. (Even though my current apartment doesn't even have a dishwasher.) Eric and I schedule a viewing on Wednesday evening, and within minutes of stepping through the door, I'm positive we've found our dream home.

"Um. We want this. How do we get it?" I ask the realtor.

"I'll give you some forms to fill out, and you can bring them to the office anytime tomorrow."

"Can we do it now?"

"There hasn't been a ton of interest in this unit, and I'd like to double-check on the dog policy, so let's stick to tomorrow."

"Okay, tomorrow it is."

The next day, Eric and I drive over to the realty office at 9:00 AM sharp with all of our paperwork.

"Oh, shooooot," the lady says, with fake sympathy. "We just rented that unit out."

You're fucking kidding me.

"We have another unit in that building available, but it doesn't have as much natural light."

Not a huge deal, but I still want to slap a bitch.

Eric and I look at each other and decide on the spot. "We'll take it."

Phew. One more life decision out of the way. Time to turn thirty.

Friday morning starts with a text from Amy: *Happy Birthday to us!*

Today is technically Kerry's birthday, but Amy's was yesterday and mine is tomorrow. This trifecta is pretty magical when you think about it. In May of 1979, the earth was gifted with three girls, three days in a row, who would turn out to meet later in life and be best of friends. How often does something like that happen?

We meet at Yolk around 10:00 AM with bellies growling for mimosas.

"Oh, I'm sorry, we don't serve alcohol," the waiter says.

"Can you come back in a couple minutes?" Amy says.

Unlike the way Eric and I handled the same situation with maturity on our first date at the Greek non-BYOB restaurant, we discuss where else we should go. Our thirtieth-birthday blowout can-*not* start with virgin orange juice.

"Well, I brought gifts. And if you open them now, this might not be such an issue," Kerry says. Amy and I peer inside our sparkly gift bags and each find a full-size bottle of vodka along with a beau-tifully bedazzled flask.

"Kerry, you're a genius. I'll go fill my flask in the bathroom quick. Stand by." Amy heads off like a hero going to save a child from a burning bar.

When she returns, we order our fatty breakfast entrées, along with three orange juices. The juice is promptly delivered, and we each guzzle a third of the glass to make room for the birthday vodka. Amy mans the flask under the table so we won't seem suspicious (even though all the maniacal giggling makes us completely suspicious). Within minutes, we are all blessed with makeshift screwdrivers. In case you haven't figured it out yet, we are classy broads.

"Here's to turning thirty and feeling twenty-two," Amy says.

"And looking twenty-eight," I add.

"And acting fourteen," Kerry says.

We clink our glasses, and just before the sweet nectar hits my lips, I see a hairy blob floating up toward my mouth.

"Uh, what the hell is *that?*"

Kerry freezes. Her first sip is already in her mouth. She looks into her glass and sees hairy clumps in her glass as well.

"What the fuck!" she says, spitting juice back into her glass.

We laugh uncontrollably. It's the kind of laughter you can't fake—the kind where you know you're making a god-awful face, but you can't help it.

"Amy, did you rinse the flask before filling it?" Kerry asks.

"No. No, I did not."

Amy simply shrugs and takes a big gulp of her dust bunny–infested cocktail.

"Welcome to dirty thirty," I say in my best Samantha voice. We clink glasses one more time and then enjoy our dirty screwdrivers.

We check into the hotel after our spa treatments and wait for the Golden Girl to arrive. When she enters the room around 8:00 PM, I'm disappointed to learn that she's smokin' hot. I've never gotten a spray tan, but I know it involves being super naked and bending over a lot. I'd rather have someone with a nickname like Large Marge looking at my dimply naked ass than someone who probably wonders what it's like *not* to be the hottest girl in the room.

She sets up a privacy tent in the corner, and then we take turns letting her spray chemicals onto our aging bodies. Amy goes first. Kerry is next. Then me. I disrobe and put on the sticky footpads she hands me. I've never felt as unattractive as I do right now. I try to act comfortable chatting with her while buck-naked in the corner of a hotel room, but the sweat bubbling on my upper lip tells another story.

She sprays on the first layer of gooey brown liquid. I have no idea where to look, so I shut my eyes. I keep them shut until she instructs me to get in the next position.

"Okay, now face the back. Stand with your legs apart and bend over, please." I take back what I said before. I've never felt as unattractive as I do right *now*.

Ten minutes later, all three of us are overly golden beauties. We lie in our plush hotel beds, watch bad Pay-per-view, and eat pizza in our robes. Heaven.

We sleep in on Saturday morning and wake up to tan bed-sheets. It looks a lot like someone literally shit the bed. Between this and the rose petal catastrophe of Valentine's Day, I will probably never be allowed in another downtown Chicago hotel again. We say goodbye and go home to prepare for tonight's party.

Court and El arrive at my apartment around 4:00 PM, and Eric comes over shortly after. We have a few hours to kill before we meet everyone at the bar, so we decide to start the party early—with absinthe. Not that silly faux absinthe you can find in American bars nowadays—the real stuff. The Czech stuff.

I was introduced to absinthe during my commercial shoot in Prague. (Same one where I almost paid for sex.) My coworker Kevin had bravely kicked the bottle years ago, so I decided I would be his partner in nonboozery on our first night in town. But the rest of our crew went at it wholehog. Absinthe was a-flowing and our curiosity was a-brewing.

"I'll try it if you will," Kevin said.

Hello, moral dilemma, I thought to myself. I wanted to say no, but ever since Kylie Minogue flew off that bottle in *Moulin Rouge,* I'd hoped to meet the green fairy one day. (She's so cute and a really good dancer!)

"Two, please," I told the waiter.

If you've never experienced absinthe, it goes something like this: A grumpy Czech waiter comes to your table, puts a sugar cube on a spoon, dips it into the absinthe, and lights it on fire. When the sugar starts to melt, he drops it into the glass and the glass catches on fire. You then blow it out and shoot it. Um, that's a lot to remember for first-timers.

We anxiously tried to remember the instructions while we waited for our shots to arrive. Then it was time. The waiter did everything he was supposed to, but Kevin and I froze and stared at each other like scared bunnies in a forest.

Our producer impatiently coached us by screaming, "Go, go, go! Drink it! Hurry fast, Go, *go!"*

Kevin and I dove into the green mystery liquid. This is where everything happened in slow motion. As I began to drink, I noticed a small chip in my glass, but it was too late to stop—people were cheering us on. Green wetness trickled down the side of my face as I tried to swallow like my throat had a built-in sifter. Just when I started to panic, I looked at Kevin. His pants were on fire. For real.

"I swallowed glass! I swallowed glass!" I sputtered, clutching my throat.

"My pants are on fire! My pants are on fire!" Kevin sputtered back, slapping at the fire in his lap.

Once the fire was out and it was confirmed that my throat was not bleeding, we tried to act cool.

"That was fun," I said.

"Totally," Kevin replied.

Amateurs, the locals growled with their eyes.

After such a lovely first experience, I brought two bottles of absinthe home with me from Prague but haven't had the balls to give them any love. Until now. I coach everyone on how to shoot it, but I'm kinda making it up because I don't have the correct kind of spoon, sugar, or glass, and I'm not an angry Czech waiter. We're all marginally concerned about the social implications of this decision, but as the green liquid swims down our throats, we forget about it. There's no better occasion to lose your mind than a thirtieth-birthday party, right?

We get to the party, and Amy tackles me.

"Baby! Happy birthday!" Amy and I have celebrated our birthdays together for the last four years:

In 2005, Amy flew in from Dallas (where she lived for two years after Miami Ad School). We had a low-key celebration at a dive bar downtown, followed by a high-key fight between me and Lazy Eye. I wasn't the best host, but Amy still got to make out with Lazy Eye's cute roommate, so all was well.

In 2006, Amy had just moved to Chicago. Hello Dave (my favorite college band) was playing at a bar in town, so we made it our own party. I brought home a guy I had been dating (we referred to him as Hot Rocker), yet I somehow woke up in bed alone—still wearing my coat. When I called him to find out *why* I was alone, he said, "Don't you remember breaking up with me last night?" No, no, I did not. But at least I didn't have to figure out a way to let him down easy.

In 2007, we threw a bash at the shady dance bar down the street. Nothing good happens at this bar, ever. Neither of us remembers how that night ended, but I woke up with a bloody foot and Amy couldn't open her right eye.

In 2008, we found a place with Pop-A-Shot and a jukebox. I bought my first dress that cost over $100 for this party. By the time I got home that night, it was covered in red liquid, thanks to a shot called Redheaded Slut. (This is why I don't have nice things.)

And now, here we are in 2009. In an attempt to be classy, we rented out the back room at a nice bar across town. There is no dancing, no Pop-A-Shot, and no random hookups—but we're okay with that because we're *thirty*. The party is over by 1:00 AM. And then, unbeknownst to us, the night *really* begins.

I give Court my keys so that she and E1 can stay at my place. (I'm in my one-bedroom apartment for another month, so my guest accommodations are nonexistent unless I shack up with Eric.) Eric and I jump in a cab and head to his loft. I notice he's in bad shape after he tells the cabbie to stop at eight random intersections that are in fact not anywhere near his loft. I'm cold and tired, and bed is the only thing on my mind, so I get pissier as time goes on. We finally get to Eric's place, and he realizes he has no cash to pay the cabbie. I scrape every dime I can find out of my purse and *clickety-clack* toward his building in a high-heeled huff. Eric fumbles around in his pockets when he gets to the door.

"Uh, I think I left my keys at your place."

Shit. My apartment is a fifteen-minute cab ride away.

"Well, I just spent all my money on that cab, so can you go to an ATM?"

"Yes, good idea," Eric slurs. I slide down the wall dramatically and sit on the cold cement. Eric returns in record time.

"Hi!" he giddily shouts.

"Hi."

"What are you doing?" he asks with blank eyes.

"Are you serious right now?"

"Let's go upstairs!" He reaches into his pocket for the keys and then stops. "Hey, I don't have my keys."

Fuck you, absinthe. Fuck. You.

"So, you didn't go to the ATM?"

"What?"

I take matters into my own hands and run like a madwoman to 7-Eleven to get cash. We cab back across town, and I tell Eric he'll be spending the night on my living room floor and I'll take the couch, since Court and E1 are sleeping in my bedroom.

I text Court when we get there. She opens the door with tears in her eyes. I see that E1 is already sleeping on the couch.

"Everything okay?" she asks.

"No. Everything okay with you?"

"No."

Court and I walk back to my bedroom without saying anything else. We leave Eric to pass out wherever he lands. I give Court the short version of what I've just been through.

"This was supposed to be *my* big night. And now I'm the one taking care of him? What the hell?"

"I'm sorry, Bree. Guys are dumb."

"What happened with you guys?"

"I don't even know. Just a stupid argument."

We take our minds off the madness by talking about fun, sisterly things. We talk about old family trips, funny elementary school stories, and, of course, our favorite Shelly moments. I almost forget that I was even mad.

But then there's a knock on the bedroom door. E1 tiptoes over to Court's side of the bed.

"Um. Eric just peed," he whispers.

I erupt from the bed. "Jesus, he's pissed his pants?!"

"No. (Awkward silence.) He peed on your coffee table."

Expletive-expletive-expletive-expletive! I don't even know what words are coming out of my mouth right now, but I know they'd get bleeped on television

I march out to the living room. I grab Eric's leg and squeeze it with all my might. He opens his eyes, completely oblivious to what has occurred.

"Hi," he says sleepily.

"You just pissed on my table."

"What?"

"You. Pissed. On. My. Table," I maniacally sputter.

He looks up at me in confusion. I almost feel bad. *Almost*. And then I remember this was *my* night. Mine. I was supposed to drink myself into oblivion and pee on things. Me, not him! I turn around and go back to bed, giving him no time to react.

I lie awake the rest of the night, livid. I hear Eric leave my apartment around 4:30 AM. Thirty is off to a pissy start.

Court, E1, and I go to brunch Sunday morning. Court and E1 are getting along swimmingly. Whatever they fought about last night pales in comparison with the golden shower my coffee table suffered. Eric and I? Not so much. I'm not ready to laugh about what happened yet, but I do crack a smile when E1 takes us through his thought process when he heard the unmistakable trickle of pee near his head.

"Bree, seriously, though, dudes do this stuff all the time," he says. "One of my buddies puked on our fence just last week."

"Well, that's reassuring. I'm starting to rethink this whole heterosexual thing."

"You know Eric's a good guy. Don't give him too hard a time."

Court and E1 leave after brunch and I spend the rest of the day alone, watching Gene Kelly sing in the rain. I know just one call to Shelly would've turned this debacle into gigglefest 2009. But without her, even a swaggering man in tap shoes can't make this day feel right.

Sometimes revisiting things you enjoyed doing with a deceased loved one, like watching a silly musical, can help bring back their spirit. But sometimes it only makes you miss them more. I ignore all phone calls for the rest of the day and assume my pathetic, sad-lady-in-a-Lifetime-movie position on the couch. *Humph*.

I head into work on Monday wearing a camel-colored pantsuit for this week's resolution. I've never worn camel-colored *anything*, but

"Welcome to Doucheberg, Doucheman, & Doucheinski, how can I be of service?"

Court and I decided that after making it easy on ourselves last week by promoting musical awareness, we'd force ourselves to "dress like a grown-up" this week. We both work in industries that allow us to be slobs, so we're attempting to step out of our very cozy comfort zone and become adults. I schedule a "power lunch" with Amy so we can break down Saturday night's drama.

"What started with hairy cocktails and spray tans ended with piss and anger," I say.

"You're not the only one. Well, pee-wise you might be the only one, but Josh and I hated each other when we got home, too." Amy has been dating Josh for a little less than a year. He's great for her the same way Eric is great for me: low maintenance, patient, and accepting of the fact that he will probably play second fiddle to the ladies in Amy's life most of the time.

"I think our thirtieth birthday is going to have to go down as a bust."

"Well, at least no one ended up walking across town carrying all their pots and pans in the pouring rain," Amy says.

"Excellent point." I burst into laughter. She's referring to another one of my infamous meltdowns with Lazy Eye. We got into an argument about which one of us came up with a certain fake band name. (Note: Neither of us was actually *in* a band; we just took pride in naming them.) This super-smart argument resulted in my leaving in an angry huff—but not without Amy by my side—and, um, not without every pot and pan I'd ever brought over to Lazy Eye's apartment.

"Oh man, *that's* the laugh I needed. Thank you," I say. Amy and I give each other a very businesslike handshake (firm grip, two pumps), and I walk back to the office.

Other than my getting more respectful glances than usual due to my professional attire, the world feels right again. Oh, how "powerful" lunch with a girlfriend truly can be. My conversation with Amy reminded me how difficult relationships were before I met Eric. Peeing on my coffee table is an unfortunate event, yes, but this is the only time I've been *mad* at Eric in the two years we've been together. And there is something pretty refreshing about that.

So let's go, thirty—you can only get better from here.

Chapter 15:
road trippin'

There will not be penis straws. I repeat, there will *not* be penis straws.

A few weeks have gone by since the thirtieth-birthday-party disaster. Eric and I are back to normal and getting ready to move in together in a few weeks. But first, it's bachelorette party time. Look out, Wisconsin, here we come.

I'm no stranger to a good road trip. My parents took Court and me camping almost every weekend when we were kids. We were encouraged to fully experience the culture, no matter where the hell we were. If there was a local specialty, we ate it. (Boiled catfish? Yuck.) If there was a local celebrity, we took a tour through his/her home. (Ever been to Carl Sandburg's house? I have.) If there was a local tourist attraction, we explored the shit out of it. (A palace? Made of *corn?*) Every Housley road trip included riding in the big blue Chevy van (Luanne), rocking unwashed hair, singing songs that made our parents want to hack off their ears, and taking the scenic route (i.e., getting lost). But when Shelly was involved, the rules changed.

Excerpt from Shelly's diary, dated July 31, 1994:

> *Hey there! Bree and I met the cutest guys* ever *this weekend. We went camping at Lake McBride in Iowa City and we almost ended up next to them [at the campsite] but Bree wanted to be in the woods.*

Yes, with Shelly, even camping was about boys. The trip to Lake McBride was the first time she joined one of our family adventures. Incidentally, it was also the first time I ever packed my pink-and-purple makeup kit with my camping gear. (When Emily came camping with us, we barely packed a change of underwear.)

Our first run-in with the oh-so-hot camping duo, Nick and Nate, was during a late-night trip to the bathroom. The raccoons at this campground were animals. Well, I guess all raccoons are animals, but this place was *their* world; we were just burning marshmallows in it. We screamed and giggled as the thirty-pound vermin ambled around the Dumpster by the bathroom door. Before we knew it, our heroes risked their lives to save us from these rabid creatures. (They threw a tennis ball and the raccoons ran away.) We thanked them and introduced ourselves. A lady never lingers for too long, so we bolted. We also bolted because we had just washed our faces and didn't have a thick, protective shield of CoverGirl to make us feel pretty.

(Shelly's excerpt, continued):

> *Anyway, on Saturday we played volleyball with them (it was Bree's dad's idea). We all ended up sitting at the electrical box and talking about the dumbest things ever . . . That pretty much ended our night. Saturday we were walking to the beach and I thought we should take the*

other way back. With all our luck, it was the longer way
back and Bree got a bloody nose.

Surprise, surprise. Bree, the nerdbomber, got a bloody nose.
But of course, Shelly walked proudly by my side as I held dirty leaves
up to my face, looking like I'd just eaten someone. Fortunately, Nick
and Nate were not around to witness this event.

We finally made it back to the campsite and hit the showers, just in case we had another accidental sighting of the boys. We
could *not* look like dirty hoboes (i.e., campers). We hot-dogged it up
with my parents and then walked down to the playground, hoping,
praying, that Nick and Nate might be there, too. They were not.
But Shelly and I seized the moment and swung on the tire swings
anyway. Just when we were ready to head back to pig out on s'mores,
we heard voices. *Boy voices.*

"Hey, guys," Shelly said casually, as if we had *not* been waiting
the last two hours for them to magically appear.

"Hey," they said back casually, as if they had *not* just sprayed on
a gallon of Drakkar Noir. This started a conversation that would go
late into the night (10:00 PM). We discussed important issues, like who
would win in a street fight between Mario and Link (from Legend of
Zelda). On our walk back to the camper, Shelly and I pondered all the
possibilities of marrying these guys in the future. It was *so* meant to be.

The next morning, we walked by their campsite, hoping to
catch a glimpse of our future husbands before we all departed. But
they were gone. The campsite was empty. They hadn't even stopped
by to say goodbye.

(Shelly's excerpt, continued):

After they left, I snuck down and took their camping
registration card from the slot so we'd have their address.
Bree and I are going to write them this week. Well, that
was probably the best weekend I've had in a long time. I'd
better go. Love, Shelly.

The only thing that could make two teenaged girls this happy? Boys in the wild. And S'mores.

We actually *did* write them. So. Creepy. But the boys never wrote us back.

Shelly framed a picture from that trip and gave it to me for my birthday years later with a poem about friendship attached. It wasn't perfectly posed and the quality was shoddy, but the joy on our faces made it one of our favorites. I look back at that photo now and think about how sacred the time we spend with our girlfriends truly is. I need more pictures like this.

To help document our weekend in Lake Geneva the same way Shelly documented our weekend in Lake McBride, Court and I vow to snap lots of photos and write a haiku dedicated to our favorite shot each day. Lazy poetry is my specialty. I can only hope my bachelorette party ends up being the "best weekend I've had in a long time."

Before bachelorette weekend arrives, I have an appointment with my personal trainer, followed by a meeting with my wedding officiant (i.e., Kerry). My personal trainer has gotten friendlier since she found out I'm at least a little bit athletic. I can't touch my toes or anything crazy like that, but I do play competitive volleyball twice a week and try to get to the gym regularly. When I mention my bachelorette party, she says I'll probably want to "up" my cardio next week for those extra couple cocktails. I don't think she's kidding when she says "couple," but I laugh anyway.

She gets back at me by focusing on butt and thighs for forty-five minutes. I don't complain—until my butt quivers and I collapse into a sweaty pile of shame.

"See you next week?"

"Sure. If I'm walking."

Lisa has the last laugh.

I replace all the calories I just burned off (and more) with a margarita at the Twisted Lizard. Kerry requested a meeting with the bride-to-be so she can start writing our wedding ceremony. It hadn't occurred to me that she'd have to put time and thought into this thing. I'd be fine if she just stood up and said, "Do you guys love each other? Do you love the same TV shows? Okay, you're married!" But I guess Kerry has more respect for making our love official than I do.

Kerry sets her notepad on the table and gets down to business. First, she asks me how Eric and I met. Easy: the meatloaf-off. Next, she asks what I like most about Eric. Easy: He's nothing like me. Lastly, she asks when I knew he was the one. Uh . . . not so easy. When *did* I know he was the one? (Sidebar: To me, "the one" doesn't mean that there is only one person in the whole world for you. That's just crazy talk. Though I *am* ridiculously happy about the idea that Eric and I will spend the rest of our lives together.)

"Please give me a moment, Reverend."

"As you wish."

I think back to how it all started. After Lazy Eye deserted me in April, I engaged in some very successful summer/fall flings. This ensemble included a musician, an improv actor, a super-young coworker, and two Yale grads. Not bad, right? Because of my impressive roster, I wasn't really looking for anything serious when Eric and I had our first date, in November. However, I couldn't ignore the fact that dinner with Eric felt more comfortable, yet more exciting, than any date I'd been on in months. But still, when did I truly know that it was more than just good chemistry and Electric Reindeer chardonnay?

Oh, wait. I totally remember.

"This isn't appropriate for the ceremony, but I'm going to pretend you're my friend Kerry instead of my wedding officiant."

I tell Kerry about Matt, a guy I met in college. Matt was insanely hot. Shelly and I were friends with him from working food service together in the dorms, so we all started hanging out one summer. After a raucous night at the Dean's List, the trashiest bar in town, where we took full advantage of Nickel Night (literally a nickel per drink), I was surprised to find myself making out with this sexy dreamboat. Eventually, it became a regular thing. Was I his girlfriend? Of course not. As expected, he dropped me and went back to his ex-girlfriend just before I started my internship in Florida.

We kept in touch over the years, but we hadn't seen each other since I left Iowa State. And then one day, out of the blue, he invited me to be his date for a wedding while I was attending Miami Ad School. I flew out to Iowa for the weekend, and our romance was rekindled (i.e., we made out). The distance kept things casual after that, and we both moved in and out of serious relationships with other people, but we still kept track of each other. When Matt found out Lazy Eye and I bit the proverbial dust, he invited me to visit him in Mexico. I had frequent flier miles saved up from all my work trips, so a free flight to Mazatlán in December (he was living there temporarily for work) was a no-brainer. I booked the trip in October and then had my first date with Eric in November.

Eric and I hadn't officially defined our relationship yet when it was time to leave for Mexico in December, but I knew I liked him. A lot. I told him I was staying with a friend from college and that I'd call him when I got back. He wrote down my flight info "just in case."

Matt was as charming as ever when I got to Mexico. He wined and dined me at the kind of beach resort I'd seen only on postcards.

My college self would've jizzed in her corduroy overalls if she had known this was what her future held. He admitted that he'd made a mistake when he let me go and that he was sure we were meant to be after all these years. Every girl dreams of hearing an old crush say this. *You win!* But oddly enough, even though I had feelings for Matt, Eric occupied my mind the whole time I was there.

I returned to Chicago at 2:00 AM on a frigid Monday. I was exhausted as I rode the escalator down to the baggage claim, but something woke me up. Eric was all bundled up at the bottom, with a coffee in each hand. My insides got all squiggly, and I couldn't contain my cheesy-ass smile. *That's* when I knew he was the one who would make me happy forever.

When I'm done telling the story, Kerry jots down some notes. "So . . . a sexy Mexican hookup brought you two together?"

"Yes, pretty much."

"That's beautiful."

I see this haiku when I check the blog Friday morning:

The truckstop pornshop.
Whose rad minivan is this?
It's us. Porn for Bree.

Oh boy. Apparently, Court and Denise have made a classy stop during their drive from Des Moines to Chicago. Maybe I should've been more specific when I said no penis straws. I would prefer a penis-free weekend. But I suppose it's the thought that counts— even when it comes to dirty truck stop porn.

My entire lady dream team arrives at my apartment, and the seven of us load into two vehicles, both equipped with playlists that would make any man blow his brains out. We check into the hotel a few hours later and hightail it to the pool before it starts to rain. The sky is an aggressive shade of gray, but you'd never guess it from the beachwear we're all sporting.

Penis straws were not invited to this party. A penis wrapped in a suit, however, can crash as long as it supplies free drinks for my pretty friends. (Left to Right: Foxy, Denise, Kerry, Amy, Penis, Christine, Me, Court.)

"Hello, ladies, these cocktails are compliments of that gentleman at the bar," the bartender says as he gives us a tray of pink drinks.

"Ooooh, thank you," we all coo in unison.

I've seen this sort of thing happen in the movies—but in the movies, the "gentleman" isn't a chubby forty-something-year-old wearing a black sport coat with navy Dockers. After two more rounds, I learn that free drinks are nice—but only when you're surrounded by pretty friends and don't have to flirt with the man who keeps said drinks coming.

We head back to the room when it literally rains on our parade.

"Time to open gifts!" Court declares. I'm secretly hoping for my first ever sexy-lady lingerie. I've always wanted to wear something scandalously see-through, but if you buy sexy lingerie for yourself, it's like saying, "I think I'm super sexy." However, if you wear something your friends bought you, it's like saying, "Isn't it hilarious how my boobs look totally hot in this teddy? Oh, look, my crotch is exposed! What a hoot!"

Instead of teddies, negligees, and crotchless-panty suits, I unwrap multiple blow job books, lube, and two packs of candy nipple tassels. Eh, well, seven amazing women surround me, and that's better than any trashy gift I could ask for. I've come a long way from that timid girl who was content with *one* friend who had the personality of ten.

We spend the rest of the weekend cocktailing, eating fried foods, dancing with random strangers, and writing haiku. And you know what? It *is* the best weekend I've had in a long time. I have the pictures to prove it. I only wish Shelly (and my pink/purple makeup kit) could've been there, too.

Chapter 16:
"she didn't make it."

A week from now, my bachelorette pad will be forever a memory. *Whoa.* I look around at all my stuff crowded into seven hundred girlie square feet. These things have seen me through just about everything. *Am I ready to move on? What do I keep? What do I leave behind?*

It's funny how some of our most meaningful possessions are junk to the naked eye. The glass ladybug on my mantel looks like a handicapped tchotchke from Family Dollar (she lost a leg when she took a tumble last year). But she carries the weight of Shelly's death on her tiny bug shoulders. I want to protect her from becoming clutter. Court embraces this thought, and we vow to "appreciate the small stuff" for this week's resolution. We'll rediscover the treasures that surround us every day, and we'll let them speak.

As I write the blog post to introduce the idea, I realize that I'm ready to share the story of what happened during the last two weeks of Shelly's life. I've kept most of my posts relatively light up until now, but these faceless strangers who read the blog have become a support group. I can open up to them without any consequences. I don't have to see worry on their faces. I don't have to endure the awkwardness of a pity hug. I don't have to hold back the tears. They deserve to hear the whole story. So here goes . . . (grab a glass of wine).

I got a call from Shelly on Wednesday, January 5. I was running late for a focus group, so I let it go to voicemail. She didn't leave a message.

Christine and I sat in a dark room all morning behind a two-way mirror and watched strangers bitch about the commercials we'd just shot. Shelly called again that afternoon, and again I was too busy to pick up. (And by "too busy" I mean I was listening to a bitter woman ask if the writer of the commercial was "retarded or something.") I should've called her that night, but Lazy Eye and I were going on a date, and I figured I'd catch up with Shelly during one of our marathon phone calls over the weekend.

The third call worried me. It was too early. Morning calls weren't our thing.

"Hey!" she said, in her usual bubbly tone. *Phew, everything must be okay.*

"Sorry I haven't answered the last few times you called. Work has been atrocious."

"Well, of course! You're a rock star advertising exec nowadays."

"You're thinking of Angela Bower. I'm just a lowlife writer." (In case you're keeping track, yes, this is my second *Who's the Boss?* reference.)

"Whatever. You're a celeb to me. Anyway, the reason I called is because I went to the doctor Tuesday and had kind of a bad appointment."

"Ohmygod, are you okay?" *Please don't say you lost the baby. Please don't say you lost the baby.*

"Well, yes and no. I'm only thirty-three weeks along, but we're going to induce labor this weekend because I have something called preeclampsia. I've been on bed rest since Tuesday."

"Oh shit, I'm such a horrible friend! How does this work? What does inducing mean? You're not due until mid-February, right?" I sat down on my bed, ignoring the fact that there was no way I'd make it to work on time.

"Well, yeah, but the only way to treat preeclampsia is to induce labor. It's usually cured as soon as the baby is born, so the doctors will just start the birthing process early instead of waiting for me to go into labor."

"Is this normal?"

"Yeah, the doctors said preeclampsia is common. I mean, I did get to ride in an ambulance from the hospital in Iowa Falls to the hospital in Des Moines, but other than that, not a big deal. I'll call you Saturday. *Don't worry.*"

Something didn't feel right, but I shook it off. Shelly had never lied to me before, and if she said she was going to be fine, then she would be fine.

Shelly called on Saturday, just as she promised. Little did we know, it would be the last phone call we would ever share.

Brad left a voicemail Sunday morning to let me know that Hailey was born at three pounds, seven ounces, but that she would be fine. "Shelly can't wait to talk to you," he said.

I called Shelly's phone immediately. Her voicemail picked up.

"Ahhhhhhh! Congratulations! I'm so excited to meet Hailey next weekend! Be sure to say my name lots and lots this week so she knows I'm important! Call me!"

I imagined Shelly was too busy cradling Hailey in her arms to answer the phone. I was wrong. Hailey had been rushed to the NICU and Shelly was in pain, lying in the critical care unit.

Brad called back Sunday afternoon, but I was at the gym, so my voicemail picked up again. "Things aren't going well. Shelly's preeclampsia has progressed into something called HELLP syndrome. Blood is pooling on her liver, so they're trying to figure out what to do. Hailey is hanging in there, though. She's off oxygen and breathing on her own. So. Uh. I'll keep you in the loop."

I didn't call Brad back. I wanted Shelly to be okay. I wanted *her* to call and tell me everything was fine. (In hindsight, it was rude not to call Brad. But you'll soon learn that most of what I did seems wrong in hindsight.) I worried all night when I didn't hear from her, but I wanted to remain positive (i.e., remain in denial), so I went on with my life per usual.

On Monday morning, I went to the editing house to finish producing my commercial with Christine after getting all the feedback from focus groups. I plopped down with my bagel and coffee and stared at the television monitor like nothing was wrong. But in truth, everything felt *extremely* wrong.

I hadn't gotten any updates on Shelly's status by the time lunch was served. Everyone else headed to the communal eating area, but I told Christine I wanted to stay in the editing suite. I didn't feel like being social. She stayed with me even though I had completely zoned out.

"What if she died and no one wanted to tell me?" I said out loud, surprising even myself. Christine froze, midbite. She jumped up from her chair and landed next to me.

"Bree, ohmygod, don't say that! She's going to be fine. I bet they're all just busy taking care of Hailey."

"I know, I know. But something just doesn't feel right."

My phone rang a few hours later.

I didn't recognize Shelly's mom's voice at first. She didn't sound sad. She didn't sound hopeful. She sounded exhausted.

"Hi. How is she? What's going on?"

"Well. (Pause.) Shelly was airlifted to the hospital in Iowa City because they are better equipped to do liver transplants. Hailey is here, too. She's doing very well."

"Shelly needs a liver transplant?"

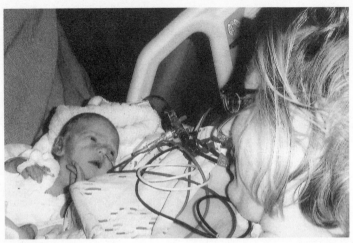

No words.

"The doctors *think* so, but they want to wait and see if things heal on their own." *What the fuck?* Either someone needs a liver transplant or they don't, right? It's not like trying to decide whether to take Advil for a headache. I was completely baffled, but I didn't want to make Brenda explain any more than she already had.

"Okay. Should I come home? I don't know what to do."

"Honey, none of us knows what to do. We'll call you when we find out more."

"Okay. I'll sit tight for now. Thanks for calling me, Brenda."

"Shelly asked me to."

"She did?"

"When they wheeled her out of the room, she whispered, 'Call Bree.'" Brenda's voice broke. I wanted to get off the phone quickly so my voice wouldn't do the same. Crying in public is not my style.

Would you believe that I didn't go home at this point? In the movies, this is where the woman speeds home to be with her best friend. In real life, this is where the woman is so fucking scared and confused, she pretends that everything is going to be okay.

I was afraid that if I rushed home, I'd be admitting tragedy.

Minda, a good friend and our former RA from Iowa State, called me on Wednesday night after the news had spread.

"I heard Shelly's in the hospital. Are you in Iowa right now?"

"No, I'm still in Chicago." I felt like an asshole. Deep down, I knew I should've been by Shelly's side. "She'd probably rather have us all visit when she's feeling better, so I'm going to wait until Friday after work," I said. *I was in no rush.*

Let me tell you what my best friend was going through while I focused on downplaying the severity of the situation. (I learned most of this from her parents after Shelly died.)

On Monday and Tuesday, Shelly had been put on dialysis to help flush the toxins out of her body. Both her liver and kidneys had been affected by the inability of her blood to clot. This is what happens when preeclampsia progresses to HELLP syndrome. (So much for that "once the baby is delivered, everything will be fine" thing.) Unless they could stabilize her and control her bleeding, she would not survive a liver transplant if that were the route they chose to take. She became less coherent as the days passed. She awoke for a moment on Wednesday and whispered, "Turn it off, Dad. Turn the machine off. It's okay." Those were the last words she'd ever say to her father.

Later that day, the doctors put Shelly in a paralytic state to reduce the stress on her body. Her vitals began to show signs of stabilizing. Nothing changed for the better or the worse on Thursday. But on Friday afternoon, Shelly's condition worsened. The doctors feared she was on the brink of total organ failure.

What was I doing during this time to help her? Well, not much. I sent her daily emails about silly things or serious things—or just things in general. That way, when she returned home, she would know I was thinking about her the entire time. Brilliant, right? Maybe, if you didn't already know how this story ends.

I left work early on Friday so I could get on the road before rush hour. I stopped at a gift shop in town for something to give Shelly

when I visited her that night. I saw that glass ladybug, the piece
of junk that now sits on my mantel, and knew it would be perfect.
Shelly had been so excited about the bug-themed nursery her Iowa
friends created for her and Brad when she was on bed rest. I wanted
to contribute in the way I always had: small, but meaningful.

When I returned to my apartment, I got *the* phone call.

"Hi, Bree, it's Minda. Um. A couple of the girls are at the
hospital right now, and I'm on my way there." She spoke in a very
careful, very intentional tone.

"Okay. I'm packing. I'll leave in an hour or so."

"I just wanted to let you know that the doctors put Shelly on a
liver transplant list. They gave her forty-eight hours."

I didn't understand the words I heard.

"Forty-eight hours for what? Like, forty-eight hours to find the
liver and then they try something else?"

Minda cleared her throat. "Without the liver, she only has
forty-eight hours to live."

My body shook when I got off the phone. *This is not real,* I
thought to myself. *She is going to be fine.* I ran around my apartment
and packed haphazardly while singing, "You're going to be okay,
okay, okay. You're going to be okay and I hope you like this song" in
that same childlike rhythm in which Shelly and I had sung, "We're
going to get a drink, a drink, a drink" sixteen years earlier.

My mom called just before I left my apartment.

"Is there someone else who could drive you home?" It hadn't
occurred to me that I was in no shape to drive alone for four hours.

"Um. Yeah. I'll find someone." Adam (Lazy Eye) and I had
been dating for only a month, but he was the first one I called.

"I'll be there as soon as I can," he said.

I didn't know what to do while I waited for him to pick me
up. I paced. I sang some more. And then I sat down and wrote her a
note. I folded it in that origami way we folded notes in junior high
and stuffed it into my pocket.

Adam and I picked up my mom on the way to the hospital in

Iowa City. I couldn't wait to breeze in and give Shelly the note and the cute bug and make everything better. I was going to be the hero who swoops in at the last minute and saves the world.

When I walked into the waiting room, people visibly squirmed in their seats. No one wanted to make eye contact with me. Even as I hugged old friends, I felt the coldness of a secret they kept inside. After five minutes of awkward greetings, Kim offered to take me to Shelly's room.

As Kim and I started to walk away, Minda stepped forward from the skittish group of acquaintances.

"Bree?"

"Yeah. . . . "

"She doesn't look like Shelly." Her face twitched. "Just know that, okay?"

I nodded, but I didn't really grasp what she had been trying to prepare me for. I peeked into each room, one by one, as Kim and I walked past the open doors. Suddenly, Kim was no longer next to me. I turned and realized she had stopped.

"She's in here."

I had looked in that room, but I hadn't recognized the person in the hospital bed as Shelly.

What I witnessed inside that room will forever haunt me. Shelly was jaundiced and puffy from the dialysis. Her mouth was partially open, crammed with tubes. Her chest pumped violently up and down with the help of machines. One blue eye was closed, one was half open—but neither was cognizant of me or anything else in front of her. *She wasn't there.* A metal probe was jammed into her skull to measure her brain activity. Half her head was shaved; the other half of that beautiful head of blond hair was mashed to her face, greasy with fluid. She looked like the victim in a horror movie—not like the vibrant, bubbly blonde I'd known and loved for so many years.

Her grandmother-in-law and another older woman were perched next to her. As I stepped closer to Shelly, an awful noise screeched and moaned. I felt goose bumps creep up my arms and down my legs. Was she trying to say something?

A nurse rushed in and fumbled with monitors and tubes and contraptions until the noise stopped. "Don't worry, it was just the machines," she said, before exiting the room. I shook my head, but I had a hard time believing that noise wasn't human.

The two older ladies got up to give me some time alone with Shelly. Her grandmother-in-law leaned in and whispered, "We've been sitting here all day. That's the first time we've ever heard that." She winked at me sadly and left the room.

It was her. I *know* it was her. She had been waiting for me to arrive. For the first time in sixteen years, *I* was the one running late. She was saying hello . . . or maybe goodbye.

"Hey, Shell, how are you?"

I felt like an idiot. What was she supposed to say? *I'm dying, thanks, how are you?*

"Sorry I didn't get here sooner. I had a busy week at—" And then I stopped. There was no excuse good enough for not getting there sooner. I touched her arm and stared for a long time. I didn't know what else to do. I placed the origami-style note in Shelly's lifeless hand and walked out of the room.

Brad met me outside the door. "Want to meet Hailey?"

Do I want to meet Hailey? Do I want to meet Shelly's tiny baby girl without Shelly there to introduce us?

"Of course. I'd love to meet Hailey," I said, forcing a smile.

Moments after I touched my dearest friend's lifeless hand, I touched Hailey's fragile fingers. I watched her delicate body expand and retract. She opened her eyes and looked at me. And everything became clear. Even if someone had told Shelly what would happen to her, if someone had held up a magic mirror to the sight I'd just seen, she wouldn't have changed a thing.

"Hello, Hailey. Welcome to the world," I whispered.

I squeezed the ladybug in my pocket and wondered if I should give it to Brad at that moment, but I decided to keep it because there was still a chance I'd get to give it to Shelly.

When I returned to the waiting area and saw all the looks of concern, I couldn't stop. I was in no mood to pretend I felt okay. I told Adam and my mom that I would be right back and fled the scene. (Poor Adam, right? *Hi, this is my mom. Please stand with her for hours in a waiting room while my best friend dies, okay? Thanks!*)

I found an empty hallway around the corner and melted into the wall. I pushed my palms deep into my eye sockets. I tried to take deep breaths, but with every breath, reality stung my lungs and I choked. I couldn't be there anymore. It was just a waiting game. Someone else, with a healthy liver, had to die in order for Shelly to live.

Now, think about this for a minute. I was literally praying for someone else's death so *my* friend could live. And not just anyone could die; it needed to be an organ donor. Shelly had been moved to the top of the list because she was a healthy young mother, but there was a whole list of people waiting for a liver. A whole list of people surrounded by family members wondering if this would be the last day of their mother/father/sister/husband's life. It was at this moment that I decided to become an organ donor. I hadn't registered in the past because one of my high school teachers freaked us out when she told us what happens to your body when they extract the organs. Well, guess what, Mrs. Barnes? I witnessed what happens when the organs of a *living* person fail, so I don't really give a fuck about what could happen to me after I'm dead. Please take the time to go to OrganDonor.gov and learn how to become an organ donor if you aren't already. It's kind of like being a superhero, but you have to die before you can save someone. Still worth it, though, right? Right.

Okay, back to your previously scheduled program.

My mom rounded the corner and found me staring out the window, holding that ladybug tightly in my hand.

"Let's go get some dinner," she said.

We didn't return to the hospital that night.

We visited the hospital again on Saturday, but nothing had changed. I went back into Shelly's room and saw that my note was on her nightstand, unopened. I pretended to be friendly when other people walked in to see Shelly, but I really just wanted her all to myself. I hated listening to people talk to her. *She's not going to answer you.*

When I couldn't take it anymore, we drove the forty minutes back to Walcott and sat down to watch TV, but no one registered anything on the screen. The phone interrupted our blank stares around 8:00 PM. I sprinted to answer it, feeling the first kick of hope I had felt all day.

"Hi, Bree, I've got some good news," John said.

"They found a liver?"

"They found a liver! They have to do some tests first, but they will prep Shelly for surgery around 3:00 AM and begin the surgery around six."

John went on to tell me they had only given her a 20 percent chance of survival, but come on, it's Shelly we were talking about here. The girl made shit happen.

I slept on the couch, curled up against Adam—too anxious, too scared, to sleep alone. There are no words for the emotions I felt as I lay there. Imagine that childhood excitement of waiting until morning for Santa Claus to arrive, mixed with the fear that Santa Claus might die instead.

I was jolted awake around 6:00 AM. I felt I'd been gutted. There was no explanation for the sudden panic—until the phone rang an hour later. This time, I didn't run to pick it up.

Timid footsteps came down the stairs. My mom peeked her head into the room.

"Bree, honey? [Pause.] She didn't make it."

And with that, my best friend, my childhood, my soul . . . died.

We went over to the Warners' shortly after we got the call. There wasn't much to say. There wasn't much to do. We just felt like we should be together. John explained that when the doctors did the CAT scan to prep for surgery, Shelly was brain-dead. The transplant would've been futile. *What a cruel joke,* I thought to myself. Locating that liver at the last hour was a miracle. To get that close, to raise our hopes that much, and then—*surprise!*—she dies anyway? What the fuck?

The funeral was planned for Wednesday, so Adam and I drove back to Chicago Sunday night. I didn't want to make him go through any more of my hell than he already had. I will always be grateful that he was there when I needed him most. The next year and a half may've been rocky, but he saved me that weekend.

When we got back to Chicago, I called Amy. I didn't feel like talking, but I knew I had to tell her what happened because she was one of the many who had left concerned voicemails. Some people have the rare talent of knowing what to say at any moment. Amy is one of these people. I'll never forget what she said that night.

"Bree, Shelly was your best friend for a long time—and I know she can never be replaced. But ya know what? I'm going to be here for you for the *rest* of your life. So . . . I hope that's okay with you."

Just before I went to bed that night, I took the ladybug out of my pocket and placed it on my mantel. I bought it to cheer Shelly up. But in the end, it was probably always meant to be mine.

Shortly after I post a blog entry summarizing the heartbreaking story, I get a blog comment from a high school friend named Sarah. (Also famous for being "Jon" in our brilliant NKOTB talent show routine.)

In high school, one of Sarah's best friends was Jerry. Jerry and I played the French horn together in band. He was eccentric and had a personality just as big as Shelly's. We gossiped like the ladies in *Sex and the City* even though we were fourteen-year-old band nerds. Well, Jerry died in a car crash in 1999. The news was devastating. Even more devastating for Sarah.

Sarah writes:

*When he was in the hospital after his car accident I had
almost the exact same reaction as you did with Shelly. He
was in the hospital in St. Louis and I didn't go down to visit
him because I kept reassuring myself that he was going to
be fine and I didn't really need to drive down to see him. It
couldn't be that serious. . . . I knew he was going to be fine.
I still regret not driving down to see him before he died and
I think you're absolutely right that everyone with great loss
has some element of that. Thanks for this post Bree.*

I've felt tremendous guilt for not rushing to be with Shelly the
first day she told me something was wrong. Or the day Brad told
me Shelly's condition had worsened. Or the day Brenda told me
Shelly asked her to call me. I could go on and on about the things I
should've done. And it eats at me every day. But Sarah's words help
me realize that I'm not a horrible person. I'm a best friend. And
sometimes, a best friend doesn't know what to do when her partner
in crime isn't there to help her do the right thing.

Just when I think my healing is at max capacity for the week,
Court posts this on the blog: "And the final reason a post like that is
a little tough is because Bree is my Shelly and I can't even begin to
imagine my life without her."

Wow. Thank you, Sarah. Thank you, Court.

Chapter 17:
we're all just visitors

Shelly would've turned thirty today. I can't treat her to a martini, or twelve. I can't buy her an ironic but totally usable gift certificate to Walgreens. I can't call her and scream, "Happy birthday, Schpelly!" obnoxiously into her ear. (We were "Bianca" and "Schpelly" for special occasions. I have no idea why.) So instead I donate to the Preeclampsia Foundation in her honor. Kind of a bummer, if you ask me.

So how do I *celebrate* her birthday?

Shelly and I were shameless tourists whenever we traveled together. We didn't know what it meant to be "over it." We were wildly excited to be *anywhere*. We swam with the dolphins at Sea-World, posed with creepy wax statues at Ripley's Believe It or Not!, ate cheeseburgers in paradise at Margaritaville, and followed cute boys around the Alamo. So I make a promise to her, on her thirtieth birthday, to spend the week enjoying Chicago the way I know we would've together.

If there was a photo op, Shelly and I posed the shit out of it. This was taken in 2002 at Universal Studios when Shelly came to visit me in Florida. We got bombed on hurricanes at Pat O'Brien's later that day.

For this week's resolution, Court and I will be tourists in our own town. We'll stop being grouchy locals and take advantage of all Chicago and Des Moines have to offer. (Oh man, this means I'll have to go places where people don't walk fast, or, even worse, where they stop right in the middle of the sidewalk without warning. I suffer from a major case of pedestrian road rage.)

The wedding is barreling toward us at a speed that makes me wanna shit my pants a little. Pizza, booze, cupcakes, and munchies have been ordered; RSVPs have been received; floral arrangements and centerpieces have been designed; and we've secured a sound system to play all of DJ Bree-style's finest tunes. We totally lucked out with the sound system. Foxy's dad is in a band in Davenport and offered to set up his sound equipment at the mansion all day and night. For free. It's almost as if he handed me a coupon that says: "$2,000 off!" Mr. Foxy is the stuff.

Speaking of music, I'm trying to figure out how to get all of my

favorite songs involved in the big day. I'd be lying if I didn't admit
I've had a page in my old journal titled "Possible First Dance Songs"
for the last ten years. (Yes, I also have a "Possible Baby Names"
list and a "Guys I've Slept With" list. You can't trust your brain to
remember *everything*.) A few tunes have come and gone from the list
over the years (sorry, Blues Traveler), but I have ten solid options to
present to Eric. He nixes only one, so there are still nine songs in
the running. Foxy will be singing during the ceremony, so I call her
for advice. Foxy's voice isn't like butter, by the way—it's better than
that. It's like butter*scotch.*

"Well, since you have a bunch of songs you like, why don't you
include the leftovers in your prelude?"

"Um, prelude?"

"Yeah, you'll need music for the prelude, the processional, and
the recessional."

"The what, the what, and the what?"

"You've probably never noticed at a church wedding because
they use hymns a lot, but you can totally go nontraditional and use
songs that mean more to you all throughout the ceremony."

"Get the fritz out. I don't have to walk down the aisle to 'Here
Comes the Bride'?"

"Nope."

"My mind, she blown."

Wow. And also, *geez fuckin' Louise.* Just when I think we're
on the home stretch of this figure-it-out-yourself wedding, we
get derailed. Foxy explains more about how the wedding day is
orchestrated. It's all news to me. We decide that she'll sing a Joshua
Radin song (yeah, yeah, it's pussy rock, but I love it) between the
prelude and the processional, but other than that, we've got a wedding to score.

I spew mouthfuls of the new lingo I learned to Eric that night
on the phone.

"Let's have Crads sing one of the other songs you like during
the ceremony," he says. Kevin Cradock, or Crads, is one of Eric's

childhood friends. I love him to death, but *songbird* doesn't come to mind when I think of him.

"Crads sings? Do you think he can do Ray LaMontagne?"

"Yeah, he's great."

"Done. And the prelude, processional, recessional, and whatever-the-hell-else-cessional?"

"Let's figure it out this weekend."

"Okay, fine."

I hang up the phone and start figuring it out immediately. If patience is a virtue, I'm a dirty hooker. I make a chart that includes a column for each part of the wedding that requires music. In case you're as lost as I was, here's how it breaks down: The prelude is a group of songs that plays while people are arriving, sitting down, and trying to avoid people from their past. The processional is the music that plays while the wedding party walks down the aisle being judged two by two (sometimes, one by one). The bride's processional is self-explanatory. Some people include music before, during, or after the vows. (That doesn't seem to have a confusing title like the rest.) Lastly, the recessional is the song that accompanies the bride and groom as they exit. So there, now you know more than I did yesterday. You're welcome.

By the end of my work session, my chart looks like *Good Will Hunting* got wasted and tried to solve a math problem using love songs. Sometimes I wish I were Jewish so I could sum it all up with one big *oy vey*.

I just ate my own nipple tassels. Does this make me a bad person?

Let me explain. I've moved most of my belongings into the new apartment. I, however, remain in my bachelorette pad with the girlie and/or embarrassing items that didn't make the cut. Lars Larsen and I are finally flying to New York next week to shoot our cookie dough campaign, so I figure I'll leave town and never return to my bachelorette pad ever again. I'm a big fan of the clean break. As I've learned, it's easier to get over a lost love when you say goodbye and one of you leaves town for a while. (Even if the other person meets someone ridiculously fast. I swear I'm not bitter. Okay, maybe just a smidge.)

I flipped on the television this morning and slugged down a Diet Mountain Dew, trying to motivate myself to report to an office on its deathbed. (Said television is a major reject in Eric's eyes. He is a technology snob and finds my nineteen-inch Magnavox hilarious. I find it affordable.) This is what I heard on the news: "Due to the outbreak of E. coli, the cookie dough has been recalled." *No, no, no, no. Please don't be my free ticket to New York. Pleeeeease.* Long story short: It was.

Lots of factors can mess up a commercial shoot. Bad weather, revisions, scared clients, poop attacks—but E. coli? *Really?* I would say this is divine intervention, but there's nothing divine about it.

I was emotionally hungry, and I needed candy, fast. Thanks to my bridal diet, the only candy available to me was in the form of nipple tassels. I contemplated whether it was wrong to indulge in my own sexy-sweet undergarments. But then I remembered that I got *two* sets of these pervtastic tassels. I mean, the first time you wear them, it's hot. The second time? Just weird.

So yeah, that's why I'm currently sitting in the middle of my living room floor, eating nipple tassels in my robe.

I get in to work around 10:30 AM. My eyes meet Lars Larsen's eyes. For a split second, I wonder whether we're going to laugh, cry, or spray Easy Cheese directly into our mouths. And then we laugh. And laugh. And laugh. There's nothing else we can do at this point. Well, except leave the office early for a not-so-happy happy hour.

We talk to our boss just before leaving and get the details. Yes, the shoot has been canceled. Yes, we will still be paid until the end of the week. Yes, we can pack our things and get the hell out of there.

Lars and I trot (actually, Lars galumphs) down to the nearest bar at 3:00 PM.

"So, how 'bout a Manhattan?" I ask.

"Is there a drink called E. coli's Nemesis?"

"God, I hope not."

Lars and I talk like old friends enjoying each other's company, not like work friends who've lost their jobs. I suddenly comprehend that I'll miss Lars and his giant chocolate-covered donuts. I know we won't keep in touch. We won't call each other or "do lunch." But I'll always remember him fondly, and I'll be thankful that, for a short while, my mornings started with a greeting from a giant man named Lars Larsen.

Since New York isn't happening, it's time to break up with my apartment. I rummage through the kitchen drawers to pack up the last of my crap, and I come across an old piece of mail from 2005. Shelly had been dead for almost a year when I got it. I hadn't cried much, other than when I visited the cemetery, and I was still having a hard time knowing how to feel about everything that went down. One not-so-significant weekend, the finality of her absence hit me— hard. I don't remember what caused this epiphany, but I sobbed on the floor for hours. The sobs turned into anger, and I yelled at Shelly, God, and anyone else I could blame. Very few are blessed with the kind of friendship I had with Shelly. Most people have a falling-out with childhood friends, or simply outgrow them. But not us. Things got difficult at times. For a while, I contemplated whether we were best friends because we said we were best friends or because our hearts were really in it. But the day she asked me to be in her wed- ding, all that doubt disappeared and I accepted that we truly were soul mates.

So how was I rewarded for my friendship and loyalty? Oh yeah, I got to stand by a hospital bed and watch her die. Not fair. I cried myself to sleep the night of the epiphany and went to work the next morning with puffy eyes. When I returned home, I halfheartedly checked the mail. The mail system at my apartment was sketch city (and highly illegal) at the time. The mailman carelessly chucked everything into a communal bin, and the four of us tenants had to dig in and hope no one stole our Crate & Barrel magazines. (Also, I was the only chick in the building, so it was never not embarrassing to get my Spanx catalogs.) In the midst of my daily mail dig, something caught my eye. I stopped digging. My heart stopped beating. I picked up an envelope addressed to Shelly Warner. *Oh no.* Had someone with her name moved into my building? What a cruel joke! But then I got a closer look and saw that it was addressed to *my* unit. Shelly and I hadn't lived together in over four years, but it was almost as if we were roommates again.

Turns out, it was junk mail. But it wasn't junk to me. I believe with all my heart that it was a message from Shelly assuring me that she'd be with me, always.

I pack the letter carefully in a box marked "important stuff" and continue loading up my car until the apartment is vacant. As I shut off the light, it's sad to see the place so empty and lifeless after I've called it home for the last four years. Never again will I walk through this door to escape the chaos of the city. Never again will I sit in front of my space heater in my flannel pj's and watch E! for hours with a pan of ramen noodles in my lap. Never again will I live alone. Maybe that's not such a bad thing? Guess I'll find out. Goodbye, single Bree—we've had some good times.

Christine agrees to meet me at Millennium Park Grille on Wednesday afternoon. The park is directly across the street from the office where we worked together for four years. It's also crawling with tourists, screamy children, and mangy hoboes.

This isn't the average lunch between friends, for three reasons: (1) I'm getting married in a week. (2) She's having a baby in two weeks. (3) I'm wearing a fanny pack. I'm still disappointed that her life-changing event will keep her from being part of mine, but she's assured me that she'll make the baby feel guilty about it for the rest of his life.

I arrive early and grab a table. Much like Shelly, Christine is habitually late. This gives me time to gawk. Welcome to Tourist Country, population: way too many.

Christine breezes in looking adorably massive and glowy.

"So sorry I'm late!" she says, out of breath.

"Really? I wouldn't even leave the house if I were your size."

"Ohmygod! Be nice!" she laughs, in her signature screech.

"Can you believe us? It seems like just yesterday we sat here in the middle of the day celebrating the first campaign we ever sold together. Now we're celebrating babies and husbands!" Not every creative team (art director/copywriter) bonds like Christine and I. Our union via workplace was the equivalent of meeting at a bar, having sex in the car that night, getting married a week later, and still being madly in love.

"Oh, I miss those days!" she laughs.

We finish our lunch and wander over to the main attraction of the park: "the bean." (Apparently, it's actually called *Cloud Gate*, though I've never heard anyone call it that and I would probably slap anyone who did.)

The bean is a reflective stainless steel structure that you can marvel at for hours without getting bored. It's mesmerizing. We stare at the city's reflection. We stare at our own reflection. We stare at each other's reflection. (We're like the old-lady version of Ferris and Cameron in the classic Art Institute scene in *Ferris Bueller's Day Off.*) And then we realize we're about to be pummeled by a very meaty family in said reflection. That's a lot of reflection for one day.

We stretch out on the grass in front of the band shell and catch up until the sun goes down. When it's time to leave, Christine attacks me with a hug that would induce nightmares if it came from anyone else. Knowing this is the last time we'll see each other before I become Missus and she becomes Mom makes this day seem even more like an adventure.

There's a turd on the floor. And it's not mine. Fortunately, it's not Eric's either. It seems that both he and his dog, Willie, show love for me through excrement. This living-in-sin thing is a lot less sexy than I anticipated. If I were a super-cool chick, I'd pick it up, since

Eric has already left for work. But in case you haven't noticed, I'm not a super-cool chick. I don't like to clean up after anyone, myself included. I've robbed myself of the joy of a pet's unconditional love for this very reason. I grew up with a cat named Biscuit. In the looks department, she gave that Fancy Feast spokescat a run for her money. However, the itchy cat hair, the sporadic barf à la Meow Mix, and the occasional pork chop bone in my bed made me a sans-pet gal. I hope to eventually bond with Willie, but for right now, he's a K-9 dick. Eric gives me permission to leave the turd "as-is" until he gets home. Disgusting? Absolutely. But I support this plan of nonaction.

I take advantage of the alone time in our new pad to organize my stuff. I realize, upon putting a few books on the shelf, that Eric was not so relentless when deciding what was worthy of making the move. I gave *Owen Meany* and *Bridget Jones* up for adoption at the Salvation Army, yet *You on a Diet* and Suze Orman's *The Money Book for the Young, Fabulous & Broke* sit prominently on the bookshelf? Something isn't calculating here. I make a mental note to go rescue my literary orphans in the near future.

As a citizen of Chicago, you're required to hate Navy Pier. But after surviving an afternoon among sweaty tourists in Millennium Park with Christine, I'm prepared to face that funnel cake–flavored hell. Amy agrees to meet me at Chicago's number-one tourist trap if, and only if, our bedazzled flasks are invited. I wouldn't have it any other way.

We class this tourist challenge up a level by wearing matching outfits because that was an awesome thing to do when traveling with the family. Amy and I choose to wear the fantastical wolf T-shirts I bought for us at the World's Largest Truckstop for our birthdays a few years ago. I pair this gem with some mom-style khaki pants that have somehow survived the move. (Who am I kidding? I totally wear these when I'm home alone.) I cinch my pants to uncomfortably cup my ass and feel as if I'm getting ready for a shift at Shoney's.

I receive a text from Amy as my cab pulls up to Navy Pier: "at entrance."

I pop out of the cab with a giddy smile on my face. The smile fades as I wander around aimlessly, having only the Native American woman and wolf on my T-shirt to guide me. Spectators glance at me sympathetically, as if I've been rejected by a blind date.

Amy and I eventually learn there are two million and five entrances to Navy Pier. We embrace dramatically upon finding each other. Those sympathetic glances turn into envy—or maybe that's just my imagination. Did I mention it's raining? Strike that, it's *pouring*. But like all good tourists, we forge ahead. Time's a-wasting—to the Ferris wheel we go!

A sign greets us: SORRY, THE FERRIS WHEEL IS TEMPORARILY CLOSED.

"Noooooooo!" I shout.

"At least we have our flasks," Amy says. We order two giant Sprites from the Completely Nuts food cart and then pose for a picture with the proud nut distributor. Whenever I flip through albums of old trips, I'm always amused by the amount of photos of people

Me and the lady on my t-shirt are PISSED.

posing by random statues, unimpressive landmarks, and employees of places with random statues and unimpressive landmarks. In fact, I have a full set of photos that I took with my 110 camera of Shelly, Emily, and me in San Antonio with SeaWorld employees. They were like celebs in our eyes.

Amy and I search for a safe place to devirginize our Sprites and discover the Transporter. It looks like a cross between a molester van and something from the original *Star Wars*.

"Excuse me, sir? What does this do?" I ask the high school dropout at the ticket booth.

"You take a trip through time," he says flatly. We wait anxiously for more info. He doesn't give it to us.

"Well, sign us up!" Amy says, in the most exaggerated mom voice ever.

We step inside. It's dark, and it smells like belly button sweat.

"I hope we don't die today," I say, only half joking.

We dump our vodka into our Sprites and brace ourselves for the ride. The molester ship jolts. Our journey through time begins. Dinosaurs and lava lurch at us from a screen. It's worse than my

If you're anywhere near a nutcart, you know you're in tourist territory.

childhood nightmares. The thing finally screeches to a halt. We hold hands across the aisle and breath a sigh of relief.

"Uh, no one is in line if you guys wanna ride again," the guy says through a speaker in the corner. After thoroughly hating the ride, we both shout, "Yes, please!" We'll never not be excited by free stuff. Ride number two is just as awful as ride number one. We exit the van holding our bellies. The pink sawdust that teachers sprinkle onto puke probably sponsors this ride. We walk the rest of the way down the deserted pier, happy to be alive.

I spent the last Saturday of my single life at Navy Pier, in the rain, wearing a wolf T-shirt. Jealous? You should be.

While I gallivant about Chicago, enjoying vodka-soaked tourist traps, Court visits *educational* places like the Iowa State Capitol and the Clive Historical Society. If you're fascinated by birth order psychology, you would have a field day with the two of us. We decide to reverse our dumb sister/smart sister roles for our last excursions. Court checks out giant plastic cows, courtesy of the Anderson-Erickson Dairy Headquarters, but still ends up accidentally learning when she goes in search of a giant buffalo. Said buffalo lives at the National Wildlife Refugee *Learning* Center. Good try, Court.

I plan to check out a local museum. I also plan to make Eric come along with me.

"So, what do you have going on today?" It's Sunday, and we usually have TV, movies, and frozen pizza going on today. He looks at me suspiciously.

"Uh. Depends. Why?"

"Let's get to know the neighborhood. How's about we visit the Ukrainian Museum?"

Eric hesitantly rolls off the couch and puts on some pants. We stroll over to the museum in the panty-soaking heat. We're the only people there, and, based on the hostess's enthusiasm, we're probably the only visitors this week. She goes to fetch the angry tour guide, Yelysayeta.

While I appreciate the authenticity of Yelysayeta's accent, we can't understand a word she's saying, and I'm afraid to ask her to repeat. We pretend to listen and mosey around the rooms. We learn about fancy Easter eggs called *pysanky* and a sweet-ass musical instrument called the *bandura*. According to the pictures, only people with beards play this instrument.

On our way out, the hostess chirps, "Come back again! Bring your friends!" I imagine a bunch of us playing drinking games on a Friday night. "Hey, who wants to go to the Ukrainian Museum?! Last one there's a rotten *pysanka!*"

I never got to show Shelly around my town. She died only five months after I moved here. We wanted to wait until she wasn't pregnant. We wanted to wait until I knew my way around better. We wanted to wait until—it doesn't matter. Don't wait. Do things. Do them now. You'll be glad you did.

There's no shame in being a tourist. At the end of the day, we're all just visitors on this earth anyway, right? Happy birthday, Shelly.

Chapter 18:
wedding week!

Shelly wrote the following note to me on the back of her ninth-grade
school picture:

> *Well, after six years we're still friends. It's amazing how
> time flies! I'll never forget everything we've gone through,
> doggie . . . Hopefully we'll be B/F/F and you'll be at my
> wedding and I'll be at yours and Charlie's.*
> *Love Always, Shelly.*

    Both Charlie and Shelly are dead now. Neither of them will be
at my wedding. This milestone will be the hardest one to pass without Shelly by my side, but I'm trying not to think about it—because
that's the last thing Shelly would want me to worry about.
    On Shelly's wedding day, she didn't care that her cham-
pagne toast was *toast* because she was secretly pregnant. Or that
her dress was too tight and she had to get an extra panel inserted

at the last minute. Or that one of her bridesmaids (me) ended up with zigzag cornrows after hours in the salon. (There was a bit of a misunderstanding. If a sista ever asks you if you like "twisties" in your hair, she is not referring to a French twist.) Shelly only cared about sharing the greatest day of her life with the people she loved most. Wedding week's resolution is simple: Don't freak out. Ask, "What would Shelly do?" when obstacles arise.

Our new mantra comes into play much sooner than expected. I've avoided high-maintenance bride websites thus far, but with the wedding just five days away, curiosity gets the best of me. I google "wedding day checklist" and I have a mini–heart attack when I see an entire checklist devoted to "vows." *Gulp.* How, exactly, do those work again? Do we write our own? Do we have to memorize shit? Can we use the *Family Ties* theme song? (I do. *Sha-la-la-la.*) As a wedding guest, I've never paid much attention to vows. I devote that sacred time to trying to decide which wedding-party member is the most hungover (or which ones might bang later).

You know what Shelly would do in this situation? She would call *me* for the answer. And then, when I'd tell her I didn't have a clue, she'd reach out to her entire legion of friends and acquaintances. So I turn to the blog.

My post is very dramatic and to the point: "Vows—Do we write our own? Do we have to memorize? What did you do? Heeeeeelp!" And then I go to bed.

But I can't sleep. Instead, I think about important things like facial hair. I have a waxing appointment scheduled for tomorrow, but I wonder, *Is yanking hot wax off my face four days before the wedding risky? What if I look like a burn victim again? Is it better to be a 'stachey bride or a rashy bride? Sleep, sleep, sleep. Just go to sleep and figure it out in the morning.* I try to count sheep, but then I stylize each sheep. One has on biking shorts, one wears a cummerbund, one even sports the tennis shoes that light up—show-off. *Ugh, now I'm more awake than I was in the first place.*

Well, hello, Tylenol PM, nice to meet y . . . (snore).

I wake up in a funk. *Who am I? Where am I? Why is there a corn nut in my hair?* I check my phone for any miscellaneous calls I may've made under the sleeping-aid influence. This type of call can be much more hazardous than a drunk dial because instead of old boyfriends, you call your parents. Or J.Crew.

Phew, call log is empty.

I check the blog next, and I am delighted to see some good answers to my questions. Seems like the best bet is to write our own vows and have Kerry read them in a repeat-after-me format so we won't have to memorize. Sure, we still have to figure out *how* to write vows, but come on

Brad and Shelly on wedding day. As happy as it gets.

. . . I wrote dialogue for *the* Cap'n Crunch himself for three years. (Humble brag.) Pretty sure I can handle some wedding vows.

In the midst of the wedding madness, I still have to deal with the unemployment issue. *Ugh.* I got a letter from the unemployment office saying there was an error with my application. Eric and I are jet-setting to Belize on Monday, so I need to make sure I'll be compensated for the hours I put in drinking piña coladas by the pineapple-full.

Seven phone calls and four hours later, I have yet to speak with anyone. Instead, I get a recording that says, "Voice mailbox is full. So hang up, chump." (Without the second part.) Maury Povich's viewership is probably at an all-time high. I, however, will not be indulging in any paternity test tomfoolery today. It's off to the unemployment office I go! (I'd much rather be off to the principal's office with Young MC.)

I grab a number and sit down in a row by myself. I feel like I'm in a very sad deli, waiting for roast beef. This is almost as traumatizing as the time I went to traffic court after running over a pedestrian. Oh, I didn't tell you about that?

Quick sidebar: It was a stormy Sunday night, less than a year after Shelly died. I was still dealing with some anger, so I went to thrust away my worries with gay men at the gym. (I go to the Bally's in Boystown. I never get hit on, but I *was* approached by a young man who wanted legs like mine. Awesome.) On my way home, I had to make a complicated backward-diagonal turn. I waited for a break in oncoming traffic and then gunned it. Midgun, a cute blond girl appeared in my headlights. *Thunk.*

I just hit a human being. This is happening, I thought to myself. *This is how hit-and-runs occur.* I definitely thought about speeding away for a solid six seconds. When I got out of my car, some pompous buns-hole screamed at me about how I shouldn't be on the road. People accidentally drive their cars into other three-thousand-pound cars every day, but I hit a 105-pound pixie and I'm the worst driver alive? Screw you, dude, you shouldn't be on the planet. Fortunately, she was fine. In fact, she was *thankful.*

"Um, I just called my date to tell him I'd be late because I got hit by a car. You know what he said?" I murmured something unintelligible. "He asked me if I'd still be able to pick up dinner."

We agreed to flee the scene and pretend it never happened. However, the fuzz pulled up as we were saying goodbye. *That buns-hole called it in!* I ended up in traffic court with the scum of the earth a month later. Everyone there had been picked up for driving without a license, driving without insurance, or driving without pants. I pleaded guilty to hitting a pedestrian in a roadway. It's fifty smackers just to park on the wrong side of the street in Chicago. I was terrified to find out how much it costs to hit a cute girl.

"You got $30?" the judge asked.

"Yes."

"Okay. Done."

Here's the kicker: When I looked at the receipt, the actual fine was only $5. The rest was court fees. So, if you're ever looking for something affordable to do in Chicago, you can hit a family of four and still have enough money left over for deep dish.

Okay, back to traffic court's inbred cousin, the unemployment office. Two hours go by, and my number is finally called.

"I'm getting married this weekend, so I need to get this taken care of ASAP."

The personality-less woman types something into her computer. "What's your zip code?"

"Six zero six two two."

"Okay, that's all we need. It was listed incorrectly on the information provided to us by your former employer."

"I tried to call all day. Why couldn't this be done on the phone?"

"Oh, sweetie, no one answers the phone here anymore."

I want to be upset, but that statement is just too depressing. I gather up my stuff and turn to leave.

"Brianne?"

"Yeah?"

"Congratulations on the wedding. Enjoy yourself."

Whoever said, "Don't talk to strangers" was just talking to the wrong ones. I'm probably the only person to leave the unemployment office with a smile on my face that day.

I make it to my waxing appointment within a whisker of time and then go home to create the best wedding reception playlist this side of the Mississippi. (I can only hope it will be just as successful on the Iowa side.) I include a three-song block of Shelly's favorites so we can honor her through dance. I got the idea from Kim's reception. I truly felt Shelly's energy in the room as we flailed away to Jimmy Eat World's hit song "The Middle."

Things finally feel like they're falling into place. (That's like a woman in a romantic comedy saying, "I won't trip over something and be adorable at any time in the next hour and a half.")

And I do speak too soon, because on Wednesday morning I find tiny red bumps decorating my forehead. That's what I get for trying to tame my unruly brow monsters! (And maybe a rogue chin hair, or three.) I've transformed myself into an eighth-grade boy. Not the *one* fresh-faced boy all the girls crushed on (who later became your gay best friend), but the one who was referred to as Pizza Face.

Once again, I turn to the blog for answers: "Magical cures for acne? Ready, go." Meanwhile, Court blogs about worries of her own. Mostly maid-of-honor-speech worries. We are not public speakers. It scares us more than a midnight picnic with both Freddy *and* Jason. (I have a sneaking suspicion they are funny dudes when they're together.) Our "Don't Freak Out" resolution has become an "Ask the Blog Readers" resolution. For two girls who like to keep to themselves, we're certainly reaping the benefits of reaching out to others this week.

While I wait for a magical acne cure (which turns out to be cortisone), I attend my last personal training session before wife-hood. I imagine it will be like the last day of class and my trainer will bring Rice Krispie treats and sign my yearbook with something like "Hey girl, watching your ass quiver during squats was boss. Stay sweet!" Not the case. The workout makes me sweat like a dude on steroids, and she barely says goodbye when I walk out of her life forever. Oh, I felt the burn . . . right in my heart muscle.

Eric heads out early Friday morning to golf with the guys. We got into Walcott last night and were treated to a small cookout at my parents' house before all the wedding festivities commence.

I have time to kill before Court, Amy, Foxy, Kerry, and I meet for mani-pedi appointments in Davenport, so I walk down to the cemetery. For the first time, I bring a flower for Shelly. (The only other thing I've ever put on her grave was a Laffy Taffy I had found in my pocket. Something about it just seemed right. When

I returned four months later, that Laffy Taffy still sat prominently among her gifts, even though it had snowed multiple times.)

"Hey, Shell. I'm getting married tomorrow." I set the flower on her headstone. "I hate that you're not here to be part of it. I thought we'd do everything together," I whisper.

My cell phone rings, and I jump a mile out of my skin. It's AAA Rentals.

"Would you mind stopping by to supervise the setup at the mansion?"

"Supervise?"

"We just want to make sure we get everything in the right place."

Seriously, what the hell? I made two previous trips to Iowa to meet with them *specifically* for this reason. Bollocks! Wait, I'm in Iowa. Hogwash!

"All right, I'll be there in a half hour."

I turn my attention back to the rock in the ground. "I'll miss you more than ever tomorrow. I love you."

Court meets me at the mansion to help keep my sanity in check. The good news: They haven't set up anything in the wrong place. The bad news: They haven't set up anything, *period*. Court and I walk them through the floor plan and then sit side by side on the front steps, just like we used to do back in the day. Even though it's almost one hundred degrees and we're witnessing what it might look like if drunk toddlers ran a rental company, there's something nice about this moment.

One of us learned how to sit like a lady. One of us ignored that lesson and chose to sit like Al Bundy.

The tent still isn't set up an hour later. (I would make a perverted joke here about knowing how to pitch a tent, but I'm too annoyed.) The jackholes promise us they can figure it out without supervision, so Court and I leave. This gives me just enough time to speed back to my parents' house, shower, and then get back into Davenport for our mani-pedi appointments.

"Brianne!" my mother shrieks from outside the shower door. *Can't anything go smoothly today?*

"What are you doing in here?!" We are *not* the kind of family that canoodles in the bathroom. Those families creep me out.

"The rental people are on the phone and they're confused!"

"Can you tell them I'll call back?"

"They need to talk to you *now!*" And then she does something inexcusable. *She opens the shower door.*

"*Mom!* Ohmygod!" I shrivel up into a tiny, naked, wet ball and shield my sexy parts. She turns and looks in the opposite direction and shoves the phone at me until I turn off the water and grab it.

Tromp, tromp, tromp. She's gone again.

The dummies just wanted to let me know that it costs extra for them to set up the tables for us. I don't want to give this company any more money, so I call Eric and ask if the guys can set up the tables tomorrow while the ladies get hair and makeup done.

"Sure, no problem!" he says. I'm mildly annoyed that I've had to deal with this company all day while he golfs, but an hour of hard labor tomorrow will make up for it. I put on clothes and text Court: "Mom just saw me naked. Donkeys are smarter than AAA Rentals. See you at the salon."

Court and I both get to the nail salon right on time to meet Foxy, Amy, and Kerry. When I see their happy faces, my frustration dissipates. *We* are the girls screaming with joy. *We* are the girls popping champagne at 1:00 PM. *We* are the girls I've always wanted to be.

The rest of the day goes without a hitch. The rehearsal is quick and painless, and the rehearsal dinner is more fun than rehearsal dinners are supposed to be. Eric and I don't even get to bed until 1:00 AM, but I don't care. Something tells me I won't be tired in the morning.

Holy geez, I'm getting married today.

I expect to have cold feet. Not because I don't love Eric to pieces, but because I'm the most indecisive person in the world. I can't even order a taco without wondering what life would be like with a chalupa. But I'm proud to say that as of right now, my feet are sweaty with confidence.

In order to avoid confusion, here are some wedding day logistics:

- Wake up. (Check!)
- Girls go to the salon for hair and makeup.
- Guys go to the mansion and set up tables. After that, they grab lunch and discuss things like Meg Ryan (Eric's biggest childhood crush) and lot lizards (truck stop equivalent of hookers).
- After being primped, the girls go to the mansion and finish getting ready. Guys will stay out of the way.
- Eric and I meet on the balcony off our bedroom window at 4:00 PM for some alone time—with the photographer.
- The entire wedding party meets in the foyer for group photos.
- Wedding ceremony begins.

Any questions? Yeah, me too. Fingers crossed.

Our salon visit feels like a slumber party from the junior high days. We show up with magazines, food, drinks, and way too much energy.

Once I look like a shorter, brunetter Heidi Klum, I text Eric to make sure the guys are on schedule. I don't want to take the chance of running into him before the big reveal on the balcony. I find out that yes, the guys are at lunch. But no, they did not set up the tables. I take a deep breath and call him, trying to keep my cool in front of the girls.

"Um, you're kidding, right?"

"We'll do it after lunch."

"You won't have *time*. There's a reason I made a detailed schedule and passed it out last night. That wasn't a fun little art project."

"Sorry. We'll figure it out."

Awesome. Once again, "we'll figure it out" means *I'll* figure it out.

We hang up, and I try to keep my blood at a gentle simmer,
but it *really* wants to boil. *Okay, Shelly would not freak out. She would
laugh about it and figure out a way to make it better.* When I pull up
to the mansion with the girls, my worry dissolves. The tables are
indeed already being taken care of—by the two women from Des
Moines who helped with my wedding design/decor (I barely know
these women) and a crew of my parents' best friends. My heart
floods with gratitude. It's one thing when your friends lend a helping
hand, but when people who owe you *nothing* step in and get sweaty
just to help make your day perfect, well, there are just no words
for that. (This still doesn't absolve the men of neglecting their *one*
responsibility for the day, but I guess I'll let it slide—for now.)

When it's time to put on *the* dress, I ask the girls for privacy.
Being naked in front of others whom I will not later bang is just
not my thing. I slip it on and can't believe my eyes. I'm a *bride*. As I
admire myself in the mirror, there's a tap on the door.

"Yeah?" There's no answer. "Who is it?"

I don't want to blindly open the door in case it's Eric. Or a burglar.

"It's Hailey." My heart melts. I open the door to her and
Shelly's mom.

"Hi, sweetie!" I give her a hug, and she looks up at me like I'm
a fairy princess.

"You look pretty," she says.

"Not as pretty as you."

"She was just *dying* to see you," Brenda says.

"Well, ya know what, Hailey? I'd love it if you could be in the
first picture of me with my wedding dress on."

We lean in close and pose exactly the way I would've posed

Like mother, like daughter. Have you seen a cuter flower girl?

with Shelly at this moment: cheek to cheek, smile to smile. Thank god for waterproof mascara.

An hour later, I climb out onto the balcony. I feel like I'm on some sort of bride-groom game show where the lady gets all beautified and then the guy gets to decide whether he really wants to marry her based on her beauty decisions.

"Eric, come on out and see your fiancée! Is she a keeper or do you wanna . . . "

"Ditch . . . the . . . bitch!" the studio audience would scream. (I'd totally watch that show, by the way.) The photographer leans out the window and tells me Eric's coming. I try to look casual, but it's sort of impossible in a dress that costs almost as much as my car. (Oh, settle down, I drive a Civic.)

"Wow," Eric says as he climbs gracelessly through the window. We stare at each other like nervous teenagers with advanced-aging issues. This is our wedding day, yet somehow I feel the emotional rush of a first date.

"You ready?" he says.

"Yep. You?"

He kisses me. The photographer takes some shots, and then we join our friends in the foyer. Here we go.

I'm worried about having nothing to worry about. It's thirty minutes before the ceremony, and other than the wedding table conundrum and realizing we never made name tags for the dinner seating assignment, everything has happened according to plan. (Thank you, Em and Holly, for springing into action on the name tags—crafty bitches!)

"Hey, Bree, you look gorgeous!" I turn around and see the face of a wedding guest. *Wait, what?* Guests are not supposed to be hobnob-bing with the bride before she walks down the aisle. This isn't a god-damned mixer! Our ushers were instructed to seat people *outside* upon arrival. I panic. I do not do what Shelly would do. But Amy does. She grabs my hand and guides me upstairs without saying a word.

When we get up to my room, she hands me a water bottle. I know Amy well enough to know it's not water. "Baby, I brought this in case of emergency."

I laugh, teary eyed. I need this. Not so much the alcohol, but the one-on-one time with a dear friend before I take one of the big-gest steps of my life. We spy on arriving guests through the slats in the shutters of the window. I will always treasure this moment. Just two girls, a water bottle filled with vodka, and the best seats in the house to see my own wedding begin.

Amy and I join the rest of the wedding party when it's time to line up. Court is nowhere to be found. This is not like her. She has the same obsession with punctuality as I do. She rushes out of the mansion at the last minute and gives no explanation. If my brain were capable of doing any sort of pondering, I would be suspicious. But all I can think about is walking down that aisle.

I watch the most important people in Eric's and my lives walk down the aisle, two by two—until it's just my dad and me. We're pretending not to be nervous, but the profuse sweating and shaking give us away.

The first beats of Mason Jennings's "Be Here Now" blare through the speakers.

"All right, this is it," I say, with a confident tremble.

The walk down the aisle is surreal. Think about it. Your closest friends and family surround you, but they are all crying and staring at you, and you can't stop and say hello to anyone. Fortunately, Eric and Kerry are at the finish line, so I focus straight ahead.

"Who gives this woman to be wedded to this man?"

"My her mo—her mother and I do." (I get my failure to speak in full sentences when I'm nervous from my father.)

When I'm a wedding guest, I always get weepy during this part. As a bride, I still do.

Kerry begins the ceremony. To be honest, we really had no idea if she'd be good at this gig or not. She could've bombed. She could've done the whole thing in pig Latin. She could've broken out into the dreaded chicken dance. But she didn't. She wrote a ceremony so personal and so respectful of our love that there wasn't a dry eye in the house.

Just before we recite our vows, Kerry introduces Crads to sing. He struts up with his guitar slung around his back, wearing sunglasses like a rockstar. *Oh boy, this could be a disaster.* Why didn't we make him record a demo? Or at least sing at the rehearsal?

He plays the first few measures of Ray LaMontagne's "Shelter," and I'm relieved that he knows chords and stuff. But then he starts singing. *What. The. Fuck.*

It's killer. I look at Eric in shock. He gives me a charming *I told ya so* grin. But then something else catches my attention, and I stumble—hard. I see Hailey sneak quietly over to be by her mom's side. *Michelle's* side.

Here's where I lose it.

Here's where surreal fades and reality stings.

Here's where I mourn the loss of my best friend all over again.

Oh, it got so much worse. At least the groom held his shit together, and looked pretty handsome doing it.

I sob. Not pretty-bride tears, but twisted-face, sputtering tears. *Where can I hide? I don't want to be up here anymore.* Court turns around and sees me struggling. So she starts crying. Emily hears Court crying, so she starts crying. Tears spread like wildfire while Crads continues rocking the shit out of the song. Eric puts his hand on my shoulder and looks me in the eye. *I can do this.* I take a deep breath and finish marrying the love of my life.

Phew, the hard part is over. Time for the balls-out celebration to begin. Court grabs Eric and me before we join everyone for cocktails and guides us up to our bedroom.

"Thought you guys might want to share a little 'holy shit, we're married' moment before the party starts. The night will be over before you know it." She shuts the door behind her.

Eric and I turn to find a bottle of champagne and a smorgasbord of all our favorite childhood snacks. *This* is why Court was the last one to line up. And *this* is why I have the best sister in the world.

The reception is better than any party I've ever attended. Perhaps it's the massive amounts of pizza on fancy platters. Or the colorful centerpieces and decor made by my mother. Or the mansion owner playing a keyboard while bartending. But I'm pretty sure it's the people enjoying those things that make this party so great. All of them. When the block of songs dedicated to Shelly plays, I'm amazed at the ferocity with which people bust it on the dance floor. Jumping, stomping, high kicks—and that's just the dudes. Some of our wedding guests knew her, some didn't, but *everyone* catches the fever of Shelly's spirit.

Shelly is gone, but I still have a circle of love. I have a circle of support. I have a circle of amazing friends. Oh, and a pretty kick-ass husband. (Squeee!)

Off to Belize we go!

Oh, wait—flight delay? *Dammit.* We get out of Chicago late, so one of our five nights in Belize turns into one night in Dallas, complete with Bennigan's for dinner. (Yes, our first dinner for two as Mister and Missus involves a Turkey O'Toole and fries.) The next morning, we head straight to Belize. And by "straight," I mean a 747 commercial airliner to a twelve-seater puddle jumper to a golf cart to a boat.

Hello, La Isla Bonita. Madonna may have dreamt of you, but we're gonna be inside you. We spend the first few days sitting, hammocking, floating, spying on our neighbors, drinking, eating, eating, eating, and eating.

On Thursday, we decide to use our special walking powers. We don't get very far before feeding time. We're on an eat-your-face-off-every-two-hours schedule. We follow our noses to the closest restaurant on the water. The place is eerily quiet.

"This is how horror movies start, except I'd have high heels on with my swimming suit," I say.

"And I wouldn't have a gut the size of a beanbag chair," Eric says.

A smokin' hot chick (the kind who *would* be cast in said horror flick) appears and welcomes us by telling us we're not welcome.

"Sorry, we're closed. Our kitchen staff is catering an event tonight." The thought of not being fed for twenty whole minutes

Other than the fact that we're fully clothed and not slurp-kissing in public, this private restaurant on the beach is a total dream date from *The Bachelor*.

hurts my feelings. She notices my fat-kid-with-no-cake disappointment. "There might be some burritos in the back. Hold on."

We aren't sure what to make of this, but burrito news is always good news. She returns after a few minutes. "Yep, we've got burritos. Take a seat wherever."

We have the entire restaurant to ourselves. I feel like I'm one of those unrealistic dates on *The Bachelor*. And then she turns on music.

"This is the first day of my life . . . " It's the Bright Eyes song. The same one I heard the first time I visited Shelly's grave. The same one I heard at Potbelly during "live music" week. We're in Belize, in the middle of nowhere, in a *closed* restaurant, eating leftover burritos, and *this* song plays. *Goose bumps.* Again, maybe it's just a coincidence, but I feel like it's yet another message from Shelly, letting me know she's been here all along.

When the honeymoon is literally over, we ride back on the boat, to the golf cart, to the puddle jumper, to the real world on a 747.

Chapter 19:
let's not forget about the food

"Through thick and through thin, we'll always have each other . . . and the food, let's not forget about the food!"

When Shelly's parents gave me her old scrapbooks to dig through after she died, I was delighted to see she'd kept the postcard I sent her back in '93 with the above message on it. Truer words have never been spoken (or slapped on a postcard). Food was a main theme in our friendship. Lots and lots of sugary food.

Shelly's biggest addiction was candy. Especially Easter candy. I'll never forget the Great Easter Candy Caper of 1999. It was our sophomore year of college. Shelly and I always looked forward to the three-hour road trip home from Ames to Walcott. It was our time to be alone, just the two of us—like the old days. We stopped at the gas station to fill up before hitting the interstate. What we filled up *on* isn't what her mother had intended when she gave Shelly the family gas card.

This whole gas card phenomenon was completely foreign to me. I was dumbfounded as Shelly stockpiled Snickers Eggs and Cadbury Creme Eggs at a speed at which I'd never seen her move. She was a maniac! She paused for a moment and said to me, as if it were common sense, "I have my mom's gas card. We can use it on candy!"

Sixty dollars later, we were on the road experiencing an intense sugar high. I've never seen so much fake sugary egg yolk— and I hope to never see it again. A month later, I overheard Shelly on the phone.

"*Mom,* it was for gas."

(Pause.)

"Well, we got some candy, too."

(Pause.)

"Yeah I know it only costs twenty dollars to fill up my tank, but it was *Easter!*"

She got off the phone and we burst into laughter. Her mom's gas card statement had arrived, instantly busting us on our $40 candy spree. Our gas card privileges were revoked—forever.

I first tested Shelly's devotion to our friendship back in 1992. We were at the mall, waiting for my mom to finish enrolling in the JCPenney Bra & Panty Club. (The word "panty" sent us into fits of giggles, so my mom handed us $10 and told us to go get some ice cream.) Shelly looked stylish in her County Seat sweater; I looked like an escaped mental patient in my aqua spandex dance pants.

"Wanna prove you're my best friend?"

"Yes!" This was a true testament to Shelly's willingness to do anything—even for ridiculous reasons. If I had asked her to dunk her head in a sink full of dirty dishwater, she would've done it. And actually, a year later, she did.

"Okay. Stick your teeth into your ice cream for a full minute.

Ready, go." I looked down at my faux Swatch watch and timed her. Her face turned red, her eyes watered, and then she laughed so hard she snorted. As absurd as this challenge was, it proved she would do anything for me. *Did I prove that to her?*

If not, I will try to now. Since the wedding, Court and I have gone boozeless, we've written snail mail to people who would least expect it, and we've even babysat *real* kids—for free. But this week, in honor of Shelly's adventurous love of food, we're putting our guts to the test. We must each eat as many new (and possibly scary) things as we can stomach. Bon appétit!

"Four beef tongue tacos to go, please."

The girl behind the counter at Flash Taco looks at me with an expression that tells me no one orders these before 2:00 AM. Or when sober. Pretty sure I heard, "Shit, we got tongue?!" from the back of the kitchen.

I return home with my bag o' tongues. Eric has bravely offered to join me in this questionable taste test. We unwrap the tacos with very little anticipation.

"It has taste buds!" Eric says.

"Mine also seems to be salivating," I say, noticing something oozing off the side.

We decide to attack in a "One, two, three, *eat!*" fashion so neither of us can wuss out. As I chew the warm, gamey tongue, I wonder if my own tongue feels like a cannibal. At best, it tastes like a cross between pot roast and—tongue. I will not be ordering these ever again. Unless they're for our dog. Willie totally finished them off.

My next foray is not as venturesome as beef tongue tacos. However, it's Halloween, so I attempt to make pumpkin soup, from scratch—with a real pumpkin. Me trying to cook something home-made is awfully dangerous on its own.

After a stressful jaunt to the grocery store, I put on the super-cute apron Shelly's mom and sister gave me for my wedding shower, and I get to work. So, first things first: What the hell do I do with a pumpkin? The recipe starts as if I already have the pumpkin out of its shell. I go online and search "cooking with pumpkins." Apparently, I've purchased a "field pumpkin" and not a "baking pumpkin." Well, I believe that with encouragement this so-called field pumpkin will shine like a baking pumpkin. And also, I'm too lazy to go back to the store. I cut through the orangey thickness, pull out the guts, and then scrape all the stringy junk out. This takes a *long* time— plus, I almost murder myself eight times.

When Big Daddy Pumpkin is finally cut into cubes and ready to go, I put it on the stove and tend to my salad. Ten minutes later, I add a bunch of spices to the soup and pour it into fancy bowls. I've never had nice dishes in my life, so the idea of having different plates and bowls made specifically for soup and salad is mind-blowingly exciting. It might even inspire me to cook more, but probably not.

I serve our lovely dinner on TV trays so Eric and I don't have to miss a minute of *So You Think You Can Dance*. And also because we eat on TV trays *every* night. We each go in for our first bite of soup. It's not good, but Eric pretends it's good. *Stupid field pumpkin, you'll never be as good as your baking-pumpkin brother!* The soup tastes like watery, chunky nothingness, but I eat a whole bowl of it. Eric concentrates on the salad part of my gourmet meal. Shortly after we're finished, I catch him microwaving a White Castle gut bomb. Oh well, maybe next time.

I signed on with a creative recruiting agency this week. I don't want Eric to think he married a lemon. From what I can tell, here's how it works: The recruiter sets me up with freelance gigs, or interviews for freelance gigs, and then steals all my money while I do the work. Fabulous!

I put on my game face (and my favorite yellow heels) and head to my first interview, at a small shop I've never even heard of. I usually interview fairly well, but that doesn't stop me from being terrified every time. When I get there, I stand awkwardly in the doorway, as there is no reception area. *Is it too late to turn around and run home?* Before I have time to answer myself, the executive creative director (i.e., head honcho) walks up and introduces himself as Paul. *Guess I'm doing this thing.*

We hit it off right away. It's crazy how much respect being from the World's Largest Truckstop wins me in situations like this. (Or at least gives me something to yammer on about.)

"Well, you'd be working on toilet paper," he says.

"Awesome! I—know a lot about that." *Did I really just say that?*

"It's not as bad as it sounds. Kimberly-Clark is one of our clients. They want to do an umbrella campaign that covers all their products. I just like to say toilet paper."

"Any chance you know Joe Kardel?" I'm totally that person. If there's a 2 percent chance someone might know someone else, I *will* ask. Joe lives in Neenah, Wisconsin, and I know he does something for Kimberly-Clark, but I have no idea what.

"Wait, really?"

Now I'm scared. I can't read this reaction.

"Yes?" I say with the facial expression of a toddler who isn't sure if she's doing something she'll get punished for or not.

"He's one of our main clients. We love Joe."

Whoa, whoa, whoa. This is f-a-t-e. I've known Joe my whole life. He, too, is from the World's Largest Truckstop. We went to school together from kindergarten through *college*. And we're reunited by toilet paper? *In-freaking-sane.* And get this—he was Shelly's first kiss on the twirly slide. He grew up on a turkey farm near Shelly's farm, so they got to know each other on the bus when Shelly first moved to Walcott. Joe always said Shelly and I shared a brain, which made me feel cool because I knew how much he liked her.

I tell Paul about my twenty-five-year friendship, and he's just as flummoxed as I am about the severity of the coincidence.

"Well, I guess we have no choice but to hire you."

So, my freelance career has officially started, with the help of Shelly's fourth-grade boyfriend.

The beginning of the age-old Halloween costume conundrum: Dude, what if one of us hooks up tonight? (From left to right: Rachel, Drew, Me, Court.)

I'm a sucker for Halloween. When Court and I were kids, Mom made all of our costumes by hand. She would spend at least four entire episodes of *Falcon Crest* creating elaborate disguises for us to wear while pandering for candy. Oh, how we longed for plastic-faced She-Ra costumes from Farm and Fleet like all the other kids, but *no,* we had to wear insanely adorable, totally original costumes. One year we were Crayola Crayons. I was pink, Court was yellow, and our friends Rachel and Drew were red and blue. Sure, you've seen a crayon costume in your lifetime, but we weren't four loose colors of the rainbow tramping around town. We were contained in an exact replica of the Crayola Crayon box. The box was made of wood and probably weighed more than the four of us put together. Court and Rachel (the more mature crayons) each had one of their arms poking through a hole in either end, while Drew and I toddled in the middle and complained about the houses that passed out pennies and chocolate-covered raisins. The following year, Court was the tooth fairy, complete with a giant wooden toothbrush, and I was a tooth. We won multiple costume contests that year. And I cried because I was a tooth and I wanted to be a Snork.

You should always stretch before consuming fourteen Ameretto Sours and a sloppy gyro from the dirty guy on the corner at the end of the night. (A tip you'll never hear from Jane Fonda.)

The day you realize you're too old to dress up is a sad one. Shelly and I refused to give up completely, so we painted our faces like haunted whores and handed out candy to the neighborhood kids when we were in high school. Then suddenly in college, it's cool to dress up again! (And eat Frosted Flakes. And play kickball.) Our senior year, Shelly and I dressed up like '80s marathon runners and ran laps around every bar in Ames. We even moisturized with Ben-gay before going out. I ended up making out with a guy that night and had to warn him that he might feel the burn. It was my favorite Halloween ever, though I'm pretty sure we annoyed an entire town with our drunken wind sprints.

Amy and I have dressed up in "couples' costumes" for the last three years:

- Her first year in Chicago, we were Tom Cruise and Katie Holmes. I jumped around on furniture wherever we went

while she held her pregnant belly and a Starbucks cup.
Sometimes the best ideas are the easiest to execute.

• In 2007, we dressed as bacon and eggs. The costumes
  were attached by Velcro, so we moved about town like the
  Two-Headed Monster from *Sesame Street*. I'm not usually
  one for pickup lines, but when we heard a guy shout, "I
  want *that* for breakfast in the morning," we couldn't help
  but blush. And then repeat it over and over all night.

• In 2008 we were polygamists. We bought our dresses
  from the Latter Day Saints website. It was the scariest
  costume I've ever worn.

This year we're going to be gorilla ballerinas. It's your typical
gorilla suit—with the addition of a pink tutu and a shimmery bra
because, ya know, ballerinas *always* wear shimmery bras. The gorilla
mask is the best part. I've never felt so much power in anonymity.
The two of us start aggressively humping people (and each other) the
minute we get to the bar. We "Night-at-the-Roxbury" men, women,
men dressed as women, and, yes—even naughty nurses. Turns out,
sexually harassing people makes me sweat like a pig in heat (or a
dancing gorilla in a bar). I strip the hairy beast off my body until I'm
down to my sweatpants and T-shirt. Five minutes pass, and Foxy
says the words that every married woman fears.

"Hey, Bree. Um. You had your wedding ring on, right?"

I look down at my left hand.

My stomach turns.

I want to vomit.

No engagement ring, no wedding band, no dignity. I drop to
my knees and crawl through the obliterated crowd of slutty Little Bo
Peeps. My hands scale the sticky, wet dance floor. Foxy, Amy, and
Kerry join me, bellies to the ground. I've single-fingeredly ruined the
night for everyone.

Foxy finds my wedding band, the *family heirloom* that Eric slid onto my finger just months ago, under a table. My engagement ring, however, is still MIA.

"You guys? If I get a divorce tonight, will one of you OD on candy corn with me?"

"Are you kidding? I planned to do that anyway," Kerry says. I tremble with shame as I dial Eric's phone number. I lose it when I sputter the words "lost" and "engagement ring." I hate myself. I know he's about to hate me, too.

But he doesn't.

"Wait, what happened? Where are you? Are you okay?" he asks.

No one should be held responsible for what happens while inside a gorilla ballerina costume.

This is when I realize that marriage truly is like the best of friendships. No matter how ridiculously stupid you might be, there is someone who loves you anyway, just the way you are.

Fortunately, Eric had the ring insured, just in case. The sentimental value was compromised, but Eric and I agree that losing the original while wearing a gorilla ballerina suit is sentimental enough.

I just ate an ox's ass.

I may've failed at being a good wife this week, but I still have a chance to succeed at the resolution. Eric and I walk down the street to a Cuban restaurant we've been curious to try since we moved to the neighborhood. I opt for the most questionable thing on the menu: oxtail.

In case you're not already gagging, here's the definition of oxtail (which I didn't look up until after dinner): "the culinary name for the tail of cattle. Formerly, it referred only to the tail of an ox, a castrated male. Oxtail is a bony, gelatinous meat, and is usually slow-cooked, often stewed or braised."

When the dish arrives, it looks like three floppy balls of meat swimming in an unidentifiable sauce. My first attempt at digging in results in fork to bone (or cartilage or whatever) contact. I loathe eating any type of meat off any type of bone. I think back to Shelly's tooth-to-ice-cream contact and try again. I fork around until the meat unhinges itself. It turns to mush in my mouth. I push the meat/bones/cartilage around the plate like I did back when my mom made me eat lima beans. Even though my entrée makes me want to vomit, the dinner experience is still delicious. Eric and I discuss everything from *Quantum Leap* to elementary-school teachers who didn't seem creepy when we were little but totally seem creepy now.

I can only hope this week's dinner disasters make up for the one-minute brain freeze I caused Shelly so many years ago.

Chapter 20:
the crazies

Okay, I admit it, sometimes Shelly annoyed the shit out of me. She was the spazziest of spazzes. Her nonstop energy was amusing—most of the time. But some days, strangling her with her own vocal chords was tempting. Living with someone who is constantly turned up to eleven can wear on your nerves, especially when you usually hover around four or five. As with every friendship, there were days when we complained about each other, days when we gave each other the silent treatment, and days when we just flat-out hated each other. But no matter how serious the spat, it could always be cured with a good old-fashioned dance party. It takes a big person to apologize when she is wrong, but it takes a crazy big person to break out into dance when she is wrong. It was our own unique form of apology. Sure, it only reinforced my fear of expressing my feelings vocally, but it was always fun.

So now that we're inching closer to the end of our fifty-two weeks, Court and I know that we must pay homage to that fearless/spunky/sometimes irritating side of Shelly's personality. We've been avoiding one particular resolution on our list of must-do's all year. It rhymes with *maraoke*. We both agree to sing one song, alone, in public, and upload video evidence to the blog.

There are two kinds of people in the world: those who love karaoke and those who don't even learn how to spell it (until they have to when they're writing a book). While Court and I know our rabid fear is entertaining, it's very real—and very deep. This is our ultimate dedication to who Shelly was. Failing is *not* an option.

Can one truly die of embarrassment? Well, I guess we'll find out.

Even though it's below zero on Monday morning, I choose to walk instead of drive to my toilet paper gig. (The agency is a little over a mile away from our apartment.) I need time to sift through my Christmas music to find the best song in the key of "yell." I'll be committing my vocal crime at Piece Pizzeria tomorrow night during their annual Christmas karaoke charity event. All proceeds go to PAWS (Pets Are Worth Saving), so at least I'll be helping at the same time I'm hurting.

I waddle out of the house wearing bright yellow boots, red mittens, a poopish-brown coat, a multicolored scarf, and an orange hat. I look like a paper doll for the color-blind. The first couple steps outside are the most brutal. The cold air chokes me. I head toward the sunny side of the sidewalk, which is really just a brighter version of the wicked-cold side I just escaped. *When was the last time I felt this mothertrucking cold?* I think to myself. My eyes water. I'm not entirely sure if they're cold tears or emotional ones. I'm leaning toward the latter because I realize the last day I felt this cold was almost a year ago, when I pounced on a stranger on the train platform. I think about how much Court and I have been through this year. Even though it's been a huge inconvenience at times, I'm sort of sad it's all coming to an end. Being a crazy person at least once a week has become a normal part of my life.

I shiver and push on. Further down the road, a teenage girl bolts out of a building in front of me. She's excruciatingly loud, so I instinctually roll my eyes. (I do this on the inside because she looks like she could beat me up with her pointer finger.) But then she does something incredible. She reaches down, *barehanded*, and picks up a pile of snow. *Holy hot pockets! You crazy, girl!* But then I see "the boy" running after her. Ah, she's *flirting*. I suddenly find her adorable. Oh, to be young again. Instead of trying to impress bosses and clients and people who don't matter, we just tried to get the boy with the rattail or the girl with the rainbow barrettes to notice us. Picking up snow with your bare hands in this weather is completely asinine. But when compared with the crap we put ourselves through to impress people who don't even give us moths in our stomachs, let alone butterflies, it's genius. Other than the bitching cold on my face, this walk has become quite pleasant.

I have no peripheral vision due to the hat I'm wearing, so I'm startled when I notice somebody walking next to me. Thank goodness I wasn't singing along to "Good King Wenceslas." Especially because I can't pronounce the word "Wenceslas." It's a girl who looks to be around my age (which means anywhere between twenty-two and forty-five). She, too, is bundled up in ridiculous layers of ugly, mismatched winter wear. We give each other a nod that says, *Can you believe we're actually walking in this shit? We are badasses.* And then she passes me up. This silent conversation energizes me. It makes me happy. Once again, a cold-weather interaction brings warmth to my day. Sometimes I forget that when you don't drive through life so fast, things happen. And most of the time, things are good.

I'm an icicle by the time I reach the office, but I'm confident I've found the perfect song for tomorrow night's event. I bet if you try really hard, you can guess what it is. Does "Funky, Funky Christmas" sound familiar? If you were an NKOTB groupie, it does. What better way to make Shelly proud than to reprise my role as Jordan Knight? Although this time, I'll also have to be Donnie, Danny, Joe, and Jon.

I meet my workmates and instantly feel like I've made new friends. *What's my problem lately? Why am I so damn loving?* I blame the blog project. It's making me look at people in a new light. My judge-at-first-sight attitude is waning. I don't question *why* people are being nice to me anymore, I'm just happy that they are. People can be pretty amazing sometimes. This is starting to sound like a children's book. Can someone punch me in the face or something?

I get the okay to work from home on Tuesday. And work I do—on my karaoke performance. (I'll just work double time on toilet paper later tonight when I'm puking in the toilet.) I've recruited a friendly support group to witness my demise, but if any of them knew I was practicing in front of the mirror right now, they'd probably ditch me. An hour before the event, I call Court for a pep talk. I wish I were going to Iowa for Christmas so we could face our fear together, but I've agreed to spend it with Eric's family in St. Louis this year. It'll be my first Christmas away from my family. We seriously contemplate forfeiting, but then agree that it would make the last fifty weeks a sham. Singing is what brought Shelly and me together; I can't wuss out on this one.

"Well, good luck. *Please* call me when you're done. Or text. Or something. I just need to know you're alive," she says.

And then it's showtime. Almost.

Eric and I get to Christmas karaoke around 8:00 PM. Foxy, Kerry, Kelly, Lea, Jim, Brandan, Maggie, and Tommy join us shortly after. (This totally sounds like an imaginary group of friends, but I swear they're real.) Much to my horror, the pizzeria is packed wall to wall. I ease into performance mode with a couple of red and green Jell-O shots. (Ya know, for charity.) With every passing minute, skipping this resolution feels like the responsible thing to do. These innocent people shouldn't be punished for simply wanting to support homeless puppies and kitties. But Lea sees right through me.

"Bree, which song do you want to sing? I'll go sign you up."

Dammit, why do friends have to be so fucking supportive?

"Oh, I don't know. Maybe 'Funky, Funky Christmas,' by New Kids on the Block?" I pretend this is a spur-of-the-moment song decision and not something I've already choreographed dance moves to.

Lea returns much too quickly and plops a giant songbook onto the table. "They don't have it. What's your backup?"

The ounce of confidence the Jell-O shots had given me evaporates. My plan is ruined! I'll have to wing it. I've never been capable of winging anything. I even practice ordering pizza before I make the call.

"Um, how 'bout 'Snoopy vs. the Red Baron'?" Court and I love this song to an irrational degree. Our third-grade music teacher, Mr. Farwell, made us sing it every day from Thanksgiving break until Christmas. (We also had music class in a trailer behind the school, and Mr. Farwell was obsessed with Mary Lou Retton, but that's beside the point.) I may not be able to do a song that was special to Shelly and me, but I'll be damned if I can't make Court proud with an obscure Royal Guardsmen hit.

"Is that really a song?" Lea asks.

"Duh," I say, slamming somebody else's beer. (This is something I do when I'm nervous. It's not a great habit.)

Lea looks at me with mild concern and then flips through the book as if I told her to look for something by Chris Brown.

"They have it."

Before I have time to gulp uncomfortably like they do in cartoons, Lea signs me up. I strongly believe that if she hadn't, the show would most definitely *not* have gone on.

"Next to the stage is . . . Bree Housley. Is there a Bree in the House—lee?"

Oh, come on, dude—I am so not amused by your "clever" play on words right now. Obnoxious hoots and hollers fill the air—all from my table. Clearly, they want to see me ruin my life.

When I get onto the stage, front and center, I face my audience and I realize everyone is young, drunk, and sloppy. I can totally do this.

The music starts.

I stand uncomfortably, waiting for the vocal track to kick in.

The music continues.

Words race across the screen.

I march in place like an old-timer, still waiting for that vocal track.

The music keeps going; words keep racing.

"Go, go, go! *Sing!*" The DJ screams from his booth.

Oh god. There's no vocal track? What. The. Fuck.

I've already missed the first verse of the song while *marching*. If you were wondering, *what's the worst-case scenario?* Well, this is it. I would run off the stage right now, but I don't want to disappoint my adoring fans (i.e., the people who are cringing right now).

So I go for it. I don't even wait for the next line; I start midsentence. I'm more off-key than I thought possible. *Voice. Is. Broken.* But that's not the worst part. You know how sometimes the sync is off when you watch TV and the actor's mouth is moving way faster than the words they are saying? Well, since there's no vocal track, and because I'm more nervous than a fourth-grade boy during sex ed, I sing at forty-five times the speed of the actual music. It's uncomfortable for everyone. I want to shrivel up and die right there on the stage.

But then I hear the kind of sexy girl-scream that you'd hear at a Bon Jovi concert. It's my friend Kelly, and it's all I need to loosen up and enjoy the moment. Tonight, she's my Shelly.

Enter hoppy jazz squares. And hoppy hip rolls. I can't stop hopping! And now I hear *more* cheers! *People love hopping!* I'm a star! A star who switches keys every few words or so. The true test is coming up. For the billions of you not familiar with the song, there's a part where Snoopy cries out, "Merry Christmas, my friends!" Audience participation, folks. Either it's going to be dead silent (and I truly *will* shrivel up and die onstage), or this will be the best moment of my life.

Please sing with me, please sing with me.

"And then Snoopy cries out—" I scream, holding one hand to my ear like a gay WWF wrestler.

Note the word "Dysfunctional" displayed prominently behind me. Foreshadowing?

"Merry Christmas, my friends!" The crowd roars. *Holy shit. People love me. I'm famous! Oh god, when is this song going to be over? Another verse? Please, just end already. I wanna go home. I want to eat cheese in my pajamas.*

The music finally trails off. The audience screams in adoration. (Okay, they clap.) I take a deep breath, clutch my heart, and place the microphone back on the stand.

It's over. I did it. And it only proves that the scarier the challenge, the sweeter the victory. I hope Shelly is proud of me, or at least laughing her ass off, wherever she is.

I text Court: "Done. Alive. Barely."

The next morning, Eric and I watch the video before I post it to the blog. I can't help but laugh. And cringe. And then laugh again.

"Well, I'm just glad it's over. And that I didn't take any clothes off onstage."

"Um. About that . . . " Eric says.

I stare at him, eyes wide.

"Do you remember backup dancing to that Run-DMC song?"

"Shit. I'm going back to bed."

Court massacres "Billy Jean" in Des Moines later that night. She, too, misses the first verse, but her crotch-grabbing dance moves more than make up for it. I guess the Housley girls are just born to dance. If you're into jazz squares and crotch grabbing, that is.

I *love* that Court and I faced our karaoke nightmares. I haven't felt that scared, nervous, alive, or exhilarated in years. Shelly and I sang all the time when it was just the two of us. My only regret is that we never took our show to the masses. If I were given one more day with her, there's a million things I'd want to do—but singing Clay Aiken in front of a drunken audience together would definitely be in the top five.

Will I ever sing karaoke again? Probably not. But I'll never forget the way I felt during those three minutes and nine seconds. And I have Shelly, Court, Lea, Kelly, Tommy, Maggie, Brandan, Kerry, Jim, Foxy, and Eric to thank for that. It takes a wacked-out village to raise a nutcase.

Chapter 21:
the ultimate payback

I had a toast planned for Shelly's wedding. I wanted to thank
her for making me laugh for fifteen years. I wanted to thank her
for being there through all the adolescent humiliation, and for
letting me hide behind her whenever I got scared. But most of
all, I wanted to thank her for making me who I am. So much of
the courage in my heart comes from winning the acceptance of
someone who could've spent her time with dozens of adoring fans
but who chose to spend most of it with me instead. I'll never know
why she picked me that day in fourth grade; I'm just glad she
did. I practiced what I would say in that speech a million times. I
couldn't wait to finally express with words how much she meant to
me. But when the time came, I regressed into that shy girl with the
bad bang perm all over again. My nerves got the best of me, and
I sat on the sidelines and watched the other girls in the wedding
party speak on the microphone.

Five years later, the blog has put that microphone into my hands. While I may not be able to tell *her* all those things, I can tell everyone else in the world. More than that, I can tell them that we should treasure the relationships that are important to us because you never know when they'll be taken away. It's an old lesson that gets thrown around a lot, but people really can disappear from your life in an instant. "Hello" one day, eternal silence the next. (I won't preach that you should leave nothing unsaid, because if someone you love dies suddenly and you have nothing more you would've said to them, then you're just not human.) Show your friends you love them, laugh with them, cry with them, eat candy and ice cream with them, because once they're gone, it's those little things that you'll wish for.

Now it's time to pay Shelly back for inspiring us. This week, we'll raise $500 for the Preeclampsia Foundation in her honor. We're perfectly aware that the world is broke after Christmas, so we simply encourage (gently beg) people to give that weathered dollar they find in the washing machine, or the six bucks a new nonsmoker would've spent on a pack of cigarettes. We decide to use an Iowa-based savings tool called Smarty Pig to collect the donations. They don't add any processing fees; plus, we get an adorable Pig-o-meter widget to put on the blog.

We receive our first donation just minutes after posting the resolution: "Hailey is giving some of her Christmas money to Mommy Shelly." If that isn't more precious than a puppy wearing argyle, I don't know what is. The donations continue to roll in. New friends, old friends, casual acquaintances, complete strangers, ex-boyfriends, friends of ex-boyfriends, preeclampsia survivors, family members of preeclampsia victims—all of them eagerly chip in. We reach our goal of $500 in one day. Unbelievable.

Even though Court and I were blessed with the confidence of field mice, we raise the goal to $800. After all, our pride is the only thing at stake here, and that's partly what this year of resolutions has been about anyway. Eight hundred dollars comes and goes, so we take

a giant step and raise the bar to $1,500 on Friday. We're probably set-
ting ourselves up for failure, but in my mind, we've already won.

By midnight on Sunday, we're at $1,350. Meh. We shouldn't
be disappointed, considering our original goal was $500. That's
like ordering a cheeseburger, receiving a Big Mac, and then getting
pissed when the Big Mac is missing a pickle slice. But I *am* disappointed. Shelly always went above and beyond. And I got caught
up in that spirit—only to be let down. I'm happy to donate the
final $150, but I might as well call myself Sally Sallerson and get an
extra box of Thin Mints.

Monday morning, I have *nine* emails from Smarty Pig. Funds can't
be transferred on Sundays. *Duh.* People didn't just kick in at the last
minute; they kicked in like the Rockettes on ephedrine. I call Court
to share the news.

"We got a few more donations. Guess how much?"

Her voice perks up. "Did we get up to fifteen hundred?"

"More."

"Seventeen hundred?"

"More."

"Just tell me already!"

"And the retail price is: two thousand, two hundred thirty-five
dollars," I say, in my best Bob Barker voice. (I know donations aren't
retail, but it deserves to be stated with game show–like enthusiasm.)

"No way!"

"Yep. We did it."

"And it was *so* much easier than karaoke."

There's no better feeling than honoring your BFF by raising
money to help save *other* people's BFFs, mothers, daughters, grand-
daughters, and babies. And when you get to do it alongside the sister
who has held your hand throughout your entire life? Well, that's just
the cat's pajamas.

Shelly did so much to make me who I am, and I've never felt I
could repay her for that. For the first time, I do. And as with a lot of

things in life, I have Court to thank for helping me do that. Court and I are closer than we were one year ago. We aren't just sisters; we are best friends. And I don't care how precious that sounds. Without her, I would've most definitely taken a wrong turn—or hit another girl with my car.

It's hard to believe a year has passed since the accidental brainstorm for fifty2resolutions with Foxy and Kerry. The idea, which seemed fatuitous at the time, became one of the most profound experiences I've ever had. It brought Shelly back into my life. I had a place to talk about her, to remember her—to confess how much I miss her. It was the therapy I didn't want to admit I still needed. In a way, I had finally accepted her death. I always knew I wanted to tell our story; I just didn't have a happy ending yet. But now I do.

That feeling of accomplishment quickly fades. I lie in bed, wide awake, feeling guilty. *Was this too much about me? Would Shelly truly approve of everything we've done this year?* Court and I have been telling ourselves how much she'd appreciate our silly antics, but what if she wouldn't have? What if she doesn't really want me to heal? A best friend never wants to be replaced, right?

And then something unbelievable happens. (For real: You won't believe it, and I don't blame you.) I feel a hand brush through my hair. I turn toward the calming touch, and my hair gently falls back onto my face. No one is there. *Am I awake right now?* I look at Eric: He's sleeping. I look at Willie: He's sleeping. I pinch myself: I'm awake. Love and reassurance wash over me. *She approves.*

"Goodnight, Shelly. I love you."

I will always have a Shelly-size hole in my heart. However, thanks to the peaks, valleys, and potholes I stumbled upon this year, my heart is no longer broken. Shelly and I taught each other the definition of true friendship. It's up to me to continue teaching that lesson to others. It exists in many forms, from the girls who make you

December, 2004. The last photo we took together. (Shelly was, of course, an hour late to lunch.)

laugh and dry your tears, to the man who loves you unconditionally, to the sister who does all of the above and then fills in any of the leftover cracks.

While I'll never be a social butterfly like Shelly, I will be the most social moth you've ever seen. I will take more chances, make more random eye contact, and maybe even indulge in some chipper morning elevator conversation every once in a while. *We* make life a gift. Otherwise, it's just something given to us—like a pair of Wigwam socks or a flier for 50¢ off chicken wings.

Don't get me wrong: I will still be slightly odd and somewhat introverted, and I'll consume caffeine like it's my job. Because in the end, Shelly picked *me* for a reason. And I always want to be the girl she picked. I'll just be a better version of that girl.

Saturday, January 16, 2010 marks Shelly's five-year deathiversary. I'll say goodbye to her as I have for the last four years. But this year will be different. This year I'll say goodbye knowing I've done something to make her proud of choosing me as her Hillary, her Cagney, her Shirley, *and* her Miranda fifteen years ago.

Epilogue:
where are they now?

I'm a sucker for these segments on TV. There's nothing I love more than seeing one of my childhood idols all washed up with a feral-cat habit. Unfortunately, my update will not be nearly as exciting.

It's been almost three years since Court and I completed the project. Writing this book has become yet another unforeseen step in my healing process. Sitting alone in my office, crying into my red wine every night, might not sound healthy, but the giant exhale I took when I finished the last chapter felt better than anything I've ever experienced. I'm extremely fortunate to have gotten the opportunity to introduce Shelly, and all her craziness, to those of you who never got to meet her. I do apologize if there were a few more f-bombs than you prefer (Mom), but I wanted to write with my gut—and my gut has a filthy mouth sometimes.

I still live in Chicago with Eric and Willie. Court still lives in Des Moines with E1—and a new baby! We were ecstatic to welcome Eleanore Josephine to the family on January 13, 2012. As I'm sure you can imagine, the due date made me a nervous wreck. Court was originally due on January 18, just two days after Shelly's

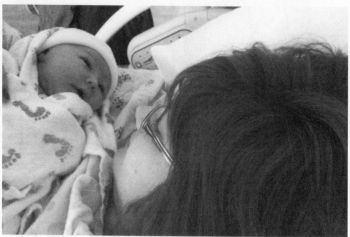

Court and Baby Eleanore. (Happy sigh.)

deathiversary. When I opened up to Kim about my anxiety via email, her response made me smile: "I wouldn't be worried. I'm sure that Shelly is sick of us being sad around that time, so she decided that's when you should become an aunt. Sounds like something she would do." And Kim was absolutely right. Court was induced on January 12 due to issues with gestational diabetes, and she gave birth to our perfect angel on Friday the thirteenth.

Amy married Josh in September of 2010. While I did not supply her with a magic water bottle full of vodka on the wedding day, I was flattered to be her maid of honor. And this time, I didn't cower from the microphone.

While we're on the subject, I'd like to take this moment to thank everyone who helped make our wedding one worth writing about. When you're in that crazy-bride state of mind and all you can see are dollar signs, it's difficult to express how much the little things (and big things) really mean to you. And then, when you're writing about it a year later, you think to yourself, *Did I ever send them a gift? Or a thank-you? Or anything? Man, I'm such a dick!* And then you spend a few sleepless nights worried that people hate you. Or is that

The beautiful bride, Amy, and her maid-of-honor who may or may not have fallen into a bush while out on the town the night before.

just me? Anyway, I owe many generous people a lifetime of gratitude. But for now, I'd like to thank those who put in some hard labor behind the scenes: Courtnee and Eric Carstens, Mom and Dad, Jack and Margo Sahrmann, Holly and Chris Duncan, Craig and Carrie Sahrmann, Denise and Nate Miller, Kerry Craig, Sarah Constantino, Heather Creswell, Maya Boettcher, Dan and Mary Fox, Kathy Heaps, Bobby Folsom, Ami Fox, Kevin Cradock, Jackie Huston, Matt Abramson, Alex Fendrich, Georgia and Gary Bower, Scott and Shannon Kenneally, Diane Soppe, Christa Anderson, and Christine Richman (who couldn't be there but designed our lovely invitations). From creating centerpieces to pumping up the jams, you all made it a day/night we'll never forget.

My belief in the power of friendship has only gotten stronger, and I want to do everything I can to keep our girlfriends alive. In fact, I no longer dread the Preeclampsia Foundation fundraisers, for this reason. It's not about *me;* it's about all of us banding together to make a difference. Please visit Preeclampsia.org to learn more about the disease that kills over seventy-six thousand women and five hundred thousand babies each year, globally. And while you're there, why not donate a few bucks in memory of Shelly Bridgewater? Yeah, that sounds like a spectacular idea! Also consider visiting OrganDonor.gov to learn more about saving others with your body parts.

Lastly, call someone you love, right now.

acknowledgments

Let's start with a caveat: I know I will accidentally forget people, and I'll probably sound like a rambling ass at some point. Bear with me.

First of all, thanks to Shelly for inspiring everything this book is about. I love and miss you more than words can say. (Although I tried—with seventy thousand of them.)

I didn't know the first thing about writing a book. My editor, Brooke Warner, and my literary agent, Laney Katz Becker, took the time to guide me like every day was my first day on the best job ever. Thanks for your patience, knowledge, and wit, ladies.

I'd also like to give special thanks to the late Jeffrey Zaslow, who had the kindness in his heart to respond to an email from a clueless first-time writer. He continued to give me advice while finishing his final two books. His untimely death was yet another reminder that the good ones can be taken away from us at any moment. Also, thanks to Mike Benoist, Michael Zadoorian, and Jeffrey Wise, who offered helpful words when I didn't even know where to start.

Also, big thanks to Ami (Foxy) and Kerry for unknowingly helping to come up with the idea that made this book possible; to Shelly's family for providing me with Shelly's photo albums and diaries and also for encouraging me to tell our story; and to Amy, Christine, Kelly, Megan, Cassidy, and Lea for joining me on many of the adventures throughout the year.

Thank you to each and every person who read the blog, especially those who wrote comments that kept us going; to all the friends and strangers who donated to the Preeclampsia Foundation in Shelly's honor over the year; and to anyone who has ever taught me anything about friendship, especially my oldest and dearest friend, Emily.

Most of all, I'd like to thank Eric for letting me do my thing, and for cooking amazing dinners while I did it. Thanks, Mom, Dad, Eric (E1), Georgia, Gary, and the rest of my family (both old and new) for being there for me every day and for supporting my lunacy with open arms. And thank you, Courtnee, for voluntarily jumping into the trenches and holding my hand through it all.

So, wait.

what exactly is preeclampsia?

One of my goals in writing this book was to increase preeclampsia awareness. So now that the fun part is over, here are the facts.

According to the Preeclampsia Foundation, preeclampsia is a disorder that occurs during pregnancy and the postpartum period and affects both the mother and the unborn baby. Affecting approximately 5–8 percent of all pregnancies, it's usually a rapidly progressive condition characterized by high blood pressure and the presence of protein in the urine. Typically, preeclampsia occurs after twenty weeks' gestation, though it can occur earlier. Symptoms to look for:

• Swelling of the hands or face

• Sudden weight gain

• Unrelenting headaches

• Visual disturbances

• Nausea or vomiting

If you just feel like something *might* be wrong, please, *please* visit your doctor, even if those symptoms turn out to be nothing. By conservative estimates, preeclampsia and other hypertensive disorders of pregnancy are responsible for seventy-six thousand maternal and five hundred thousand infant deaths each year.

Now, what is HELLP syndrome?

HELLP syndrome is a life-threatening pregnancy complication usually considered a variant of preeclampsia. The letters stand for:

- H (hemolysis, which is the breaking down of red blood cells)
- EL (elevated liver enzymes, an indication of liver damage)
- LP (low platelet count)

The symptoms are very similar to those of preeclampsia and can also include:

- Nausea/vomiting/indigestion, with pain after eating
- Abdominal or chest tenderness
- Shoulder pain or pain when breathing deeply
- Upper abdominal pain
- Shortness of breath
- Bleeding

Of the 5–8 percent of U.S. women who develop preeclampsia, 15 percent develop evidence of HELLP syndrome.

There is no surefire way to prevent these illnesses, but the best thing to do is:

- Get yourself in the best physical shape possible before getting pregnant.
- Have regular prenatal visits.

- Inform the doctor about any previous high-risk pregnancies or family history of HELLP syndrome, preeclampsia, etc.

- Understand the warning signs and do not delay reporting them to your doctor; trust yourself when "something just doesn't feel right."

The Preeclampsia Foundation's mission is to combat these life-threatening disorders of pregnancy by providing patient support and education, raising public awareness, catalyzing research, and improving health care practices. One of the best ways to get involved is to participate in or start a Promise Walk for Preeclampsia™ near you. Please visit the Preeclampsia Foundation's website at Preeclampsia.org for more information.

© Eric Sahrmann

about the author

Bree Housley is a freelance writer who grew up in Walcott, Iowa (a.k.a. the World's Largest Truckstop). She now lives in Chicago, where she spends most of her time cocktailing with friends or sitting in sweatpants and watching movies with her husband and their dog. She is not named after a French cheese.

selected titles from seal press
By women. For women.

P.S.: What I Didn't Say, edited by Megan McMorris. $15.95, 978-1-58005-290-0. For the friend who's been there for you through everything, the friend you've lost touch with, or the friend you've wished you could help, this thought-provoking collection of unsent letters expresses the unspoken.

Dancing at the Shame Prom: Sharing the Stories That Kept Us Small, edited by Amy Ferris and Hollye Dexter. $15.00, 978-1-58005-416-4. A collection of funny, sad, poignant, miraculous, life-changing, and jaw-dropping secrets for readers to gawk at, empathize with, and laugh about—in the hopes that they will be inspired to share their secret burdens as well.

Wanderlust: A Love Affair with Five Continents, by Elisabeth Eaves. $16.95, 978-1-58005-311-2. A love letter from the author to the places she's visited—and to the spirit of travel itself—that documents her insatiable hunger for the rush of the unfamiliar and the experience of encountering new people and cultures.

1,000 Mitzvahs: How Small Acts of Kindness Can Heal, Inspire, and Change Your Life, by Linda Cohen. $16.00, 978-1-58005-365-5. When her father passes away, Linda Cohen decides to perform one thousand mitzvahs, or acts of kindness, to honor his memory—and discovers the transformational power of doing good for others.

Kissing Outside the Lines: A True Story of Love and Race and Happily Ever After, by Diane Farr. $16.00, 978-1-58005-396-9. Actress and columnist Diane Farr's unapologetic, and often hilarious, look at the complexities of interracial/ethnic/religious/what-have-you love.

How to Die in Paris: A Memoir, by Naturi Thomas. $17.00, 978-1-58005-364-8. The edgy, poetic memoir of a young middle-class black woman who escapes a tortured past in New York to pursue a new life in Europe—only to find herself broke, desperate, and contemplating suicide on the streets of Paris.

Find Seal Press Online
www.SealPress.com
www.Facebook.com/SealPress
Twitter: @SealPress